QUEERING LORCA'S DUENDE
DESIRE, DEATH, INTERMEDIALITY

LEGENDA

LEGENDA is the Modern Humanities Research Association's book imprint for new research in the Humanities. Founded in 1995 by Malcolm Bowie and others within the University of Oxford, Legenda has always been a collaborative publishing enterprise, directly governed by scholars. The Modern Humanities Research Association (MHRA) joined this collaboration in 1998, became half-owner in 2004, in partnership with Maney Publishing and then Routledge, and has since 2016 been sole owner. Titles range from medieval texts to contemporary cinema and form a widely comparative view of the modern humanities, including works on Arabic, Catalan, English, French, German, Greek, Italian, Portuguese, Russian, Spanish, and Yiddish literature. Editorial boards and committees of more than 60 leading academic specialists work in collaboration with bodies such as the Society for French Studies, the British Comparative Literature Association and the Association of Hispanists of Great Britain & Ireland.

The MHRA encourages and promotes advanced study and research in the field of the modern humanities, especially modern European languages and literature, including English, and also cinema. It aims to break down the barriers between scholars working in different disciplines and to maintain the unity of humanistic scholarship. The Association fulfils this purpose through the publication of journals, bibliographies, monographs, critical editions, and the MHRA Style Guide, and by making grants in support of research. Membership is open to all who work in the Humanities, whether independent or in a University post, and the participation of younger colleagues entering the field is especially welcomed.

STUDIES IN HISPANIC AND LUSOPHONE CULTURES

Studies in Hispanic and Lusophone Cultures are selected and edited by the Association of Hispanists of Great Britain & Ireland. The series seeks to publish the best new research in all areas of the literature, thought, history, culture, film, and languages of Spain, Spanish America, and the Portuguese-speaking world.

The Association of Hispanists of Great Britain & Ireland is a professional association which represents a very diverse discipline, in terms of both geographical coverage and objects of study. Its website showcases new work by members, and publicises jobs, conferences and grants in the field.

Founding Editor
Trevor Dadson

Editorial Committee
Chair: Professor Catherine Davies (University of London)
Professor Stephanie Dennison (University of Leeds)
Professor Sally Faulkner (University of Exeter)
Professor Andrew Ginger
(New College of Humanities at Northeastern University)
Professor James Mandrell (Brandeis University, USA)
Professor Hilary Owen (University of Manchester/University of Oxford)
Professor Philip Swanson (University of Sheffield)
Professor Jonathan Thacker (Exeter College, University of Oxford)

Managing Editor
Dr Graham Nelson
41 Wellington Square, Oxford OX1 2JF, UK

www.legendabooks.com/series/shlc

STUDIES IN HISPANIC AND LUSOPHONE CULTURES

Queering Lorca's Duende

Desire, Death, Intermediality

❖

Miguel García

l

LEGENDA

Studies in Hispanic and Lusophone Cultures 49
Modern Humanities Research Association
2022

Published by Legenda
an imprint of the Modern Humanities Research Association
Salisbury House, Station Road, Cambridge CB1 2LA

ISBN 978-1-78188-724-0 (HB)
ISBN 978-1-78188-728-8 (PB)

First published 2022

Copy-Editor: Dr Ellen Jones

CONTENTS

❖

A Fina López,
la madre más *queer*.

ACKNOWLEDGEMENTS

❖

This book would not have been possible without the invaluable help and support of my doctoral supervisors, Sarah Wright and James Williams. You have been my inspiration and I will never thank you both enough for helping me be more assertive and believe in my ideas the way you both have done. I would also like to thank Legenda and the MHRA for their incredible support with this project, especially Graham Nelson and, most especially, Trevor Dadson, who sadly passed away as the book was being finalised. May this work serve as a humble testimony of all his care and support to countless academics like myself: Trevor, you will be sorely missed.

I am also very grateful to the Fundación Federico García Lorca in Madrid and the Centro Federico García Lorca in Granada for all their kind assistance during my research visits, and especially to President Laura García-Lorca for her generosity and kindness and for granting me permission to use Lorca's images in the book. Special thanks go to Maria M. Delgado and Federico Bonaddio for their invaluable advice in the process of turning my PhD thesis into this book. The good advice I received from Jackie Rattray, Tom Whittaker, Chris Perriam and Stephen Roberts also deserves special thanks.

I would like to thank everyone at the Department of Languages, Literatures and Cultures at Royal Holloway for their continued support during this journey: Arantza Mayo, Lidia Merás, Alba Chaparro, Abigail Lee Six, Avril Tynan, Anna Kingsley, Aïda Antonino, Ruth Hemus, Ruth Cruickshank, Hannah Thompson, Karina Berger, Ann Hobbs, James Kent, Colin Davies, Jon Hughes, Miriam Haddu, Odile Rimbert, Sarah Midson, Helen Thomas and Giuliana Pieri. I also thank my students for everything I learned from them in the past years, their progress and encouragement inspire me to keep teaching.

Thanks to all my colleagues from the HiPLA Department and the School of Modern Languages at University of Bristol, you've all made me feel welcome and incredibly valued despite the online obstacles and pandemic uncertainty. Special thanks go to James Hawkey, Jo Crow, Matthew Brown, Rachel Randall, Gustavo Infante, Madalena Pires, Caragh Wells, Albertine Fox, Bethan Fisk, Paco Romero Salvadó, Xavi Mas Craviotto, Ana Suárez Vidal, Aris Da Silva Contreiras, Becky Kosick, Elisabeth Bolorinos Allard, Mark Biram, Pete Woollaston, Goya Wilson Vasquez, Paul Merchant, Jose Lingna Nafafe, Marga Menéndez López and Andreas Schonle.

To all my fellow early-career academic colleagues, my most important pillar during these challenging years, I am eternally grateful to you for all those long and sometimes panicky coffee breaks and study sessions and for the privilege of witnessing your talent and intelligence: Jessica Wax-Edwards, Katie Cattell, Laura Ventura Nieto, Clarissa Hotchkiss, Michelle Clarabut, Serena Alessi, Ambra Anelotti, Amélie Boubaker, and especially my dearest and admired friends Lucy Hill and Lauren Faro. To my lovely housemates, Al, Anna and Irene, for putting up with me all these years and always giving me new things to think and talk about in as many languages as possible.

Finally, I thank my family for their unconditional love and support, I am who I am because of you: Mamá, Papá, Isabel, os quiero hasta el infinito y más allá; Fraggles, sin vosotros duele más: Sánchez, Espa, Toñi, Ginés, Sando, Aynara, Adri, Álex, Antonio, Jacopo; Toni, gracias por el cariño y apoyo; Óscar, thanks for transgressing confines from London to 'la huerta'; mi querida Laura Cogorro ('no saben terrible'), mi Mari voluta, mi poema hecho carne Laura Fernández y mi eterna compañera y hermana de alma, Maite.

To magicians everywhere. Reach for the moon.

M.G., August 2021

ABBREVIATIONS

❖

DRAE   Real Academia Española de la Lengua. 2014. *Diccionario de la Real Academia Española de la Lengua*, 23rd edn (Madrid: RAE) <https://www.rae.es> [accessed July 2021]

DT   Federico García Lorca. 2018. *Diván del Tamarit*, ed. by Pepa Merlo (Madrid: Cátedra)

MHRA   Modern Humanities Research Association

OC   Federico García Lorca. 1986. *Obras completas*, 22nd ed. by Arturo del Hoyo, vols. I, II, and III (Madrid: Aguilar)

OED   *Oxford English Dictionary*. 2021. *Oxford English Dictionary Online* (Oxford: Oxford University Press) <https://www.oed.com> [accessed July 2021]

PC   Federico García Lorca. 2013. *Poesía completa*, 6th edn (Barcelona: Galaxia Gutenberg)

TC   Federico García Lorca. 2016. *Teatro completo*, 2nd edn (Barcelona: Galaxia Gutenberg)

LIST OF ILLUSTRATIONS

❖

INTRODUCTION

❖

Duende's Mysteries

El duende... ¿Dónde está el duende? Por el arco vacío entra un aire mental
que sopla con insistencia sobre las cabezas de los muertos, en busca de nuevos
paisajes y acentos ignorados: un aire con olor de saliva de niño, de hierba
machacada y velo de medusa que anuncia el constante bautizo de las cosas
recién creadas. (García Lorca OC III: 318)

Queer is by definition *whatever* is at odds with the normal, the legitimate, the
dominant. *There is nothing in particular to which it necessarily refers.*
(Halperin 1995: 62)

Queer Lorca

Federico García Lorca (1898–1936) is today considered one of the most prominent
figures in Spanish literature and culture of the twentieth century: his status as 'a
national trademark' (Delgado 2008: 2) has been confirmed by a vast amount of
scholarly and artistic works and cultural events celebrating him throughout most of
the last century and increasingly in the present one. From the 1980s until the late
2010s, Lorca has been reclaimed as a literary treasure and his production has become
an unquestionable part of the canon. His national and international recognition
began to grow with the multiple homages around the climactic centenary
celebrations of his birth in 1998 and which included events in Spain, the United
Kingdom and the United States.[1] The multimedia centenary tributes ranged from
conferences, museum openings and exhibitions to stage and musical productions
and performances.[2] On screen, following a 1976 documentary and a TV mini-series
in 1987, the Hollywood film production *Muerte en Granada*, directed by Marcos
Zurinaga (1997) and starring Andy García, depicted for mainstream audiences
the tragic events leading to Lorca's assassination. *Lorquiana* (1998), an album of
Lorca's poems and songs performed by Spanish singer Ana Belén, was also released
to great acclaim at this time. Since then, Lorca has been referenced and adapted
by contemporary Spanish filmmakers like Pedro Almodóvar or Paula Ortiz and
international artists such as Philippa Goslett or Nilo Cruz.[3] Amongst the most
recent tributes is an album compilation of flamenco songs inspired by Lorca's works
entitled *Lorca Vivo* released by *El País* (Limón 2016), and theatre productions of
Lorca's plays are still very prolific both in Spain and abroad.[4] Now that the rights to
his *oeuvre* have legally become public domain (Ruiz Mantilla and Koch 2017) eighty
years after he died, Lorca's legacy still lives on through a multiplicity of cultural
channels and practices.

In addition to the multifaceted nature of his artistic production and his canonical status, the interest in Lorca has expanded in such a global way due to the mysteries surrounding his death and to his identification with heterodox desires and identities. His brutal assassination by the insurgent armed forces of the Nationalist Right at the outbreak of the Spanish Civil War in 1936 granted him the status of Republican martyr and made him a symbol of all those oppressed and executed during the war and the subsequent forty-year dictatorship in Spain. Recently, a group of Spanish and British archaeologists has tried in vain to exhume Lorca's lost remains through various excavations aided by the 'Ley para la recuperación de la memoria histórica', but his disappearance and execution by Nationalist supporters is still a dark and saddening chapter of Spanish history 'haunt[ing] the national imaginary' (Delgado 2015: 178).[5]

In parallel, the many works examining the connections between Lorca's life and work and ideas of sexuality, gender and sexual orientation also attest to his uniqueness and importance as a 'gay icon' (Walters 2007: xxiv) with immense seductive powers.[6] Sahuquillo claims that 'Federico García Lorca's homosexuality is no longer questioned among those professionally involved in literary criticism or biographies' (2007: 14) and Garlinger suggests that 'in many cases his sexuality is inexorably linked to his literary production' (2002: 710). Nonetheless, the issue of sexuality is, like Lorca's death, also enveloped in mystery and controversy. Following the polemics surrounding Lorca in the past, there now seems to be a consensus amongst scholars and the public that gender and sexuality are areas likely to be explored and scrutinised in his life and work.[7] On the other hand, conservative critics still take issue with readings or statements looking at the author through the prism of heterodox desire, considering that if aspects like (homo) sexuality or sexual orientation are explored or taken into account, a critical analysis of Lorca's work would be merely biographical, somewhat frivolous or even devoid of academic rigour.

There have been extensive studies, such as those by Binding (1985), Sahuquillo (2007) and Herrero (2014) arguing that Lorca's homosexuality was expressed, disguised or encoded in his texts.[8] Works like *El público*, *Así que pasen cinco años*, *Oda a Walt Whitman* or *Sonetos del amor oscuro* have been considered clear signs of Lorca's inclusion in a homosexual subculture in Spain. Sahuquillo defines the *culture of homosexuality* or *homosexual culture* as 'the linguistic and aesthetic cultivation of all that refers to the expression of homosexual love and its problematics' (2007: 26), and notes Lorca's ability to share the extent of his homosexual experience with homosexual audiences and those in the know while hiding it from hostile others. Similarly, Carlos Jerez-Farrán (2004) analyses Lorca's 'impossible plays' and especially *El público*, attending to the dynamics of veiling and revealing a spectacle of homosexual tendencies in the play, while Cordero Sánchez examines a group of Lorca's plays establishing correlations between the 'meta-author' characters and Lorca's biography to argue for the playwright's 'opening or acceptance of his homosexuality' and his 'partial coming out of the closet' (2012: 143). Lorca's biographer, Ian Gibson, has postulated the poet's homosexual relationships (1999,

2009) and revealed extensive research into his much-debated affair with Salvador Dalí.[9] Further evidence of Lorca's male lovers and companions has since been discovered (Tremlett 2012), with the concomitant application of some of these accounts to the study of his work. All of these examples corroborate Paul Julian Smith's critical argument that there often is an 'equivalence of life and work' (1998b: 65) in Lorca studies, so the poet's life events have often been used to analyse his texts or vice versa and the circumstances of his death have sometimes overshadowed his work. On both fronts, nevertheless, Lorca still remains 'a locus of contested meanings and significations' (Wright 2000: 1) and the many mysteries contributing to his strong power of seduction also make his exploration of sexuality and the life-work relationship far from clear.

These mysteries and their causes, while problematic and very particular in Lorca's case, are not unprecedented. As Cleminson and Vázquez García note, 'the mid nineteenth century was a period in which the sexual came to represent the key to a person's mind, body and actions. Sexuality became the secret to be explored and discovered as the truth of the person and indeed of society itself' (Cleminson and Vázquez García 2007: 219), a notion which continued to prevail well into the twentieth century. There were accounts representing the homosexual as a 'tragic, suffering and ultimately failed (or even suicidal) personage destined to self-destruction', a vision which tended to accept 'rather unquestionably the new pathologising, if naturalising theories of psychiatry and the sexual sciences' (Cleminson and Vázquez García 2007: 274). Lorca's taste for fatality and the tragic and his recurrent representations of death — as well as the connection usually made between these and his own assassination — have been aligned with these theories and taken to reveal 'a symbol for the desperate struggle to express his love as an equal; a poet [...] who names the reality of his fears made flesh in revelatory folding screens [...] and visual images of castrated desire' (Peral Vega 2015: 4). Generally, pathologising articulations and representations of homosexuality, containing a prominent element keen to essentialise sexual identities, were brought into question later in the twentieth century after the post-Stonewall emergence of new gay paradigms that affirmed a more positive vision of homosexuality and of queer individuals and communities in an effort to achieve visibility and social and legal equality.[10] Gay and Lesbian studies from the 1970s to the 1990s tried to rescue historical figures from the silence that had surrounded homosexuality until then and which tended to obliterate sexuality altogether from an author's life and work or to avoid delving too deeply into desire and sexual identity (Mira 2004: 247–62). Alberto Mira insists on the academic and political value of the visibility that the gay paradigm offered (2011: 124) but suggests that applying contemporary western mythologies on homosexuality to earlier or non-western authors can lead to inaccuracies and questionable conclusions, like postulating a transhistorical homosexual identity (2011: 125). Ideas and discourses like 'the closet', 'finding one's true identity' or 'expressing one's own self' can prove anachronistic or impose limiting paradigms if applied directly to an earlier time like Lorca's. In the 1990s, Queer theory was consolidated and approaches to homosexuality and other heterodox desires became more concerned with the fluidity and performativity of genders and sexualities, so the study of individuals and works preceding this model became more complex than a mere hetero/homo identification or a search for clues in texts attesting to the author's own sexual identification. Biographical studies of authors like Lorca have tended to reduce the life and work to a more limiting and easily assimilable gay paradigm (Binding's otherwise remarkable work applies this paradigm too narrowly at times), but the advent of a more fluid queer approach can offer new enlightening insights and discourses. This study, without denying the invaluable effort of biographical approaches to Lorca or the necessity of LGBTQ activism, will suggest that looking at Lorca through the queer lens is necessary to comprehend more fully the mysteries of his poetics. Queer approaches, typically enquiring into the politics and aesthetics of subjectivities, are especially suited to explore the Lorquian intersections between processes of subject formation and the reappropriation of multiple aesthetics in order to question and recreate norms.

Cleminson and Vázquez García identify a variety of discourses in the early twentieth century theorising and categorising homosexuality which at times challenged previously established essentialising notions. Alongside the trope of the homosexual as victim and of homosexuality as death and disease, there emerged other discourses, especially in Mediterranean countries such as Spain or Italy, which advocated an unstable form of bisexuality and questioned, usually in playful and irreverent terms, any essentialisation of homosexuality through biology or psychiatry. In this so-called 'Mediterranean model' of sexuality, same-sex relations 'take preference over any strong expression of identity' (Cleminson and Vázquez García 2007: 275) and operate in literary and artistic discourses by means of suggestions, irony, metaphors and silences.[11] There is evidence of established social circles in Spanish cities in the early twentieth century (Granada, Cádiz and Barcelona among them) whose members, however overtly, acknowledged their awareness of heterodox desires and of the transgressive nature of their discourse, often necessitating a negotiation between expression and silence. In this study I shall argue that Lorca can be included in the Mediterranean model, since his poetics often goes beyond the binary distinctions homosexual-heterosexual and male-female and resists a narrowly biographical approach. Lorca's life-work dichotomy and the issues of sexuality explored in his works are areas full of nuances. There is not a clear identity between Lorca the man and Lorca the poetic persona, let alone a stable (sexual) identity that can be ascribed to the further personae in his poems and plays.[12] Lorca's quasi-obsessive exploration of the limits of love, desire and mortality will not render easy and unequivocal interpretations; rather, in its emphatic resistance to be categorised, his work is more aptly described as anti-normative or *queer*. Full of suggestions and silences, his works displayed a combination of avant-garde experimentalism, intermedial practices and a sense of self-consciousness as an artist and thinker. This reveals an aesthetics whose significations go beyond the morbid ironies of his tragic death and the correlations between his life experiences and his poetic images. In his important study on Lorca's legacy, Jonathan Mayhew aptly considers Lorca a 'poetic thinker' whose 'radically modernist hermeneutics and poetics [...] remains particularly resistant to unitary interpretations' (2018: 25–26) which tend to oversimplify or condescend to his poetic thought.[13] In particular, Mayhew underlines the importance of Lorca's performative poetics and of the pragmatic and spiritual dimensions of his poetic thought, all crucial aspects of the poet's works examined in this study.

The difficulties in identifying the relationship between Lorca's life and his work, the complex nature of his poetic thought and the problematic dynamics of sexuality and gender call upon the need to introduce a more nuanced theoretical perspective to the study of his *oeuvre*. If queer is understood as that which has fallen from the normative and is opposed to it, thus denying notions of essential or immutable identities based on sex, gender or sexuality, then Lorca's works, never easily categorised or delimited by norms and often actively trying to contest normativity, can offer a queer poetics in their own right. In other words, speaking of Queer Lorca and queering his poetics will not consist of simply pointing to potentially gay and lesbian characters or motifs or insisting on the sexual identity of the author; rather, it will involve revealing in his works the incoherencies between sex, gender and sexuality and placing them against the normative discourses from which they emerge as different and subversive. This book is an effort to navigate the complicated terrain where biographical accounts of Lorca and scholarly criticism on his works converge in the similarly complex and obscure exploration of queer desires and sexualities.

Lorca Post-New York: Avant-Garde Boundary Crossings

Queering Lorca's Duende proposes a queer reading of Lorca's later works produced after his sojourn in New York in 1929–30 and which belong to what might be called his late corpus. It has been said about Lorca that 'more so than any other twentieth-century Spanish writer, he remains a paradoxical embodiment of the local, the national and the global' (Delgado 2008: 2). Indeed, the particular mixture of Andalusian folklore and avant-garde experimentations found in Lorca's works is one of the main reasons for his canonical status within Hispanic studies, although the varied and multifaceted nature of his *oeuvre* also complicates the task of categorising it or identifying clear-cut periods or phases within it. In the early 1930s, Lorca's international fame and recognition — and his economic independence — grew thanks to the success of his poetry and plays in Spain and in America. This final chapter of his life (1930–36), following his momentous trip to the United States and Cuba, is an eventful and multifaceted one. Although the argument for a clear line of evolution in Lorca's oeuvre is controversial and perhaps irrelevant, the innovations in his work and his self-recognition as an artist are palpable in the 1930s.[14] His association with traditional literary styles such as Romanticism and Spanish *Modernismo*, with gypsy culture, and with Andalusian folklore was decidedly challenged through his adoption of elements from the European avant-garde, while his burgeoning national and international acclaim was valid proof of his transient status between the local and the universal.[15] The intense period leading to his abrupt death, just after the outbreak of the Civil War, saw Lorca travelling around the American continent, establishing connections with artists from across the globe and immersing himself in a variety of creative practices, while also receiving praise and influence from artists and scholars both at home and abroad. However, although his work at this time granted him the financial independence from his family he had long sought, the late corpus is far from stable and unified. It contains many unfinished poetic and dramatic projects or works that were never published in his lifetime, and is multifarious in terms of thematic and stylistic elements as well as of popularity and commercial viability.[16]

Starting out as a music student and pianist, Lorca focused on poetry very early in his life and has reached audiences far and wide through his theatre. Not stopping there, he also became a graphic artist and illustrator, a theatre actor and director, a puppet master, a music composer, a literary theorist and a film scriptwriter. In addition, his incursion into multiple creative practices is complemented by the constant crossings of media boundaries within his works. It has often been noted that he was 'a master of visual imagery in his poems and plays [...], characterized by a vibrant use of color, unusual descriptions, and insightful juxtapositions of imagery' (Cavanaugh 1995: 13). His plays make use of lyrical verse or cinematic terms;[17] his poems use musical references and usually play with the musicality and visuality of linguistic images and connections through poetic devices;[18] and many of his drawings fuse and combine language and image.[19]

Lorca's diversification into numerous media can be inscribed in the framework of avant-garde artists working in literature, painting and performance simultaneously at this time. A quintessential example of this multimedia artistic production in early twentieth-century Europe is the French artist Jean Cocteau (1889–1963), whose work bears many resemblances to Lorca's in its negotiation with Surrealist elements and in the similarities found in both their aesthetics. One of many particularities that bring both artists together is Cocteau's transmedial approach to the arts:

> [Cocteau] referred to practically all of his work as 'poésie'. His plays were 'poésie de théâtre' ('theatre poetry'), his novels 'poésie de roman' ('novel poetry'), and his drawings 'poésie graphique' ('graphic poetry'). When talking about his first-ever film, the experimental Le Sang d'un Poète, he once said: 'I used film as a vehicle for poetry in order to show things that I cannot say'. (Phillips 2000: 1117)

Whether Cocteau was a direct influence on Lorca's work is open to debate (although it is documented that Lorca knew Cocteau's work and vice versa), but it is undeniable that both of them were aware that artistic creativity did not have to be limited to only one medium.[20] Like Cocteau's use of film as an alternative means of poetic expression, Lorca claimed that at times his drawings helped him express what he could not put into poetic language.[21] He sought other artistic ways to express and represent his ideas through new channels of transmission, sometimes through many at once. The later Lorca, very much like Cocteau, refused to be stopped by media limits, and the spirit of the avant-garde he experienced at the Residencia de Estudiantes suited him very well in this respect. Recent studies have looked at the 'cross pollination' taking place between the arts and the sciences at the beginning of the twentieth century, revealing that artists and scientists alike became aware of the 'relational, nonrigid nature of the universe' (Gala 2011: 2). The inter-artistic collaborations and intermediality so characteristic of this moment in time became more and more prominent in Lorca's late works, in that he made conscious use of disparate elements associated with particular media and included them into other media.[22] Crossing media boundaries becomes in Lorca's poetics an act of transgression, a process of (re)creation, extracting new aspects from the conventional by disrupting it, but also a way out of the conundrum posed by the limitations of a given artistic medium.

Among the definitions of medium emerging from current discourses and discussions of intermediality, Wolf (2011) proposes a distinction which hinges on the semiotic organisation of information as well as on the cultural conventions that regulate its perception as a medium. In this broad sense, a medium 'is a conventionally and culturally distinct means of communication, specified [...] by particular technical or institutional channels' and 'by the use of one or more semiotic systems' (Wolf 2011: 2). Lorca's poetry can be considered a distinct medium in opposition to his plays, his drawings or his film script, attending to what they transmit and how they transmit it through one or more semiotic systems (language, image) and their technical and institutional differences (materials used, publication or exhibition, adaptation to cinema, potential for performance, etc.). It is also understood, as Elleström suggests, that 'all kinds of sign systems and also specific media productions and works of art must be seen as parts of a very wide field including not least the material, sensorial, spatiotemporal and semiotic aspects' (2010: 4), which he calls the four modalities of media. Intermediality thus implies 'any transgression of boundaries between conventionally distinct media' (Wolf 2011: 3), as well as 'a bridge between medial differences that is founded on medial similarities' (Elleström 2010: 12). In Lorca's later corpus, characterised by its multimodality and, more precisely, by its awareness of media transferences and combinations, there is both a transgressive aspect and an intention to move beyond a reductive or restrictive vision of the arts, favouring instead a sense of fluidity and similarity among them. He combines what is considered 'other' with the normal or conventional, developing a poetics of boundary crossings which establishes a transmedial dialogue among his various works.

In spite of these aesthetic developments and of the global recognition some of his later poems and plays have received (especially his so-called rural trilogy), many of Lorca's post-New York works have been treated by scholars and the public as inaccessible, obscure and difficult to interpret, which has led to their less canonical status within the late corpus.[23] Lorca's later poetry, particularly his poetic collection *Diván del Tamarit* and the sonnet cycle *Sonetos del amor oscuro* (1934–36), are the climactic poetic works in his final years.[24] Due to their posthumous publication and the textual and editorial problems concerning the manuscripts of both works, they continue to be a rather mysterious and sometimes controversial part of Lorca studies, despite revealing Lorca's mature lyrical approach to love experiences, desire and death through poetic forms until then unprecedented in his poetics. Andrew A. Anderson's (1990) seminal work is still the main point of reference on these later works, although there has been an increasing scholarly interest in them in recent years.[25]

Lorca's drawings have recently started to receive the attention of scholars, although they have often served as a tool to illustrate his poetic or dramatic works, especially in the works by Oppenheimer (1986), Cavanaugh (1995) and Plaza Chillón (2008, 2014, 2016, 2019).[26] Lorca's film script *Viaje a la luna* (1929–30), a fascinating intermedial artefact, despite being written around the same time as the much-acclaimed *Poeta en Nueva York*, was lost for most of the twentieth century and not realised as a film until 1998 as part of the centenary celebrations. Scholars like Laffranque (1980, 1982), McDermott (1996), Felten (2005), Puyal (2011), and Anderson (2017) have acknowledged the importance of Lorca's *Viaje a la luna* within the poet's oeuvre, especially in relation to Lorca's negotiation with Surrealism in his late works and the influence that contemporaries Luis Buñuel and Salvador Dalí had on his work.[27] Nonetheless, the film script, assessed in the context of Lorca's later corpus, his transgressive aesthetic theory and ideas of intermediality, is still open to fruitful interpretative possibilities. In parallel, the so-called *teatro irrepresentable*, the term even Lorca's contemporaries used when he first invited some of his friends to private readings of *El público* and *Así que pasen cinco años*, has received more scholarly attention recently and has in the late twentieth and early twenty-first centuries been proved as far from impossible to stage.[28] The innovations and avant-garde aesthetics of these two plays have been corroborated and, being so close in time and aesthetically to Lorca's other later works, they offer a great opportunity for an intermedial dialogue with the poetry and the visual works.

These later works produced through four artistic channels — poetry, theatre, drawing and film — and their particular specificities are, in sum, as representative of Lorca's avant-garde period as the more canonical works, not only because they present formal and thematic innovations to varying degrees, but also insofar as they reveal intermediality as a key aspect of his poetic project and they delve in varied ways into processes of destabilisation and transgression of limits and norms. This study aims to examine them closely and in their own right as well as comparatively in order to show that their importance within the later corpus confirms Lorca's awareness of his growth and confidence as a multifaceted artist.

Lo insólito del duende: The Limits of Desire and Death

An insightful entry into Lorca's final years is his first-person discourse reflecting on his poetics, understood as 'the theory developed by the poets themselves to reflect upon their art form' (Mayhew 2018: 54), a discourse which can be found in his lectures and prose texts as well as within his poetic and dramatic works. In the 1930s, Lorca's sense of authority as an artist and thinker and his awareness of the avant-garde's innovations were instilled into his lessons on poetry and art. The academic lectures, also somewhat marginal within his production, aim to articulate and disseminate his artistic thought and aesthetic theory and are proof of his (self-) recognition. Mayhew (2011a, 2011b, 2018), Quance (2011) and Martínez Hernández (2011) have focused on the lectures to argue for the need to consider the poet's thought and aesthetic theory as fundamental to the study of his poetic and artistic production. *Juego y teoría del duende*, delivered in Buenos Aires on 20 October 1933 at the *Sociedad de Amigos del Arte*, is probably the best-known among them. A clear example of Lorca's mixture of traditional and avant-garde elements and of the local and the universal, the *duende* lecture is an enlightening signpost to his later works. Its lyrical and playful approach and its daring mixture of genres, styles and multiple references to European philosophers, artists and Spanish popular culture situate intermediality and the transgression of spatiotemporal and artistic limits at the centre of the poet's later production. Teasing out these aspects and reassessing Lorca's later corpus offers an opportunity to map his final years as a crucial period in his career.

Stemming from Lorca's original understanding of a notion taken from Andalusian folklore and flamenco culture and used to qualify artistic creation and performance, *duende* is defined as a mysterious and ineffable charm or enchantment, 'encanto misterioso e inefable' (*DRAE* <https://dle.rae.es/duende> [accessed July 2021]), as well as 'an impish household spirit' (Maurer 2007: 35) or naughty sprite.[29] Lorca's appropriation of this seemingly obscure term in *Juego y teoría del duende* serves a double purpose that relates precisely to the two aspects of the title (play and theory) as well as the two senses of the word *duende*. The fantastical and supernatural spirit which in folkloric tales is said to cause mayhem and play tricks on humans mirrors Lorca's play with poetic images to explain and communicate his aesthetic thought. Simultaneously, the performance of *duende* and its perception hinge on its mysterious and malleable nature, shapeshifting and crossing boundaries as the impish creature would change form and hide people's belongings in a mocking game. In this same vein, Lorca sets about explaining *duende* as a simple and lighthearted lesson on poetry but tricks his audience into attending a lecture on twentieth-century aesthetics, European philosophy and intermediality, as well as a poetry recital.

Lorca had travelled to Argentina to attend the production of his play *Bodas de sangre*.[30] From the perspective of a now renowned poet and playwright, he was in an authoritative position to theorise about his own work. However, Lorca's tone in *Juego y teoría del duende* is determined to sound conversational and colloquial to his audience, speaking as a friend or fellow student rather than as a lecturer or professor, a practice he often employed in his public lectures. As Mayhew insightfully notices, 'Lorca prefers to explain his poetics through concrete yet often contradictory metaphors rather than through abstract, systematic reason' (2018: 39). He opens his speech with an anecdote about his student days and the usual boredom he experienced attending tedious lectures at Madrid's Residencia de estudiantes. He establishes two different styles (of lecturing and of making art) inscribed in different times: his own experience at the Residencia, where old Spanish aristocracy attended lectures, is deemed a boring and ash-ridden experience. Against this old time, his lecture is meant to represent a new era: all that is old, conventional and obsolete needs to be replaced by a new aesthetic approach, a new artistic style. The poet thus proclaims *duende* as the spirit of this new era. He situates it in the Spanish peninsula (by locating the land between four Spanish rivers roughly encompassing the whole national territory) but also in Argentina, near the Plata River. The ever-expanding description of *duende* as the lecture progresses gradually opens it up to Europe, to Ancient Greece and Rome and to America, so it ends up losing its original Hispanic specificity and gains a universal aspect. Roaming between the concrete and the abstract, playing with space and time, and jumping across borders and boundaries, Lorca's *duende* honours its shapeshifting trickster ancestor and becomes nothing but elusive and mysterious.

Comparing the old and new styles, the latter led by *duende*, Lorca describes the artistic process as a battle with this mysterious spirit, applying it to poetry and philosophy; to painting, theatre and film; musical performance in singing, dancing and composition;[31] even to the bullfighter's performance in the traditional Spanish *tauromaquia*.[32] He finds a common ground in all these different media and practices: the transgression of norms and canons and of edges and limits, and the physical wounds that cut bodies open. Lorca perceives signs of *duende* in artists like Goya, El Greco, Zurbarán or Picasso in that they broke away from canons and conventions and created new forms never seen before. Zurbarán's use of *chiaroscuro*, for instance, inspired by Caravaggio's paintings and Spanish polychromatic sculpture, created a dramatic sense of mystery and *tenebrismo* in his reproduction of martyr figures.[33] Goya's obscurity and vividness in his depiction of images of horror — which he painted, Lorca claims, using his knees and fists — also exemplify the transgression of canons of beauty in art. Lorca posits that the inspiration required to create an artwork does not stem from imaginary external forces like angels or muses, but from the physical and spiritual violence that *duende* brings about within the artist.

A key notion that Lorca develops in the lecture is a transference and collaboration among the arts, a wish to contest the clear-cut distinctions usually ascribed to them:

> todas las artes son capaces de duende, pero donde encuentra más campo, como es natural, es en la música, en la danza y en la poesía hablada, ya que estas necesitan un cuerpo vivo que interprete, porque son formas que nacen y mueren de modo perpetuo y alzan sus contornos sobre un presente exacto. (OC III: 311)

In spite of his emphasis on performative media in *Juego y teoría del duende*, his claim that all arts are capable of acquiring a poetic dimension which can transgress norms and cross boundaries, spatiotemporal, corporeal and artistic, is a groundbreaking notion marking the precepts of his later works. Crucially, this idea is also applicable to media which could be considered less performative: I shall argue that some of the still unexamined specificities of his poetry, his drawings, his plays and his film script will show Lorca's queering of limits and boundaries, to which the intermedial use of poetic expression adds a further layer of transgression and novelty.

Death, another key aspect of the lecture, is ubiquitous in Lorca's *oeuvre*. From the elegiac tone of some of his long poems to the pervasive tragedy in his plays and his constant use of ominous and deadly symbology, Lorca's production shows an intimate and unique involvement with mortality. Virtually every work devoted to the study of Lorca has examined or mentioned death to some extent.[34] One of the most relevant to this study is an early work by Salinas which asserts that 'the vision of life and man that gleams and shines forth in Lorca's work is founded on death. Lorca understands, feels life through death' (1962: 102). In *Juego y teoría del duende*, Lorca establishes an intimate relation between art and life, but that relation includes a clear awareness of — and even a need for — mortality. Yet the link between these two poles is far from clear-cut in his works. Recently, Óscar Enrique Muñoz (2013) wrote an extensive philosophical-poetic study on the many meanings of *duende*, its origins and pervasiveness in Spanish literature, and some of its articulations across Lorca's production. He suggests that Lorca's *duende* is a poetics of the limit and the liminal (Muñoz 2013: 49), of desire as the moment of transit — which remains perpetually suspended in time — from life to death and from the virtual idea to the created form. *Duende*'s transgressions and boundary-crossings are characterised by an acute sensibility towards the limits of desire and mortality.[35] The supposed clear-cut distinction between living and dying, pleasure and pain, or love and destruction is heavily distorted and destabilised. The Lorquian aesthetics of death relates to the immanence of mortality in human imagination and to the poetic force that death's interrelation with human life (especially with the impulses related to desire) brings about. Any symbol of life processes and energies acquires a more powerful contrast when confronted with death and that coalescence of radical opposites is sought as a factor of subversion and novelty. What Lorca calls *lo insólito* encapsulates what an artist must achieve with their work. He wants to create poetic images that can offer unprecedented associations of meaning, drawing on aspects of reality that, beautiful or gruesome, are familiar in their evocation of destruction and creation but add new aspects that have not been experienced before and will never be repeated.

Perhaps the use of the term *duende* in close relation to flamenco culture,[36] a sense that still survives today, has not only contributed to enhance Lorca's folkloric roots and Andalusian flavour worldwide, but has also led to the overlooking of his extended use of the term to encompass all the arts and transcend specific genres and styles.[37] In his lecture Lorca created a 'new aesthetic category' which unites 'life with artistic creation' (Martínez Hernández 2011: 94) in that it shows the psychic and existential effects that art can have on an audience. Attending to both the thought processes behind an artwork and the performative aspects of its transmission and reception, there is an emphasis on what art *does* rather than what it *is*. On performance rather than essence. In Quance's view, 'it is precisely because "duende" names an event and not a thing in the world that it is elusive and that Lorca himself did not strictly speaking represent it in a text but, rather, suggested its effects' (2011:182). What *duende* does, however, is bring life and death together through art.

As such, *duende* implies a transgression of established norms by reinterpreting a certain work of art or style or purposefully distorting or reconfiguring an artistic canon or model.[38] It is a quality ascribed to the creator of a work of art, an inherent force which possesses and takes hold of the artist's body to infuse in it the capacity to produce the artistic work. Additionally, it is a quality that *must* be sensorily perceived by the reader/spectator/viewer for the work to be deemed good or worthy of being an art form. Lorca describes this interaction between the artist and the spectator as the necessary qualitative condition of creative practices, which must offer immediacy, vivid sensory stimulation and an aspect of novelty. The artefact created or performed under the influence of *duende* is alive but short-lived and ephemeral, a 'forma viva' which as a result is faced with an imminent death. Each act of performance aided by *duende* 'rechaza toda la dulce geometría aprendida, [...] rompe los estilos' (*OC* III: 310). In breaking the norms associated with a creative medium, the artist performatively rearticulates that normative system and creates something unprecedented, shocking or subversive, which will emerge as anti-normative, odd or, indeed, *queer*. Lorca's poetics favours the creation of bodies, personae and images which cannot quite fit into the normative, but whose identities fluctuate and metamorphose, constantly mutating to adopt a state of liminality or becoming. The relationship between life and death, being and non-being, is therefore a *queer* one.

Duende acts as a dual desire, or a dual drive in the psychoanalytical sense, towards life and death. Lorca scholars have often acknowledged the relevance of psychoanalytical discourse in their analyses of the poet's work, especially in the recurrent interrelation of desire and mortality: the notion of *eros* and *thanatos* in Sigmund Freud's terminology.[39] While the purpose of this study is not to offer an exhaustive psychoanalytical reading of Lorca's poetic discourse based on Freud's theories, the ubiquity and interweaving nature of desire and death in Lorca's late poetics requires a careful consideration of this trope in its wider context.[40]

Lorca explores the notion of the Freudian drives in relation to artistic expression, the sense of selfhood and erotic desire.[41] The Lorquian *eros*, associated with pleasure, sexual desire and sensory perception, is presented as an overpowering human instinct transcending and superseding ideas of sex, gender and self-identification. *Thanatos* coalesces with *eros* in that the poet often longs for a state between life and death, for a wound bringing the limits of both together. The intertwining of *eros* and *thanatos* conveys *duende*'s liminality.[42] In *duende*'s search for *lo insólito*, desire and mortality acquire a prominent aesthetic stance and their values are interrelated and subverted. A mortal yet regenerative wound signifies the circular and spiralling process in which desire is always inscribed.

Queer Spatiotemporal Transgressions

Because Lorca's poetics creates and exposes transgressions of limits through artistic performance, it can be read as a queer strategy. It underlines the constructed and normative nature of art, especially in its articulation of the supposedly rigid limits of life and death and in its ostensible representation of stable identities. *Duende* figures the paradoxical coalescence and incoherency between desire as a creative impulse and a destructive one, the site in which the seemingly linear progression from life to death gets disrupted and the apparently discrete nature of bodies, genders and sexualities gets blurred.

To examine Lorca's later works in light of the poetics of *duende* and its queerness, I will have recourse to a number of contemporary queer approaches. Hinging on its oppositional nature and its state of constant formation, queer's performative and transformative aspects relate to a great extent to Lorca's poetics: both performatively challenge and transgress established norms that promote fixed visions of identity, the body and existence. Lorca's poetics — understood as *poiesis* or the creative production of a work of art through whichever medium — tries to contest this fixity by destabilising subjects and objects and presenting them as fragmented, conflictive and in constant mutation. As a result, the poetic images through the lens of *duende* fail to be categorised as canonical or conventional: they produce shock and appear queer and unfamiliar, *lo insólito*, due to their anti-normative nature.

Queerness, as Lee Edelman characterises it in his application of Lacanian psychoanalytical discourse to queer theory, insists on '[opposing] itself to the logic of opposition' (2004: 4) and therefore on negating the very system from which it emerges as different, aberrant or abnormal. In destabilising norms relating to bodies, genders and sexualities, the queer exposes both the regulatory power and the constructed nature of normative discourses. In parallel, *duende*'s creative function implies a process of constant (trans)formation and redefinition of norms and whatever falls from the norm. Always mutable and liminal, this is a process which never ends, a desire that is never fulfilled and a wound that never heals. *Duende*, in its cyclical destruction/recreation of (hetero)normativity through its never-sealed wound, actively subverts the very notions of stable identities and meanings, suggesting ever-changing new aspects emerging 'not as innate or essential but as always in construction and in conflict with its environment' (Kramer 2008: 15). Bodies are fragmented and face destruction, but they are also recreated and reassembled, enlivened by their wounds, eluding stasis and ontological stability.

The emergence of the queer will suggest 'a refusal — the appropriately perverse refusal that characterises queer theory — of every substantialization of identity, which is always oppositionally defined, and, by extension, of history as linear narrative [...] in which meaning succeeds at revealing itself — *as itself* — through time' (Edelman 2004: 4). Lorca's *duende* creates subjects and objects in constant formation, defying spatiotemporal fixity. Rather than presenting essential aspects or immutable identities, they revel in endless metamorphoses and are always in the process of becoming. Simultaneously being destructured or disintegrated, wounded or about to die, they swiftly become something other and shape-shift in a constant cycle of regeneration. Any substantiation of identity is therefore difficult if not impossible.

Edelman's theorisation of queerness in its inextricable relation to temporality, especially futurity, and death, will be an invaluable framework in this study's analysis of Lorca's later works. *No Future: Queer Theory and the Death Drive* (2004), drawing on Lacan, positions the queer as the surplus which evades the 'reproductive futurism' of heteronormativity and thus negates the possibility of future as the eventual realisation of meaning as complete and absolute, instead standing for the Lacanian death drive.[43] The foreclosure of any possibility of fulfilment and therefore of the meaning promised by that fantasy of fulfilment announces death as the point of inflection towards which the open wound tends.[44] The Lacanian twin drives that lead the subject to both libidinal fulfilment and self-destruction pose a threat to the very ideas of identity and meaning, and therefore to the construction and validity of sexual identities. Indeed, Lorca's poetics not only disrupts norms of gender and sexual desire; it also questions the reliability of language to produce any meaning which is stable or immutable, in turn questioning the linearity of time and its supposedly stable and continuous succession. Life does not necessarily lead to death. This supposed linear journey is disrupted and reversed, and at times becomes cyclical or remains crystallised or unresolved.

The intrinsic relationship between subjectivity/identity and temporality has been considered one of the main issues concerning queer theory in recent years. McCallum and Tuhkanen conclude that 'with the notion of queerness strategically and critically posited not as an identity or a substantive mode of being but as a way of becoming, temporality is necessarily already bound up in the queer' (2011: 8). Issues of subjectivity in Lorca's complex representation of bodies and identities and of temporality in the spatiotemporal breaches and discontinuities find a point of confluence in *duende*'s never-ending transgression of norms. This resonates with the performative complexities of queerness. José Esteban Muñoz, drawing on Edelman's ideas on futurity and queer time, argues that 'straight time tells us that there is no future but the here and now of our everyday life. The only futurity promised is that of reproductive majoritarian heterosexuality' and insists that 'we gain a greater conceptual and theoretical leverage if we see queerness as something that is not yet here' (2009: 22). This implies a glimpse of queerness in futurity, not in Edelman's reproductive futurism, but in the imagining, the *fantasy*, the impulse towards a horizon of being beyond the here and now, or in that sense of becoming what is yet to come. Muñoz sees the need for queerness as a utopia, a fantasy of the not-yet-realised but potentially realisable. Lorca's representation of desire as a perpetually unsealed wound, pointing towards the potentiality of death and the potential recreation that death can bring, is a sign of a queer fantasy. The wound opens a space in which both death and life are potentialities, reversible forces that never get resolved but escape the linearity of time and remain cyclical and liminal, although inevitably elusive and mysterious.

Duende's Play in the Later Corpus

Approaching queerness as the performative transgression of normativity, this study reassesses some of the key functions of *duende* as a queer poetics of boundary transgressions, offering close readings of the later works which expose queering modes of fluidity and limit destabilisation. The book concentrates on the poetic works *Diván del Tamarit* and *Sonetos del amor oscuro* (1934–36), the plays *El público* (1930) and *Así que pasen cinco años* (1931), the drawings from 1930 to 1936, and the film script *Viaje a la luna* (1929–30), arguing that *duende*'s functions are articulated via transgressions of the notions of sex, gender and sexual identity; notions of desire, death and spatiotemporal stability; and notions of media representation, multimodality and intermediality.

The first chapter of the book is divided into two parts corresponding to each of Lorca's final poetic works. *Poiesis*, understood as the creative production of artefacts with aesthetic value, applies etymologically to poetry, the medium which Lorca favoured the most throughout his *oeuvre*. *Juego y teoría del duende* speaks of the poetic image as the basis of the artistic task, the starting point which Lorca opens up to further media, so in this study Lorca's poetry will also be the starting point. In *Diván del Tamarit*, the aloof and indeterminate poetic voice presents glimpses of a beloved who remains perpetually elusive and difficult to identify because of his/her ungendered and fragmentary identity. The poet's desire beats intensely, but the poetic voice resists the possibility of fulfilment, aligning *eros* with *thanatos* in an interrelated and ambivalent cycle of pleasure and pain defying the linearity of time and the logical route from life to death. Spatiotemporal disruptions, I argue, mirror the queering of bodies and sensory perceptions, signalling the poet's realisation that identity is constantly destructured and recreated, in a cyclical process of metamorphosis. Drawing on Edelman and Muñoz and ideas of queer futurity and utopia, I conclude that the poet and the beloved are forced to inhabit a liminal space in which ontological and spatiotemporal coordinates are suspended, unintelligible and unnameable, where the death drive signalled by the queer emerges to announce an impossible fantasy yet to come in which limits and norms cease to exist.

In *Sonetos del amor oscuro*, Lorca's final poetic project, I suggest that 'obscure' encapsulates the mysterious, inarticulable and norm-transgressing qualities of desire explored in the late poetry. The love in the sonnet cycle is neither clearly homosexual nor heterosexual, precisely because gender indeterminacy, fluidity and reversibility of roles abound. This permeability reveals the poet and the beloved entwined in a simultaneously erotic and destructive relationship as ambivalent as their elusive (sexual) identities. *Chiaroscuro* is recurrent in the imagery Lorca creates, reinforcing the pleasure/pain and being/non-being reversibility and the subversion of tropes taken from the Petrarchan and Spanish Mystical traditions, both of which are reappropriated by Lorca to create scenes in which the limits of life and death, sexual desire and spiritual suffering become destabilised and blurred. Central to Lorca's poetic works is the representation of the human body and the importance of the five senses. As this study will show, this is also true of his other creative practices and plays a prominent role in his aesthetics, as it becomes in the late works a vehicle to explore intermediality and transgress the limits of desire and death. He claimed that a poet must be a master of the five bodily senses (OC III: 229) and after his visit to New York and his experimentations with avant-garde artistic practices — *Poeta en Nueva York*'s free verse, and Surrealist or Expressionist elements are examples — he invented unprecedented ways to articulate these in his poems and prompted his increased practice of other media.

The second chapter explores the staging of both spatiotemporal and sexual instability in Lorca's most modernist plays, *Así que pasen cinco años* and *El público*. Written against the backdrop of an attempted renovation of the Spanish stage, these two works deal boldly with heterodox sexualities, presenting in shocking and innovative ways characters whose desires challenge binary identifications and instead embrace fluidity and reversibility. Meta-theatrical devices are used profusely so as to inscribe these queer identities within aesthetic debates considering the unstable interrelation of life and theatre and the ability the latter has to reveal, disguise or tap into the inner desires and identities of those involved in the theatrical experience. In *Así que pasen cinco años*, I argue that temporality is disrupted and manipulated to show the characters' efforts to delay and eschew the fulfilment of desire in order to escape the linearity of heteronormative time and the imminence of reproductive futurism and mortality. In *El público*, a conflicted view of theatre and reality is represented, mirroring the conflict brought about by the performative nature of gender and sexual identity. Queer visibility serves in the play to challenge a unitary vision of identity, be it sexual or ontological, proposing instead that multiplicity and fragmentation are more suitable principles to approach existence and its relation to theatre.

In the third chapter, I carry out close readings of Lorca's drawings from his late period in their own right as plastic poems, drawing on Bakhtin's ideas on the grotesque as the convergence of life and death. Lorca redefines in his graphic works some of the conventions associated with portraits, shifting the gaze to male figures and foregrounding unsettling details of corporeal fragmentation, bodily issue and fusions of human with animal and floral motifs. The beguiling 'Venus (Agua sexual)' presents a female body in a grotesque state of physical disintegration which conjoins the genital issue of blood with sexual desire and pain, while the spine-chilling 'Solo la muerte' depicts a monstrous figure superseding sex and gender identification and questioning the logic of sensory perception and life/death differentiation — which resonates with Lorca's liminal characters from *El público* (Desnudo rojo) and *Viaje a la luna* (Hombre de las venas). In his final drawings, severed hands, arrows and abstract human and animal parts articulate the wound, bleeding and the piercing of flesh as signs of a crystallised liminal moment in which life and death coalesce through the aesthetic pleasure and interrogation allowed by visual poetry.

In the fourth chapter I examine Lorca's film script *Viaje a la luna*, arguing that its tableau structure creates an anti-narrative in which spatiotemporal transgression leads to a spectacle of death which encircles the juxtaposed images and characters in a cycle of interwoven humour, horror, sexual desire and violence. The close reading of the film script will take into account the innovations Lorca had discovered in the early cinema he experienced when studying in Madrid, especially his homage to Buster Keaton in one of his earlier short plays. The correlations between *Viaje a la luna* and other early films also attest to Lorca's negotiations with the avant-garde and his appropriation of cinematic elements to recreate Lorquian imagery via the film medium, to make poetic images 'watchable'. Drawing on ideas of the body, the 'cinema of attractions' and Lorca's avant-garde aesthetics, I suggest that the film script repositions the queering of limits as a poetic-cinematic montage in which erotic desire and death are inscribed in a circle, a cyclical journey to the moon, leading them only to each other and leaving the potential spectator in a state of uncertainty, shock and disorientation.

The fifth and final chapter looks at the four media examined in a broader, comparative sense. The close readings focus on the recurrent word–image interactions which occur within the later works as well as on aspects derived from Lorca's aesthetics which are articulated in specific ways through each medium and transmedially; particularly motifs like roots, hands, roses and circular objects and processes like fluidity, doublings and fusions. The calligrams, *commedia dell' arte* characters, and the particularly intermedial and grotesque drawing 'Muerte de Santa Rodegunda' will offer glimpses into Lorca's poetic fluidity, not only roaming across media limits but suggesting that identity itself is too unstable and fluid to be ever delimited.

Despite the perceived complexities and indeterminacies of some of Lorca's later works, it is in the period following his New York phase where the poet achieved a clearer sense of self-assurance in his aesthetics. Following a deep existential crisis and a period of self-doubt preceding his journey overseas, with his multiple creative practices Lorca acquired new avant-garde tastes and greater recognition in the 1930s. *Juego y teoría del duende* encapsulates his aesthetic authority and epitomises the principles of his poetic project, which at this stage is no longer restricted to a single medium, but roams across poetry, theatre and the visual arts and confidently combines traditional and folkloric elements and modern formal elements and imagery. If Lorca believed that all media can participate of *duende*'s queering function and become 'formas vivas' with aesthetic value for the artist and the audience, it is worth exploring how all these media can effect *duende*'s transgressions in their own unique ways and in relation to one another.

This study ultimately acknowledges that Lorca's iconic status and uniqueness are still paired with his many facets and complexities: his legacy lives on, but he remains a figure full of ambiguities and mysteries. I will examine how the queer subjects and objects Lorca creates and their metaphysical mysteries become poetic artefacts with aesthetic value, offering the artist and the reader/spectator a substantial sensory and spiritual experience. The principles articulated in the theory of *duende* and their play in Lorca's later works will help to map the poet's aesthetics within the context of critical and biographical analyses of his later period. In addition, by focusing on the specific articulations of Lorca's poetics through his filmic, poetic, theatrical and graphic works and their intermedial correlations, this book will also propose a reassessment of his later years through the queer lens. The more 'mysterious' and challenging post-New York works must form an integral part of the vast scholarly corpus on Lorca's production so as to give the poet's entire artistic project the recognition it deserves.

Notes to the Introduction

1. The Casa-Museo Federico García Lorca in Valderrubio, Granada opened to the public in 1998, letting customers explore the space Lorca inhabited in his childhood and the personal items preserved by his family. Events in Granada, Fuente Vaqueros and Madrid, where the then President of Spain José María Aznar gave a speech at La Residencia de Estudiantes, launched one of the biggest cultural tributes ever held in Spain. A helicopter flying over Granada 'bombarded' the city with a rain of one hundred thousand leaflets with Lorca's poems, an international

conference took place there in May, and an archive in Fuente Vaqueros — the Centro de Documentación y Estudios Lorquianos — was inaugurated (León-Sotelo and Ruiz Anton 1998).

2. Worldwide adaptations of Lorca's theatre coincided with the centenary celebrations: *Bodas de sangre* was staged in Japan and *Yerma* in Egypt around that period (Doggart 1999: 19). Large conferences on Lorca and his legacy took place at Cambridge University and in Newcastle-upon-Tyne, the latter being part of the multimedia 'Lorca Fiesta', held at the Newcastle Playhouse and considered the 'largest event outside Spain to commemorate the centenary' (Doggart 1999: 19).

3. Almodóvar's *La mala educación* (2004) and his Oscar-winning *Todo sobre mi madre* (1999) both reference Lorca's life and works, while the recent *La Novia* (2015) is Ortiz's cinematic adaptation of Lorca's play *Bodas de sangre* and received two Goya awards amongst several other accolades. *Little Ashes* (2009), directed by Paul Morrison and based on a screenplay by UK screenwriter Goslett, recasts Lorca's friendship and love affair with Salvador Dalí in the years of La Residencia de Estudiantes in Madrid. Cuban American playwright Nilo Cruz, widely acclaimed and winner of the Pulitzer Prize for Drama, wrote the plays *Lorca in a Green Dress* (2003) and *Beauty of the Father* (2006), both featuring Lorca as a character.

4. *Yerma* ran until the summer of 2016 at the Young Vic theatre in London (Clapp 2016); while more recently they staged an adaptation of *Bodas de sangre* (2019). *Amor de don Perlimplín con Belisa en su jardín* was staged at La Seca theatre in Barcelona in February 2017 (Pérez Pons 2017).

5. Rodriguez Zapatero's government passed the Historical Memory Law on 31 October 2007, followed by an excavation of the Alfacar area near Granada in 2009, lacking definitive results (Tremlett 2009). In 2014, there was another dig in a neighbouring area carried out by archaeologist Javier Navarro, historian Miguel Caballero and experts from the University of Nottingham such as Stephen Roberts, but the exact location of Lorca's remains is still shrouded in mystery (Junquera 2014). A new dig was completed in October 2016, still with no conclusive results (Ruiz Mantilla 2016, 2017). There are rumours and speculation among the area's local inhabitants that Lorca's remains cannot be found because at some point they were disinterred and transferred to a safe and secret location by his family members and friends in order to be respectfully preserved and to ensure that nothing will ever be built on that ground. See the recent documentary *Bones of Contention* (2017), exploring LGBTQ repression under the Franco regime with the backdrop of Lorca's lost remains as its starting point and narrative thread.

6. Both Smith (1998a) and Wright (2000) note Lorca's power to seduce both general audiences and scholars and biographers working within Lorca studies.

7. According to Garlinger, 'the sudden appearance of a clandestine edition of the *Sonetos del amor oscuro* in 1983 irrevocably opened the closet door on Federico García Lorca's sexuality. Mailed from Granada by anonymous sources to 250 literary and cultural critics, the clandestine version confirmed that a manuscript still existed. As a result, the García Lorca family was compelled to publish an "official version", which appeared in *ABC* on 17 March 1984. The accompanying commentaries by Miguel García-Posada, Francisco Giner de los Ríos and Fernando Lázaro Carreter were anxious to assert that the word "oscuro" was not a reference to homosexual desire: they called attention to the fact that the gender of the poet's lover is not specified' (Garlinger 2002: 709–10). In his foreword to Sahuquillo's 2007 work on Lorca and the culture of male homosexuality, Mira shares an anecdote explaining the aggressive hostility he received after the publication of his own book by a well-known Lorca specialist (Mira 2007: 5). The latter was precisely taking issue with Mira's mention of the controversy around the publication of *Sonetos del amor oscuro* and of the negativity and efforts by some scholars to 'silence' the perceived homoeroticism of the collection (Mira 2004: 252–53).

8. Both Binding and Sahuquillo propose innovative and insightful close readings of Lorca's works, hinging especially on the analysis of homosexuality and homoeroticism as crucial interpretative principles to understand Lorca's imagery and symbolism. Herrero explores Lorca's homosexuality as the backdrop to his development as a young artist in the early twentieth century. The many allusions to childhood and offspring in Lorca's work are read by Binding as a fundamental trope revealing Lorca's awareness of the homophobic opprobrium destined towards those individuals incapable of biological reproduction (see Chapter 2 for a discussion of

this motif in Lorca's plays). Kramer (2008) draws on gender and queer theorists such as Judith Butler and David Halperin to articulate what he calls 'queer metaphor' in Lorca's poems, but, in a similar vein to Sahuquillo, he focuses on Lorca's endeavour to encode and hide his homosexual identity in his poetry for fear of prosecution or opprobrium. When Sahuquillo's work was first published in Spanish in 1991, homosexuality was deemed 'unspeakable' in Lorca scholarship, and his work was pioneering in the attempt to redress this unfair treatment. He finds in Lorca's letters 'the fear and desire to express something hidden and, also, the recurring appearance of motifs and themes relative to silence and to secrets in his poetic work', concluding that these phenomena are 'signs and signals of a discourse related to the expression of homosexual love' (2007: 25), inscribed in what he calls a *homosexual culture*.

9. In his biography *Federico García Lorca*, Gibson gives an account of Dalí's ambiguous and half-hearted admission in an interview that 'one day [he] gave in to [Lorca's] desires'. The painter described his relationship with Lorca as very intense and special, but he was conflicted about and struggled to delve too much into its sexual aspects: 'We tried it...It hurt me and we had to stop' (Gibson 1987: 440).

10. Following in the footsteps of the seminal work by Alberto Mira, *De Sodoma a Chueca: Una historia cultural de la homosexualidad en España en el siglo XX* (2004), a recent study by Ramón Martínez, *Lo nuestro sí que es mundial* (2017), critically traces the history and contexts of the LGBTQ movement in Spain. Some thoughts and evidence are presented in relation to queer groups and circles in the early twentieth century, including Lorca's circle of friends and intellectuals who often discussed their sense of community and their queerness in various ways (2017: 52). Also, see Ian Gibson's *Caballo azul de mi locura: Lorca y el mundo gay* (2009).

11. Cleminson and Vázquez García examine Álvaro Retana's (1890–1970) works, questioning whether we can consider the Spanish author 'a kind of precursor of today's queer theory', and adding that his work is 'the literary form of a tradition that viewed sex between men as a practice rather than an identity' (2007: 275). They also mention Lorca and some of his contemporaries, who were part of a more or less established homosexual subculture and who, like Lorca, alluded to issues of sexual heterodoxy more or less overtly in their literary works.

12. Bonaddio notices that Lorca's poetic world and his biography could be confused, but insists that 'just as there is little to be had from applying the facts of his personal life to the sonnets, his poetry in general also resists such an approach', recognising that it is Lorca the poet who 'engages with and enters his texts' (2010: 196).

13. Mayhew acknowledges the pervasive tendency by Lorca critics to treat Lorca as a 'poeta tonto', that is, not belonging to the intellectual elite of Spanish poet-thinkers associated with authors such as Luis Cernuda, María Zambrano or José Ángel Valente, among others (2018: 20–22). In parallel, he notices the mystification and sacralisation of Lorca by critics and the public, inextricably linked to his status as a 'hypercanonical author' (2018: 29) as well as to his aforementioned status as Republican martyr.

14. Lorca's brother, poet, lecturer, literary critic and historian Francisco García Lorca, was convinced that a 'clear line of evolution' in Lorca's work was extremely difficult, if not impossible, to establish, and that he went through a 'continuous metamorphosis' (1989: 232) as an artist. McDermid suggests that arguing for an 'illusory progressive development in García Lorca's thinking' is futile, proposing instead that 'the poet's writings throughout his career are driven by the same overarching concerns' (2007: 4).

15. Bonaddio notices a 'tension between the poet's adoption of a romantic rhetoric and his increasing awareness of new modes of expression; between his attraction to the sincere expression of lyric verse and his movement towards more impersonal modes — a move necessary for him to be counted amongst his contemporaries' (2010: 18).

16. See, for instance, Laffranque (1987), Hurtado Hernández (2017) and Torres Nebrera (1999).

17. *La casa de Bernarda Alba* (1936) is subtitled 'un documental fotográfico'; *El paseo de Buster Keaton* (1928) refers to cinema as a medium, to the Hollywood industry and to film celebrities; and *Bodas de sangre* (1934) appends a lullaby sung by the characters and includes a long lyrical passage recited by the Moon.

18. Notorious examples are the use of the musical term *suite* to refer to many of the poetic sequences

composed by Lorca in the early 1920s, as well as the various musical links found in the poetic collections *Canciones* (1927) or *Poema del cante jondo* (1931), which were probably inspired by Lorca's musical training and close collaboration with composer Manuel de Falla. In her monograph *In the Light of Contradiction*, Quance (2010) examines these three poetic compositions as an early project for a poetic cycle, emphasising the relation between Lorca's exploration of desire and the intermedial impulses derived from the links between poetry and music.

19. The use of free verse in *Poeta en Nueva York* allows the poet to create juxtapositions of disconnected images in contiguous and rapid visual sequences, evidencing the awareness of linguistic sound and rhythmic connections: 'Lo que importa es esto: hueco. Mundo solo. Desembocadura. | Alba no. Fábula inerte. | Sólo esto: Desembocadura', from 'Navidad en el Hudson', ll. 32–34 (1988b: 150); '¡Qué esfuerzo!. | ¡Qué esfuerzo del caballo | por ser perro! | ¡Qué esfuerzo del perro por ser golondrina!', from 'Muerte', ll. 1–4 (1988b: 183).

20. Morris relays Lorca's impressions after seeing Cocteau's *Le sang d'un poète* in 1932 (Morris 1980: 123) and Cocteau wrote a poem to commemorate Lorca years after his death, in 1953 (Morales Peco 2000: 22).

21. In a letter to art critic Sebastián Gasch dated 8 September 1928, Lorca explains his intermedial creative process to his friend: 'Ahora empiezo a escribir y a dibujar poesías como ésta que le envío dedicada. Cuando un asunto es demasiado largo o tiene poéticamente una emoción manida, lo resuelvo con los lápices. Esto me alegra y divierte de manera extraordinaria' (Cavanaugh 1995: 20).

22. Schröter (2011) argues that in the context of intermediality, it can be recognised that 'media do not exist disconnected from one another' (2011: 2). Rather than offer a univocal and general definition, he proposes a series of discourses based on scholarly debates and models which refer to different approaches to issues of intermediality. In light of this, three of them are of special relevance to the purposes of this book: 'formal (or transmedial) intermediality'; 'transformational intermediality'; and 'ontological intermediality'. Formal intermediality or transmediality is a concept 'based on formal structures not "specific" to one medium but found in different media'; 'transformational intermediality' is a model centred around the 'representation of one medium through another medium', which in turn leads to 'ontological intermediality: a model suggesting that media always already exist in relation to other media' (2011: 2).

23. For some time, it became conventional among scholars to speak of *Yerma*, *Bodas de sangre* and *La casa de Bernarda Alba* as a climactic trilogy, although there is evidence that Lorca's intention was to include *La destrucción de Sodoma*, today unfinished, as the third play. Furthermore, critics have questioned the idea that the three tragedies comprised a major project towards which Lorca was striving, since some of the testimonies before his death point to his preference for the more experimental 'impossible' plays (*Así que pasen cinco años* and *El público*, as well as the unfinished *Comedia sin título*, also known as *El sueño de la vida*), which he considered the 'real core' of his theatrical output (Wright 2007a: 42). For a fuller account, see Andrew Anderson's article 'The Strategy of García Lorca's Dramatic Composition 1930–1936' (1986b: 211–29).

24. Mario Hernández considers *Diván del Tamarit* 'una de las expresiones más acabadas y complejas de Federico García Lorca, además de uno de los grandes libros de la poesía europea de este siglo' (García Lorca 1981: 10), while Anderson claims that 'el *Diván del Tamarit* es sin lugar a dudas la colección más notable [...] Es decir, sencillamente, que el *Diván* es el libro de poemas más importante de Lorca que se fecha durante los últimos años de su vida'. (García Lorca 1988a: 14). As for the group of eleven poems known as *Sonetos del amor oscuro*, they are believed to be part of an incomplete collection of sonnets which Lorca could not finish in his lifetime, but which show his wish to stay abreast of contemporary poetic trends as young poets were now returning to traditional literary forms such as the sonnet after experimenting with avant-garde forms and creative practices.

25. Anderson (1990) examines Lorca's final poetic collections from his trip to New York until his death. His textual analyses attend primarily to the specificities of Lorca's imagery and symbology, drawing from the influence of Ancient Greece and Rome, the Renaissance, Romanticism and Arabic literature, and some biographical and historical accounts. Federico Bonaddio (2010) draws on the notion of self-consciousness to analyse Lorca's poetic collections

as a whole, devoting his last chapter to Lorca's late works. Barón Palma (1990) and Newton (1992) pay attention to *Diván del Tamarit* in some depth, while López Castellón (1981) focuses on *Sonetos del amor oscuro* within his analysis of death in Lorca's poetry.

26. Oppenheimer's (1986) and Cavanaugh's (1995) works analyse Lorca's graphic works in close relation to his poems, his theatre plays and his life. Their works offer insightful connections between some motifs in the drawings to Lorca's poems, especially those of hands and of the figure of Saint Sebastian (Oppenheimer 1986) and the reading of arabesques in both Lorca's late drawings and his late poems (Cavanaugh 1995). Cavanaugh (1995) insists that the purpose of analysing the drawings in their own right will 'provide maps of [Lorca's] thought' and 'new insight into Lorca's poems, creating a space in which they may dialogue with one another and allowing this dialogue to inform our perception and interpretation' (1995: 35). Further studies include David K. Loughran's (1978), Felicia Hardison Londré's (1984), and Estelle Irizarry's (1984), all focusing on the relationship between the drawings and Lorca's poetry and plays.

27. Puyal (2011) describes the interest that cinema had awoken amongst Spanish artists, especially in the context of the Residencia de Estudiantes in Madrid, and the knowledge and wish for experimentation many of them had about the film medium. Felten (2005) draws on the many correlations between Lorca's *Viaje a la luna* and Buñuel and Dalí's *Un chien andalou*, examining the Surrealist structural and thematic elements common to both.

28. *El público* had its widely acclaimed first staging in Spanish at the Centro Dramático Nacional's María Guerrero Theatre in Madrid in 1986, directed by Lluís Pasqual. For an in-depth account and examination of this production, see Smith (1998a: 118–36).

29. The word originates in the Spanish expression *duen de la casa* or *dueño de la casa*, and supposedly denotes 'un espíritu fantástico que habita, traveseando, en algunas viviendas, y que suele presentarse con figura de viejo o de niño' (Muñoz 2013: 12). Sarah Wright (2000) analysed the 'trickster-function' present in Lorca's plays, a phenomenon intimately related to the tricking or 'trasteador' aspect of *duende* inherited from folk tradition. The influence of the *commedia dell'arte* on Lorca's literary and visual works, palpable in his use of stock figures like Pierrot or Harlequin, may provide a further source of origin (see George 1995).

30. The production, which had had its first run at the Maipo Theatre, reopened with Lola Membrives at the bigger Avenida Theatre for its second run on 25 October 1933: '*Blood Wedding* played for several months and made a huge amount of money for the poet, to whom Lola Membrives and her husband had agreed to pay ten per cent of the takings. Lorca's letters home showed to what an extent such success was boosting his ego' (Gibson 1990: 368).

31. Lorca cites Brailowsky's piano performances of Chopin or Darius Milhaud's innovative use of polytonality, amongst others (OC III: 306–09).

32. In his exploration of bullfighting, Lorca compares the *Fiesta Nacional* with a religious ritual or a mass. The adoration and sacrifice to a deity and the imagery prominent in both scenarios is physical violence, blood spilled in sacrifice and the effects that the wound has on the audience and the ritual itself. In a Roman Catholic mass, Christ's blood sacrifice symbolises the heroic deed of the saviour and martyr, while in a bullfight, the protagonist is also a hero who battles the animal to death and risks his life in pursuit of fame and glory. In both cases, the violent and gory scene causes admiration in the audience, it produces an emotional response which Lorca equates with the aesthetic pleasure of art.

33. *Tenebrismo*, or Tenebrism, is a baroque pictorial style derived from the work of Caravaggio especially, based on the use of stark contrasts of light and shadow. In the *Diccionario de civilización y cultura españolas*, Quesada Marco defines it as: 'Estilo pictórico barroco basado en el empleo sistemático de fuertes contrastes de luces y de sombras en los que las partes iluminadas resaltan con intensidad. El tenebrismo español fue el resultado de la fusión de las técnicas del claroscuro empleadas por los pintores naturalistas — Morales, Navarrete, Roelas, Herrera, Cotán — con las de Caravaggio. El estilo y las técnicas tenebristas triunfan plenamente en la pintura de Francisco Ribalta (1564–1628) y de José de Ribera (1591–1652)' (1997: 442).

34. To name just a few, Anderson (1986) notes the influence of the Petrarchan sonnet tradition in Lorca's treatment of death as an intimate ally in the exploration of nature, human experience and love; Soria Olmedo (2006) postulates that Lorca's exploration of death is indebted to Nietzsche

and his theories on the Dionysian and the Apollonian; and there are several studies on the influences of the classical world on Lorca's use of tragedy and fatality as aesthetic principles in his poems and plays. Camacho Rojo (2006) edited an extensive collection of essays devoted to the analysis of the classical tradition present in the poetic and dramatic works by Lorca: from intertextual references and recreations of classical mythology to the influence of Greek philosophers like Plato and the use of Nietzschean theories based on classical ideas.

35. Lorca considers the connection art-life-death underpinned by duende as undoubtedly rooted in Hispanic culture: 'España es el único país donde la muerte es el espectáculo nacional, donde la muerte toca largos clarines a la llegada de las primaveras, y su arte está siempre regido por un duende agudo que le ha dado su diferencia y su calidad de invención' (OC III: 313).

36. Webster (2003) traces the relationship between flamenco and the notion of *duende* as a historical, musical and anthropological journey around Andalusia. More recently, the study by León (2018) *El duende, hallazgo y cliché*, dispels a number of myths and inaccuracies deeply entrenched in studies and discourses on Lorca's *oeuvre* and on flamenco.

37. Maurer calls the duende lecture Lorca's 'last prolonged statement on the process of poetic composition and poetic inspiration' (2007: 35), while Mayhew insists that 'one of the things that Lorca's lecture is about is the performative transmission of artistic creativity' (2011b: 167) rather than just a theory of inspiration. He posits that 'the dominance of philosophy and hermeneutics in late modern poetics tends to pull in the opposite direction from the issues of literary performance that interested García Lorca: performance brings poetry into a pragmatic context removed from the realm of abstract, disembodied thought' (Mayhew 2011a: 286).

38. Mixing the Spanish perspective with a wider, Western European one, Lorca cites Goethe as the precursor of *duende* in his praise of the Italian musician Paganini. The musician's power consisted of performing a mediocre work of art but giving it a new performative aspect that could be perceived and felt by an audience as unprecedented.

39. Paul Julian Smith (1998a) was one of the pioneering scholars to take this approach, which Feal Deibe (1973) and Martínez Nadal (1988) foreshadowed in their Freudian readings of Lorca. *Diván del Tamarit* represents, according to Newton (1992) and Barón Palma (1990), an overarching narrative of the loss of the beloved after his [sic] death by water. Conversely, *Sonetos del amor oscuro* reappropriates the love sonnet tradition to convey the profound instability of sexual desire and its reversibility with pain, suffering and mortality. Verónica Leuci (2008) applies *eros* and *thanatos* to her study of *Sonetos del amor oscuro* in order to articulate Lorca's construction of a love mysticism (paralleled with that of the Spanish mystical poetic tradition) which entails the union of desire and martyrdom in the form of death, suffering and physical fragmentation.

40. Freud's psychoanalytical theory explored the concepts of the 'pleasure principle' and 'the death drive' in all living beings, a theory named after the classical Greek mythical characters Eros and Thanatos. The former represents the instinct of survival, the movement towards life-preservation and creation, which finds reassurance in the 'avoidance of unpleasure or the production of pleasure' (Freud 1961: 1) and drives the subject to merge with another body. The latter is the body's tendency towards self-destruction, an inherent search for the state prior to existence, death being the endpoint of life as well as its origin. Smith argued that 'in its twin stress on the psychic and the social, psychoanalysis is particularly appropriate to the study of drama' (1998a: 9), and, more particularly, that '[psychoanalysis] has the capacity to put into question precisely the repressions and interdictions forming the basis of religious confession and societal restraint. This is vital for a figure such as García Lorca, whose works, even at their most hermetic, have often been interpreted violently as a personal testimony that betrays the secrets of their creator's soul' (1998a: 10). Martínez Nadal's (1988) work analyses the intricate relationship between love and death in Lorca's play *El público* and by extension in the rest of his *oeuvre*, while Feal Deibe (1973) analyses *eros* and *thanatos* in Lorca's poetic symbols, arguing that 'La muerte corta brusca, alevosamente, la trayectoria de la vida. Pero podría pensarse también que el viaje tiene una típica significación sexual, y entonces la muerte, (o interrupción del viaje) cobra el valor de símbolo de un fracaso amoroso' (1973: 114).

41. As López Castellón notes: 'sexo y muerte (el *eros* y el *thanatos* freudiano[s]) constituyen la trama de la existencia humana, y su poder es tan fuerte que el individuo se vive poseído por una fuerza indomable que no hará posible la responsabilidad ni la culpa' (1981: 125).

42. One possible interpretation of this liminality between the twin drives is given by Óscar Enrique Muñoz: 'el amor en Lorca es un deseo de continua liminalidad, un impulso irrefrenable a situarse en el torbellino donde la propia individualidad queda disuelta y se experimenta la continuidad con el ser amado' (2013: 179).

43. Binding (1985) and Smith (1998a), among others, have examined, albeit from radically different perspectives, ideas of offspring and reproduction as intimately related to homosexuality and sexual frustration in Lorca's works. The 'reproductive futurism' underlying these analyses theorises death as the emerging consequence of the homosexual's inability to procreate.

44. As Edelman notes: the 'constant movement toward realisation cannot be divorced, however, from a will to undo what is thereby instituted, to begin again *ex nihilo*. For the death drive marks the excess embedded within the Symbolic through the loss, the Real loss, that the advent of the signifier effects' (2004: 9).

CHAPTER 1

❖

Diván del Tamarit and *Sonetos del amor oscuro*: The Obscurity of Poetic Artefacts

¿Poesía? Pues vamos: es la unión de dos palabras
que uno nunca supuso que pudieran juntarse,
y que forman algo así como un misterio.
    (García Lorca *OC* III: 573)

Lo insólito ha desplazado
taxativamente a lo rutinario.
    (Caballero Bonald 2016: 1)

After the widely acclaimed publication of *Romancero gitano* (1928) and his year-long sojourn in New York and Cuba, Lorca returned to Spain in 1930 with a new-found awareness of his fame and recognition.[1] Apart from embarking on a series of projects such as his travelling theatre company *La Barraca*, his numerous interviews and lectures and the writing and staging of his plays both in Spain and abroad, in his final years Lorca continued to write poetry quite productively. His long elegiac poem *Llanto por Ignacio Sánchez Mejías* and his Galician-language cycle *Seis poemas galegos* were both published in 1935. They constitute the poet's heartfelt homages each in its own particular way.[2] The former is Lorca's last published poetic work and his personal farewell and lament for the sudden death of his close friend, gored to death in a bullfight in 1934. The latter pays tribute to the Galician linguistic, literary and cultural roots cohabiting with Spanish for centuries in the Iberian Peninsula as well as to Lorca's experience of the Galician community exiled in Argentina.

    The two most substantial and significant works of lyric poetry in this post-New York period are *Diván del Tamarit* and an unfinished sonnet cycle (1931–36), both published posthumously and relatively unknown to the public and to scholars during the first decades following the poet's death. *Diván del Tamarit* comprises a collection of twelve gacelas or ghazals and nine casidas or qasidas, written between 1931 and 1934.[3] The gacela and the casida are poetic forms of Arabic origin. The former is from the Persian tradition and is characterised by its short length — four to fifteen lines — arranged in couplets and with a clear rhyming pattern in which the first two lines rhyme consonantly and this rhyme is repeated in the second line of each subsequent distich. The casida, also of Arabic and Persian origin, is a much longer poem, with the same metrical structure in all lines and monorhyme. In *Diván del Tamarit*, these poetic forms are practically never adhered to and present a mixture of stanzas (often within the same poem), multiple syllable lengths with a preference for longer lines (usually seven, nine and eleven syllables) and varying rhyming patterns with the recurrent use of assonant rhyme or free verse.

In parallel, from the group of sonnets that has survived today, the *Sonetos del amor oscuro*, Lorca's final poetic cycle (1935–36), consists of eleven extant sonnets which adhere in most cases to the traditional rhyming scheme ABBA/ABBA/ CDC/DCD and the syllabification in eleven-syllable lines of verse organised in two quatrains and two tercets.[4] The *Sonetos* evidence an effort to return to more conventional metre and poetic form as opposed to the use of free verse in most of *Poeta en Nueva York* (1929–30), and the same effort can be recognised in *Diván*, although to a much different extent.[5] Despite their imagery and motifs retaining some of the innovations of their predecessor *Poeta en Nueva York* (Bonaddio 2010: 173), the gacela, the casida and the sonnet were well-established poetic forms that entailed a technical challenge in terms of composition. The sonnet is indeed the most prominent in the Western tradition. As such, it constitutes a major technical effort for the poet due to its tight structural constrictions. This added awareness of linguistic and poetic norms is particularly relevant to the paradoxical attempt to break and subvert norms underlying both poetic works, a transgressive effort that will be analysed in this chapter in relation to Lorca's queer(ing) poetics.

While *Diván del Tamarit* was published in 1940 in the *Revista Hispánica Moderna* (New York), the *Sonetos del amor oscuro* had to suffer through a lengthy delay before their publication.[6] A few of the sonnets were published in the 1940s and 1950s, but it was not until the 1980s that two consecutive editions came out, in 1983 and 1984. The first one, a clandestine version made public by an anonymous source, was followed by another edition authorised by Lorca's family in the national newspaper *ABC*.[7] Some critics believed at the time that the collection's homosexual overtones (Eisenberg 1988: 262; Mira 2007: 5; Plaza Chillón 2008: 6) were the reason that the sonnets had not been published earlier, while others suggested that the sonnet group — which belonged to a bigger project Lorca was working on — was already being prepared for publication at the time the 'pirated' edition appeared (Eisenberg 1988: 262). The title *Sonetos del amor oscuro* was 'never directly recorded as being employed by Lorca' (Anderson 1990: 305) and has come to us from a series of indirect sources and suppositions.[8] 'Amor oscuro' has been taken to refer quite overtly to homosexual desire (Anderson 1990: 305–07) but can also be seen as '"oscuro" por instintivo, por ser imposible de expresar o analizar lógicamente' (Díaz 1990: 36). While 'dark' has been the usual translation choice of scholars, I propose 'obscure' as the better option in this case, since this term opens up more possibilities to analyse the mysterious, inarticulable and norm-transgressing qualities of desire explored in the sonnets.

It is nonetheless relevant to notice the only explicitly articulated, if unsurprisingly ambiguous or obscure, reference to the beloved as male in *Sonetos*, which occurs in 'El amor duerme en el pecho del poeta':

> Tú nunca entenderás lo que te quiero
> porque duermes en mí y estás *dormido*.
> Yo te oculto llorando, perseguido
> por una voz de penetrante acero.
>
>   (*PC*: 585, ll. 1–4; my italics)

The fact that the masculine noun 'amor' refers ambiguously to both the beloved and to love as an idea or embodied agent complicates the poet's exploration of his tumultuous relationship, interspersed with secrecy, pain and the beloved's apparent disdain or lack of understanding of the poet's feelings, symbolised in the recurrent allusions to sleep. Anderson also notes 'Lorca's abiding concern to generalize' (1990: 306), in the use of such ambiguous terms as 'yo' /'El poeta' and 'tú'/'el amor' to refer to the two lovers in the poems. This may be read as an example of the secret nature of homosexual relationships in Lorca's time, but also of the difficulties of ascribing univocal terms to issues of sexuality and sexual orientation, always characterised by obscurity, indeterminacy and fluidity.

A factor that definitely characterises both late poetic works is their complexity and, again, obscurity. *Diván* and *Sonetos* are closer to modernist and avant-garde trends in their thematic and imagistic content than to the traditional poetic forms in which they are inscribed. Anderson suggests that the late corpus represents what he terms the 'obscurity of modern verse' (1990: 5) or its opaque systems of signification. This obscurity is also worth considering in parallel with Christopher Maurer's argument:

> these were the years when Lorca's poetry was turning away from the logic of traditional metaphor to images which attempt to evade rational analysis and to produce (in his words) 'poetic emotion which is uncontrolled and virginal, free of walls, a freestanding poetry with its own newly-created laws'. (1998: viii)

His poetry is, Maurer argues, a world of mysterious images 'without explainable causes and effects' (1998: viii). Anderson traces this phenomenon back to 'further development by many recent poets of techniques pioneered by Baudelaire and espoused by the Symbolists, with the concomitant abandonment of self-explanatory and "logical" styles of writing' (1990: 5). The depuration of poetic language to its basic units of signification and the primacy given to synthesis, nuances, suggestiveness and metaphorical associations are staples of Lorca's poems. Breaking from easily decipherable symbols and metaphorical references, they lend themselves to a plurality of interpretations and tend to resist clear and univocal readings. While the structure of Lorca's late poems, based on a 'logic of imagery' or 'logic of the imagination' (Anderson 1990: 5), indeed contrasts with earlier periods in its reliance on a more transgressive vision of poetic expression, I shall argue that this 'obscurity' or impenetrability reveals a resistance to stable or univocal meanings and instead revelling in the indeterminacy and artifice of poetic creation and its norm-breaking capabilities. In the vein of *duende*'s 'constant baptism of newly-created things' (*OC* III: 318), the language and imagery in the poems articulate processes of norm disarticulation and repositioning. Lorca seeks to create poetry which will defy established norms and reinterpret them to achieve the unexpected, *lo insólito*.

Both works present scenarios and images fragmented at the spatiotemporal level, in which discontinuities and asynchronies abound. The personae in the poems are also unstable at the corporeal level, with bodies wounded or fragmented and on the brink of destructuration, thus showing their constructed nature. The limits of being and non-being are distorted and the characters' emotional states are variable and fluid. These incongruities reinforce the difficulty in identifying or defining the poetic subject and its addressee and in acquiring a clear sense of temporality or logical coherence. It is as if, as Quance suggests, the poetic subject were 'an experiment in self-representation', because at the same time it is 'the *persona* that the poet projects' and also 'the reader's creation' (2010: 13). In the late poetry this often applies to both the *I* and the *you* in the poems, personae which can be considered 'subject[s] in process' (Quance 2010: 13). Following newly-created laws of logic, a sense of identity or of stable meaning that can be deciphered becomes unlikely, even virtually impossible. It is thus necessary to focus on the distortions, incongruities and fragmentations the poetic images create in order to glimpse the transgressions and recreations Lorca is carrying out. Close reading of the queer function in Lorca's poetic approach to the five senses and corporeality will reveal a repositioning of the limits of being and mortality and a contestation of norms of gender and desire.

Diván del Tamarit

In her edition of the collection, Pepa Merlo defines *Diván del Tamarit* as Lorca's 'obra culmen' and as his greatest artifice (*DT*: 11). If an artifice or artefact is the only thing which can reconstruct with veracity any aspect of reality, Merlo concludes, 'cuanto más artificial sea la realidad, más creíble resultará' (*DT*: 12). Lorca's poetics is resounding evidence of this, for his poems create vivid and veracious realities which simultaneously revel in their artificial and constructed nature. The Arabic framework of *Diván* is, as Anderson notes, 'no decorative mantle but rather an organic necessity and a clear pointer to several of the broader and more profound "meanings" of the poems' (1990: 28). It is, as will be shown throughout this chapter, a layer of the artifice created which lays bare its own artificiality, bestows upon the creation an aspect of novelty based on downtrodden forms reappropriated and repurposed.

Poesías asiáticas and *Poemas arábigo-andaluces* are the main sources from which Lorca probably drew when composing *Diván del Tamarit* (Anderson 1990: 18–19). The first, translated by Gaspar María de Nava, Conde de Noroña, contains a host of Arabic, Persian and Turkish poems, including casidas and gacelas, particularly by the fourteenth-century Persian poet Hafiz. The second anthology, translated and compiled by Emilio García Gómez — who wrote the prologue to the projected edition of *Diván*, which was never realised — was a collection of Ibn Said's poetry.[9] Lorca's admiration of the Asian, Arabic-Andalusian and Persian poetic traditions in addition to his search for ever-changing, unexpected poetic images result in his very own homage to what could be considered 'lo esencial andaluz' (Anderson 1990: 27), but turned into a particular hybrid of past and present, of tradition and modernity: 'una fusión perfecta de todo lo aprendido, con los pies puestos en un presente de ruptura, de vanguardia, de elaboración de un nuevo orden estético y la mirada vuelta hacia la tradición' (DT: 13).

The word diván, from the Arabic diwan, denotes in the Arabic, Persian or Turkish traditions a poetic collection or anthology by one or more authors (DRAE). Yet despite the common initial assumption that Diván del Tamarit tries to imitate in style or thematic content the Arabic background to which it pays homage in its title and poetic forms, on closer inspection of the texts in the collection, this is barely the case. Formally, Lorca's gacelas and casidas bear no real resemblance to their Arabic counterparts, indeed using 'typically Spanish metrical forms' (Anderson 1990: 21) in keeping with Lorca's own formal preferences. In terms of themes and motifs, while the gacela and the casida often dealt with erotic themes, this is also true of most kinds of poetry, and other themes typically present in Arabic poetry (wine, destiny, elegy, panegyric) are not explored in depth in Lorca's Diván. Furthermore, the intimate connection between desire and death is a major element in Lorca's collection, but it was rarely seen in the Arabic tradition. Diván's overt references to Arabic and Middle Eastern poetry and cultures are actually very few.[10] Nonetheless, the city of Granada — 'El Tamarit' was the name of the country estate of Lorca's uncle near his hometown — with its Arabic heritage so pervasive in Hispanic culture even today, becomes the spatial setting and protagonist in a number of poems in the collection. References to the Andalusian city and reappropriation of motifs and topoi reminiscent of the Arabic poetic repertory allow Lorca to elaborate his own imagery and tone, characterised by folkloric and neopopularist naïveté; a symbolically charged use of flowers, plants, animals and nature; his particular use of chiaroscuro and plays of opposites; and his search for shocking and unexpected metaphors and sensory interrelations.

In his seminal work Orientalism, postcolonial scholar and thinker Edward Said identifies 'the Orient' as a European invention, a discursive mode in which the Orient is thought of as 'a place of romance, exotic beings, haunting memories and landscapes, remarkable experiences' (1978: 1). Clearly influenced by Latin American Modernismo, the interest of early twentieth-century poets, including Lorca, in Asian and Middle Eastern subjects and motifs reveals both a typically modernist Eurocentric exoticisation and a search for evasion and transcendence into non-Western modes of thought.[11] Considering Orientalism as 'a style of thought based upon an ontological and epistemological distinction made between "the Orient" and (most of the time) "the Occident"' (Said 1978: 3), in Diván del Tamarit Orientalism is the backdrop to the fantasy Lorca creates connecting the geographical certainty of Granada with the uncertainty surrounding the subjectivities and images in the gacelas and casidas. The poet took great care during the composition and planning of the eventual collection to infuse the poems with that Orientalist flavour. What were originally poems conceived for other purposes were finally included in his Diván, and the order and titles of many of them were modified as Lorca prepared the collection, as noted earlier. This suggests that the Arabic atmosphere was not coincidental, although it is agreed that the poems in Diván were not 'falsificaciones ni remedos' either, but 'auténticamente lorquianos' (García Gómez 1978: 88). In this first part of the chapter, I will examine a selection of gacelas and casidas that illustrates a relationship between desire and death hinging on sensory and spatiotemporal fractures, allowing the poetic voice to explore queering aspects of selfhood, existence and identity. The ubiquitous indeterminacy and ambiguity that characterise the collection are, as will be shown, authentically Lorquian layers of the artifice.

The gacelas present brief glimpses into the poetic voice's fragmentary psyche and sensory experiences, usually addressing his beloved or other purposely ambiguous characters or entities in passages which attempt to break spatiotemporal continuity and semantic logic. It is rarely clear who the mysterious beloved is or if there is any possibility for the poetic voice to really know or articulate his/her identity.[12] The beloved's body changes constantly, as does the poet's perception of and relationship with the beloved. The poetic voice confounds the 'here' and 'now' of certain poems by evoking a remote, indeterminate Arabic-Andalusian spatiality which is in turn placed on the beloved's equally remote and baffling corporeality. Desire and death become processes — always in development and never resolved — inherent to the poet's discourse, both shaping and threatening his existence and his knowledge of reality. Crucially, these unstable processes and the difficulty in ascribing to the poet and his beloved any stable signs of identity reveal Lorca's intention to question the reliance on language as provider of such identification. Hence, the language of the gacelas is elusive, polysemic and ambiguous, full of wounds and fractures. Mystery, corporeal fragmentation and semantic incongruity are the staples of the first part of *Diván del Tamarit*, the point of entry into Lorca's post-New York poetics.

The first of the gacelas, entitled 'Gacela primera del amor imprevisto', introduces two personae who fail to interact throughout much of the poem: the poetic 'I' and his addressee or beloved. The poet is baffled and attracted by the beloved's presence and tries in vain to grasp — both to be in physical contact with and to understand — the beloved and attain a state of communion with him/her. From start to end, the beloved's identity is vague and ambiguous. It resists categorisation in terms of binary distinctions of chromosomal sex or gender. The deliberate use of ungendered forms of address and the lack of gender-distinctive adjectives and nouns reinforce the beloved's fluid identity and start to problematise the notions of sex or gender stability. Precisely this ambiguity, together with the instability of the poet's relationship with the beloved and the (failed) attempt to break spatiotemporal logic are the interweaving problems facing the poetic voice in the gacela. Furthermore, it is in the poet's use of gender indeterminacy where an important reason can be found for the Arabic atmosphere infused into the *Diván*. The homoerotic nature of much Arabic-Andalusian poetry since the tenth century hinged precisely on gender ambiguity and ambivalence:

> la descripción de la belleza de los efebos es muy semejante a la femenina, de forma que, a veces, es difícil saber si es una joven o un muchacho el descrito, tal vez en una ambigüedad buscada por el propio poeta, tanto en las imágenes como en los usos gramaticales. (*DT*: 21)

In his homage to the Arabic civilisation which was an integral part of Spain for centuries, Lorca may be alluding to the 'greater sexual tolerance and openness which resulted, among other things, in the atmosphere of indulgent, carnal sensuality often to be found in Arabic verse, wherein hetero- and homosexual love are viewed and treated on entirely the same footing' (Anderson 1990: 28).[13] The indeterminacy of the beloved in this gacela and in much of the *Diván* has a dual effect: on the one hand, the poet achieves a level of universality in which desire is devoid of gender specificity and difference. The other effect, and this is a queering effect, allows the poem to bring the reader's attention to the deliberately constructed nature of gender demarcation, and how the poet has done away with it.

The gacela's structure presents a symmetrical organisation into four quatrains and the poet's tone is straightforward throughout the text despite the sometimes complex use of imagery. These two aspects confer a logical standpoint to the poem, which is thwarted by the inaccessibility and unintelligibility which the poet ascribes to his beloved. Also, the clear and logical temporal succession of images, establishing a brief spatiotemporal interaction between the poet and the beloved, will be destabilised in the final two lines. Three of the four quatrains take place in a past time and lead to the poet's final reflections in the present, but this present time retroactively challenges the preceding linear progression. Initially, in the first quatrain, the poetic voice characterises his addressee in terms of his/her body, which possesses qualities unintelligible to everyone:

> Nadie comprendía el perfume
> de la oscura magnolia de tu vientre.
> Nadie sabía que martirizabas
> un colibrí de amor entre los dientes. (*DT*: 141, ll. 1–4)

The perpetual absence of sex and gender markers renders the beloved's body indeterminate, mysterious and inexplicable. It is situated in opposition to the norm, for its corporeality escapes rationality and articulation ('Nadie comprendía', 'Nadie sabía') and thus resists normativity's identification of gender or sex binaries. The poet's position is dictated by his desire to approach his addressee, but access to the addressee has been denied both physically and intelligibly. What 'nobody understood' was a dark place in the beloved's innermost space, within his/her stomach, where a magnolia flower, dark or obscure, produced its scent. The magnolia, characteristically white, has a primitive structure with tough tepals and carpels instead of petals. It evolved, before bees, to be pollinated by beetles, hence its sturdy structure which was capable of trapping insects. It also had a strong perfume to attract its victims (*DT*: 29), an attraction that may be mirrored by the beloved in the poem. The paradoxical dark magnolia in the gacela may be an image of 'the smooth, delicate texture and perhaps fragrant smell of the beloved's skin' or his/her genital area (Anderson 1990: 30), but darkened to symbolise the conflicting relationship and obscurity of understanding between the poet and the beloved. The ambiguity of the beloved's body is further complicated by the use of the word 'vientre', which can designate the ungendered central part of the human anatomy where internal organs are located (belly or stomach) but which can also carry gendered associations of birth and motherhood (like the English 'womb'), and therefore of femininity. The latter connotation is paired with the birth and growth of the magnolia flower and the later allusion to fertility through a 'ramo de simientes', but the indeterminacy in the rest of the stanza and the proximity of the stomach to the genital area further suggests an erotic connotation which the poet makes purposely ungendered.

The beloved's is a body capable of torturing ('martirizabas') and biting ('entre los dientes') as well as of engendering life (its fertile parts produce flowers and seeds): it is both an alluring and a feared body, even called 'an enemy' later on. Possible associations may be drawn between the 'colibrí de amor' and fellatio, due to the previous allusions to the beloved's genitalia and the phallic shape of the hummingbird. However, the physical contact between the poet and the beloved implies some physical or emotional pain, since 'martirizar' and 'entre los dientes' suggest harm and danger more than pleasure. Anderson argues that the poet may be 'casting himself as martyr, saint or even Christ' (1990: 31), which would turn the sexual allusions into masochistic practices, recalling the torture and suffering preceding death in martyrdom.

The senses are the vehicle through which the poet accesses his emotional states and the beloved's, both highly unstable. His initial state of awe and admiration of his beloved alludes to the senses of smell and taste ('perfume', 'dientes'). The sense of touch follows, signalling the poet's desire to be in physical contact with the addressee and the difficulty of such a task in the face of a limited temporality ('yo enlazaba cuatro noches | tu cintura') and of the beloved's inaccessible but alluring corporeality ('tu cintura enemiga de la nieve'). This last image extends the evocation of physical contact by contrasting sensations of coldness and heat, pairing the addressee's waist (suggestive of the genital area) with snow (which suggests the addressee's heat by opposition). The poet is confronted with the beloved's enticing body which he wants to pin down, comprehend and possess, but the battling of his desire with his awareness of time's implacable force renders the conflict futile and the beloved unattainable. The first two stanzas might also suggest the lovers' encounters are clandestine as well as brief and painful because of their secrecy, murmured 'entre los dientes' and taking place at night ('con luna', 'se dormían', 'cuatro noches') and away from others' knowledge.

The beloved's body can defy temporal laws and boundaries, since it remains suspended in a past time ('comprendía', 'sabía', 'martirizabas', 'se dormían', 'enlazaba') and the poet's emphasis shifts through its different parts and its varying connotations. Time in the gacela is both an enemy that needs to be defeated and an almighty powerful force that seems impossible to destroy. The poetic voice tries desperately to battle time, to defy its laws and its logic, but time is represented as an inescapable process causing agony and frustration. The hyperbaton and enjambement between lines 7 and 8 position the poet tying or binding together ('enlazaba') both the beloved's waist and the extent of four nights, which here suggests a short period of time or perhaps the fugacity of the lovers' carnal encounters. In his search for temporal evasion and break with temporal logic, the poet recalls past events, crystallised in the poem without a temporal resolution through the use of the imperfect tense. In so doing, he dissects the beloved's body into sensory memories. The allusion to 'Mil caballitos persas' may be providing another reference, this time clearly Orientalist, to the defiance of spatiotemporal limits. A thousand little Persian horses recall the *Thousand and One (Arabian) Nights*, in which Scheherazade attempted to escape her impending death through her series of nightly love stories (Anderson 1990: 32). In a similar vein, the poet tries to (re)capture past intimate moments experienced with the beloved, holding them in thrall, asleep on the mind ('se dormían | en la plaza con luna de tu frente'). However, the moon and its association with the beloved's forehead — alluding to his/her beauty but also to knowledge and reason — introduces an omen of mortality.[14]

The purpose of the poet's attempt to shatter spatiotemporal logic is to put an end to temporal specificity — to stop and escape time — by giving eternity as a gift to his addressee. This aspect clearly resonates with the Petrarchan tradition and with Shakespearean sonnets in which the poet sees the poetic task as a guarantee of eternal life for the beloved.[15] Yet the poet becomes aware that, by writing down 'siempre', he has ironically condemned both himself and the beloved to the material laws of language and time, to the Lacanian symbolic order and its lethal inescapability. The poet's realisation that the addressee's body is 'eternally fugitive' seems to be the resolution (or further complication) of the conflict, prompting the present temporality of the final two lines:

> la sangre de tus venas en mi boca.
> Tu boca ya sin luz para mi muerte. (*DT*. 141, ll. 15–16)

The adverb 'siempre' situates the poet against the inevitability of temporality. He is seeking a state of eternity, a space outside time itself, in which he can attain an eternal union with his beloved ('Yo busqué para darte por mi pecho | las letras de marfil que dicen *siempre*', ll. 11–12). However, immediately after this statement the poet realises the impossibility of his desire ('*Siempre, siempre*: jardín de mi agonía. | Tu cuerpo fugitivo para siempre.', ll. 13–14). Through insistent repetition, he realises this is but a fantasy. The fantasy of eternity he conjures would put an end to the fear of death and oblivion: he would like to exist forever and to be with the beloved forever. As Edelman points out: 'fantasy names the only place where desiring subjects can live', a place where the subject can not only 'exist for always', but also 'exist when others are no longer there. He wants to live longer than everyone else, and to *know* it; and when he is no longer there himself, his name must continue' (2004: 34). The body of the gacela's beloved and the poet's body, *qua* human bodies, are both inscribed in a finite spatial and temporal realm. They will not and cannot be eternal. The beloved will thus always be fugitive, in constant mutation and unable to exist outside time and space. In other words, the poet's wish is set up to fail: he will never attain an immortal or immaterial state because human corporeality is by definition material and therefore, finite and perishable. In the course of the poem, this realisation is articulated as a return to the present time, asserting the poet's acceptance of temporal specificity and, consequently, of human mortality ('Tu boca ya sin luz para mi muerte.', l. 16). The return to the present time ('ya') does nonetheless signify a more permanent union of the two lovers, which seemed impossible. The concluding lines suggest that complete temporal transcendence — and, therefore, stable and univocal meaning outside time — are unachievable, due to the 'chain of ceaseless deferrals and substitutions to which language as a system of differences necessarily gives birth' (Edelman 2004: 8). To escape time would imply escaping language as well, reaching a plane outside temporality and outside signification in which the fantasy of Being itself — what Lacan calls 'the Real' or 'the Thing' — could be realised. The break with temporality that the poet desired is thus denied by the necessary temporality of language and the ephemerality that comes with it.

If language is a temporal succession of endless deferrals in which true and absolute meaning can never be achieved and if that which language articulates is necessarily referring to something *other*, what chance does the poet have to ever grasp the beloved's elusive self? The poet's desire for the beloved is doomed. The attainment of the beloved, the fulfilment of the poet's desire cannot be realised except through the emergence of the death drive, that which is outside time, 'intractable, unassimilable to the logic of interpretation or the demands of meaning-production', carrying the 'destabilizing force of what insists outside or beyond, because foreclosed by, signification' (Edelman 2004: 9). The image of mortality at the end of the poem points to the death of the poet's fantasy: it unites the two lovers but this time it is a deadly union, the awareness of their necessary and inevitable demise. Death's emergence is signalled by an image in which the poet drinks the addressee's blood and the temporal succession of the poem has inevitably run its linear course to the present time, mixing a grotesque vampiric/cannibalistic image with sexual connotations. This image also ties in with the previous references to martyrdom and Christian imagery: the beloved's blood enters the poet's body as in a Holy Communion (Anderson 1990: 37–38). The desired union of the poet and his beloved takes place through blood and the act of eating: one body is appropriating another by orally consuming it. The proximity of the poet's mouth to the addressee's also evokes kissing or licking, a libidinal possession which is never explained or resolved in the poem due to the sudden appearance of death. This final scene represents the coalescence of desire and death, of *eros* and *thanatos*, a final denial of the possibility to either achieve a stable and immutable state transcending the incoherencies of gender identification (thus 'killing' the poet's desire to define and understand the beloved) and the insurmountable temporality of language (which kills the capacity of the poet to attain an eternal union with the beloved). However, the lack of a resolutive synthesis of these two 'enemies' or 'lovers' in the poem — i.e. desire and death — suggests that the poem reaches an alternative, queer space. This space entails, as Muñoz posits, a 'queer time' which prompts 'a stepping out of the linearity of straight time' (2009: 25). While the time in the poem seems to be linearly moving forward from past to present, towards the end the poet manages to disrupt this linear time by blurring the temporal limits of death and life. The indeterminacy of the final lines (are the lovers dead or is the vampiric/Christian scene a glimpse of an orgasmic 'petite mort'?) fails to announce either the death of the poet or the end of his time-defying fantasy. The poet and his beloved face death, but their mutual union seems to engender life (like the beloved's stomach engendered magnolias) and exude pleasure (the poet's mouth, 'mi boca', is literally placed next to the beloved's, 'tu boca', in the text). The lovers in the gacela are placed beyond these multiple incoherencies and thus figure the place of the queer. In this fantasy space in which death gives life and life means death, all norms and logic go to die.

In 'Gacela II de la terrible presencia', a similar attempt to fracture spatiotemporal and logical limits occurs. Its structure consists entirely of couplets (one of the instances in which Lorca reproduces the original gacela structure), which gives it a sense of speed and brevity but accentuates the individual images in each of the eight couplets as isolated events, which is also reinforced by the assonant rhyme patterns particular to each one (a/e, o/o, o/a, e/a, i/a, e/o, u/o, e/a). The creation of impossible or illogical images serves to explore the idea of an exceeding desire, uncontainable and uncontrollable. The poet's desire is articulated into a series of impossible wishes that would break the laws of logic and physics. This leitmotif is expanded throughout the first part of the poem, reaching a conclusion before the two final couplets, in which the poet addresses his beloved expressing his profound desire, which must remain unfulfilled.

This is articulated through a succession of different stages in the gacela. The first four couplets elaborate on the poet's imaginative and creative abilities, listing his impossible wishes beyond reason and logic:

> Yo quiero que el agua se quede sin cauce.
> Yo quiero que el viento se quede sin valles.
>
> Quiero que la noche se quede sin ojos
> y mi corazón sin la flor del oro.
>
> Que los bueyes hablen con las grandes hojas
> y que la lombriz se muera de sombra.
>
> Que brillen los dientes de la calavera
> y los amarillos inunden la seda. (*DT*: 142, ll. 1–8)

The imagery refers mostly to the natural world, as illogical scenarios play out in the rapid succession of couplets. These scenarios tend to ascribe qualities to natural objects which somehow contradict their conventional or logical definitions: oxen are given the ability to speak and the night, which is given human eyes, gets blinded. Worms, which normally live underground, are killed by darkness and the ominous image of a skull is given sparkly shiny teeth. From these incongruous desires, the poet moves to a change of tone in couplets five and six. His use of the present tense ('Puedo ver', 'Resisto') signals his attempt to be more descriptive and engage with logic, so the metaphors subsequently become more coherent and decipherable, although they still revolve around temporality. The battle of the wounded night against noon, the green poison from sunset and the broken arches where time suffers reveal the poet's recurrent use of *chiaroscuro* and his plays of opposites to anchor his conflicting emotions and suffering in the inescapable passing of time. Addressing the beloved, the poetic voice now makes it clear that this emotional conflict relates to the experience of desire:

> Pero no me enseñes tu limpio desnudo
> como un negro cactus abierto en los juncos. (*DT*: 142, ll. 13–14)[16]

Whilst the rest of the poem has established the poet as a desiring being, he now consciously tries to set limits to his desire, which at this point is clearly erotic and carnal. The body of the beloved, reminiscent of that of the first gacela, is also indeterminate and lacks sex and gender markers. It is exuberant and appealing but simultaneously harmful or dangerous: its clean nakedness suggests erotic attraction but its darkness and likeness to a black cactus open by the river reeds seem to frighten or hurt the poet, hence his reluctance to look at it. The beloved's mystery and ambiguity are analogous to the conflicting emotions and overpowering desire the poetic voice felt in the previous couplets. What is most significant about this gacela is the use of vivid but complex and unexpected images inserted into a regular and fast-paced structure, which gives the poem an apparent simplicity and accentuates the series of conflicts proposed through the imagery and their lack of resolution or logical synthesis.

Fulfilment in the gacela would mean the end of the poet's life and the end of his poetic discourse, so the poetic voice endeavours to keep that desire open, to stay in a constant state of liminality, of in-betweenness: 'Déjame en un ansia de planetas, | ¡pero no me enseñes tu cintura fresca!' (*DT*: 142, ll. 15–16).[17] The word 'ansia' retrospectively sheds some light on the title of the poem. The terrible presence of the beloved provokes in the poet a state of eagerness, urge, impulse, longing. His desire is 'terrible' in that it is overpowering but also unsettling, producing anxiety and even fear. Desire is kept unfulfilled, on the edge of completion or realisation and thus on the brink of destruction, 'an intermediate position between a full relationship and the emptiness of rupture' (Anderson 1990: 44). This is a desire to keep desiring, which resonates with the impossible wishes earlier in the poem.

'Gacela de la terrible presencia' contains a metapoetic statement on infinite linguistic and imagistic capabilities, although it also deems language an endless chain of meaning deferrals where meaning itself is nothing but elusive. Lorca's thought in the *duende* lecture emerges from this idea. The location of *duende* in the constant baptism of newly-created things (*OC* III: 318), in the perpetual creation of the unprecedented, must come from an unquenchable desire, for desire's wound is ever open to facilitate the experience of art. This wound, however, denies the possibility of any linear future in which that open space might be closed and in which fulfilment or an absolute and unchanging meaning might be achieved. It must also announce death as a result.

The liminal and indeterminate space situated between desire and death and between existence and destruction brings about an unsettling sense of disorientation but it simultaneously creates a site of infinite potentialities: 'un ansia de planetas'. This somewhat paradoxical or contradictory plane responds, in Anderson's view, to a tension between 'la insatisfacción emocional (y hasta cierto punto física) que repetidamente encuentra el poeta en las relaciones amorosas y la insistencia en su deseo de cumplir precisamente esos anhelos' (1986: 498).[18] The poetic voice sees in this unfulfilment a way to poetic creativity. By suppressing the denouement of the lovers' conflict, the poet offers the chance for the unarticulated resolution to become a sign liberated from any restrictions, able to be transformed and redefined in myriad ways. The lovers in the gacela can transcend time, sexual identities and gender differences and become fluid processes mutating *ad infinitum*. They inhabit a queer time characterised, as Edelman posits, by the endless deferral and difference — the *différance* — of the symbolic. This timeframe offers no possibility of a future to seal the wound open by desire: 'like the lovers on Keats's Grecian urn, forever "near the goal" of a union they'll never in fact achieve, we're held in thrall by a future continually deferred by time itself, constrained to pursue the dream of a day when today and tomorrow are one' (2004: 30). Stepping outside time as a linear succession points to the infinite potentialities that the wound creates, so poetry becomes the path to creative eternity.

In the 'Gacela V del niño muerto', a further disruption of spatiotemporal limits takes place. The poet reflects upon the inexorable passing of time and, throughout the gacela, destabilises logical oppositions between life and death and their inscription in a linear temporality, in a 'straight time'. The fluidity of bodies finds an imagistic ally in the flowing of water and wind and in the blurred spaces and times:

> Todas las tardes en Granada
> todas las tardes se muere un niño.
> Todas las tardes el agua se sienta
> a conversar con sus amigos.
>
> Los muertos llevan dos alas de musgo,
> el viento nublado y el viento limpio
> son dos faisanes que vuelan por las torres
> y el día es un muchacho herido. (*DT*: 145, ll. 1–8)

Death is invoked as a commonplace phenomenon, accepted into the space of the living as ordinary and habitual. Inscribed in the poet's space, Granada, through the anaphoric structure 'todas las tardes', the image of sunset becomes the death of a day and that of a child; the end of corporeality, of existence and of childhood and innocence. However, the linear temporal succession is inverted in the poem, beginning with present, habitual events and then travelling back to the past from l. 9 onwards. The poetic voice is aware of the inevitability of death but simultaneously tries to revert its temporal process. The allusions to childhood in the title and throughout the gacela point to this intended reversal, as they simultaneously suggest childhood as the poet's early life and as his reproductive future. As Domínguez Gil notes, Lorca identifies childhood with a period in which 'la inocencia, la sabiduría y el sentido poético, perdidos con la llegada al uso de la razón, [vienen] a ser lo mismo' (2008: 23). Adulthood is considered the death of poetic creativity, perhaps a consequence of the awareness of sexuality and of mortality that comes with the end of childhood innocence.

The correlation of temporal processes and bodily processes evokes the poet's concern with temporal specificity in 'Gacela del amor imprevisto'. The bodies represented in this poem are also in a liminal state, in a mean between life and death, between time and eternity. A dying boy and a wounded young man are projections of the poetic voice onto a timeframe that resists to be specified but remains cyclical. Water and wind are articulated as analogous to life's progression towards death: in the first quatrain water 'sits down', presumably stops flowing, as the child's death is happening; in the second quatrain the dead have mossy wings and are followed by two currents of wind identified as two pheasants flying. This correlation is extended to the next section, in which images are intermixed to convey a similar analogy:

> No quedaba en el cielo ni una brizna de alondra
> cuando yo te encontré por las grutas del vino.
>
> No quedaba en la tierra ni una miga de nube
> cuando te ahogabas por el río.
> Un gigante de agua cayó sobre los montes
> y el valle fue rodando con perros y con lirios.
>
> Tu cuerpo con la sombra violeta de mis manos
> era muerto en la orilla un arcángel de frío. (*DT*: 145, ll. 9–16)

The timeframe has now moved to the past through what seem like the poet's recollections. An encounter, remembered or imagined, with the beloved in a wine cave underground is linked to absence and quietude, which are articulated through the image of absent larks in the sky.[19] Water and wind/air thus reappear transformed into wine and birds respectively, followed in turn by 'crumbs of clouds' absent from the earth and a river drowning the beloved. The poetic personae, by juxtaposition, mirror these watery and airy images flowing betwixt and between them in the stanzas. Finally, death is invoked again, but this time the beloved's dead body has replaced that of the child from the beginning: water once more flows as a giant rolling down the mountains amongst dogs and irises, both images of death (Anderson 1990: 56), but it stops again at the end as the poet sees the body of the beloved dead by the riverbank like a cold archangel. Anderson posits that the 'whole articulated chain of death by drowning: the river, the storm, the sudden torrent, submersion, downing itself, the riverbank, forms an extended metaphor for love-making' (1990: 58), which serves to further confound any certainties about the poetic personae and the poem's coordinates.

Once more, the spatiotemporal and corporeal transformations fused in the gacela resist fixity; situating bodies, time and space on a liminal plane between life and death. The bodies inhabiting the poem ('niño', 'muchacho', 'tu cuerpo', 'un arcángel') present increasing levels of ambiguity. While 'niño' and 'muchacho' are grammatically masculine, their anonymity, multiplicity or indeterminacy are highlighted through the spatiotemporal elements presented. The repetition implied by l. 2 suggests the poet is referring to multiple children dying as multiple afternoons pass, therefore eliminating the gender specificity and identity of the child. Similarly, the 'muchacho herido' is anonymised through the metaphor equating the wounded young man and the passing of time. Anderson suggests that both these images are one and the same (1990: 54). Indeed, in the same way as time in the poem resists linearity, so do the bodies resist identification. Both 'tu cuerpo' and 'un arcángel' reiterate this resistance, since they cannot be identified or ascribed sex or gender marks beyond the grammatical masculine, and in addition, they map a liminal stage located somewhere between living and dying and between earth/nature and air/heaven. The images intertwining both realms abound in the gacela: 'el aire', 'las grutas', 'la tierra', 'de nube', 'los montes', 'el valle', 'el viento'; reinforced by allusions to nature ('musgo', 'faisanes', 'alondra', 'perros', 'lirios') and to the supernatural ('los muertos', 'un gigante', 'un arcángel'). It is as if the poetic voice wanted to create a space and a time which, while consisting of terrestrial and spiritual elements, is neither earthly nor heavenly. In this strange spatiotemporal realm, the poet creates another indeterminate beloved who is floating between desire and death and defying spatiality and temporality.

The mutability of all the bodies in the poem, flowing like water and wind, highlights their queerness, insofar as their specificity lies in their mysterious, ambivalent nature which fluctuates between an alluring sexuality and a precipitation towards death. They become agent bodies in the poem insofar as they are wounded ('un muchacho herido'), dying ('se muere un niño', 'te ahogabas') or already dead ('los muertos', 'tu cuerpo [...] muerto en la orilla'), while contributing to confound the coordinates through which the poem moves ('Granada', 'tardes', 'agua', 'viento', 'se sienta', 'vuelan', 'las torres', 'el aire', 'las grutas', 'el río', 'los montes', 'el valle', 'la orilla'). They are opposed to the logic of opposition which would make life and death mutually exclusive, since they inhabit an indeterminate space between both, a place 'beyond the distinctions of pleasure and pain, a violent passage beyond the bounds of identity, meaning, and law' (Edelman 2004: 26). By denying a logical temporal completion and blurring ontological limits, the poet suggests that *eros* and *thanatos* are difficult, if not impossible, to separate. As it disrupts linear time, the poetic voice denies any possibility of future as the advent of meaning, proclaiming the wound — the transgression where life and death coalesce and where binaries cease to be opposed — as the access to what lies beyond meaning and is inexpressible and unnameable. Granada in this poem becomes the place of a queer time, in which children die every day, the dead can fly, water stops flowing, and past and present get confusingly blurred.

The final gacela in this chapter, 'Gacela IV del amor que no se deja ver' offers a further poetic approach to the recurrent spatiotemporal and sensory disruptions, re-appropriating the city of Granada and repurposing its folklore. These become 'the everyday material that is represented in a different frame, laying bare its aesthetic dimension and the potentiality that it represents' (Muñoz 2009: 9). From its start, the poetic voice establishes a clear sensory distinction between sight and sound, but it plays with and reverses their values throughout the poem. The main premise introduced in the title speaks of a 'love that cannot be seen', while each of the main stanzas in the poem begins with the poet's desire to hear a bell toll (specifically, 'la campana de la Vela'). According to Andalusian folklore and popular tradition, the bell atop the 'Vela' tower in the Alhambra was rung by young girls (and occasionally young men) of Granada every 2 January in the hope that it would bring them love and marriage within the year (Pedrosa 2012: 330).[20] The parallel structure 'Solamente por oír | la campana de la Vela' (2018: 144) is repeated in the two first lines of the first, third and fifth stanzas, whilst the second and fourth stanzas serve as choruses, refrains or repetitive chants.[21] These refrains also present a parallel structure, beginning with the city of Granada and a simile that transforms it into a moon and a doe-deer respectively. Interspersed with the main stanzas, they give a sense of traditional folkloric song, which in the context of *Diván del Tamarit* and the Arabic tradition it references, situate Granada and its Arabic influence in the midst of Lorca's passionate love poem. As Pedrosa posits, the poem's echoes of traditional songs and poems are seamlessly integrated into Lorca's innovative efforts, which expand on the existing lines (well-known in Granada and Andalusia) and transform them to accommodate the poet's longing and anguish (2012: 335).

The parallelism occurring in the first two lines of each main stanza corresponds to actual lines from popular songs dedicated to the Vela Tower and its bell, staples of the Alhambra and the city of Granada (Pedrosa 2012: 331–33). However, the final lines of the first and third stanzas ('te puse una corona de verbena' and 'desgarré mi jardín de Cartagena'); while also partially echoing pre-existing poems and songs — they are taken from popular songs and nursery rhymes sung in Granada and used in other Lorquian poems — introduce both the poetic voice and his addressee, thus anchoring the poem in the poet's reality and modifying the re-appropriated traditional language.[22] In the final stanza, this modification becomes even more noticeable as Lorca introduces two new lines ('me abrasaba en tu cuerpo | sin saber de quién era', ll.13–14), thus transforming the tercet into a quatrain and departing from the borrowed poetic framework altogether. These additions consist of lines of different lengths from the 'recycled' lines, longer in the first and third stanzas and shorter in the last one. Their tone is also much less general and presents the poetic voice in a more intimate manner. The 'Vela' bell and its ritual associations with love, marriage and desire serve the poet to express his own desire for his beloved, whilst also suggesting its complex and unstable nature and therefore its resistance to adjust to the norms in which it has been inscribed.

In the first stanza, the poet speaks of his beloved, whom he has given a floral crown ('te puse una corona de verbena'). The poet's obsessive desire is suggested by the repetitive longing for the bell's sound and, in this first stanza, by the poet's idolisation and adornment of the beloved. 'Verbena' can refer to a scented plant or to a traditional local celebration in Spanish culture, usually characterised by music, colourful ornaments and sometimes costumes. The verbena flower has also been known in Spanish tradition to carry erotic connotations, such that the flower was believed to have invigorating and aphrodisiac qualities (Piñero 2008: 17). Thus, the poetic voice idolises and transforms the beloved through a floral ornament which suggests their contact in some form of disguise; such that, while his love cannot be seen as the title claims, it can be heard like the bell and wears a colourful flowery crown worthy of a party or ball. In her seminal work *Gender Trouble* (1990), Judith Butler argues that gender and sexuality should be thought of as cultural fictions, performative effects of reiterative acts: 'Gender is the repeated stylization of the body, a set of repeated acts within a highly rigid regulatory frame that congeal over time to produce the appearance of substance, of a natural sort of being' (1990: 33). Fittingly, in the gacela both the poetic voice and the beloved perform (the latter even in costume) a queering process against the backdrop of Andalusian folkloric norms, imitating, in Butler's performative sense, the sounds so characteristic of the songs sung there and the bell chimes evoked. Simultaneously, this imitation turns these norms on their head as it becomes evident that both the poem and the beloved's identity are distorted and disguised, as difficult to see as the love in the title. Presenting the borrowed material 'in a different frame' (Muñoz 2009: 9), the poetic voice savours the imitation but exposes it as an inadequate frame, rewriting and adapting it to suit the poem's unseen love.

Sound and also the smell of the ornamental flowers replace sight as the sensory key to the beloved, whose identity remains hidden from view and is disguised in uncertainty. This sense correlates with the final lines of the poem, in which the poet laments his burning desire for his beloved's body without knowing to whom this body belongs. The poem ends with the uncertainty of the poet, which in turn clarifies his claim in the third stanza that his garden is torn ('desgarré mi jardín de Cartagena'), the ambiguity of the line suggesting some sort of emotional and physical pain caused by the turmoil in the lovers' relationship. 'Tear' is used to modify the trope of the Cartagena garden, borrowed from popular tradition but given in the poem an ambiguous value. Both lovers in the poem are made to inhabit a downtrodden space (that of Andalusian folklore and of the garden) but their performative duties do not quite fit within this framework and therefore they are progressively torn and disrupted (both figuratively as the poem gradually departs from the recycled images and literally as the garden is destroyed) by the poet.

As for the couplets or choruses (ll. 4–5, 9–10), the focus moves from the poetic voice to a more general or omniscient voice, simulating a mysterious chant or refrain that underlines and simultaneously disrupts the main stanzas in the poem:

> Granada era una luna
> ahogada entre las yedras.[...]
> Granada era una corza
> rosa por las veletas. (ll. 4–5; 9–10)

Both these apparently simple couplets offer, however, complex and multi-layered metaphors to do with perception and perspective. With a parallel structure occurring in both refrains ('Granada era una...'), the city is transformed into a moon and a doe-deer and then personified/animalised — given the abilities to drown and to bleed. These transformed images are depicted in the throes of an impending death: the moon is drowning amidst the ivy and the doe has been pierced by lances and has turned pink from bleeding. Starting with the image of Granada, the moon which would inhabit the city's sky is by metonymy transposed to encompass the former. Subsequently, what would be the moon's reflection on the water is personified as a dying entity, so the initial visual perspective of the moon is decentred to create an anthropomorphic image of death. Conversely, the second couplet animalises Granada to evoke a further deadly image, but again it is through the visuality of the doe's pink colour that this meaning is connoted. The word 'veleta', which also graphically and phonically resembles the Vela bell, is in itself ambiguous: it can denote a weathervane as well as a lance, so the visual image of Granada's Alhambra and its pointy towers (such as the Vela bell) is twisted to resemble pointy lances piercing an animal's skin. The sense of angst and suffering in these couplets is evoked and disguised by the ambiguity and brevity in which the imagery is depicted, conveying a sense of uncertainty and lack of completion. Only by exploring their sensory meanings and their reversed perspective can their connotations be accessed. The microstructure created in the couplets thus establishes a system of meaning deferrals, simultaneously producing a series of constructed images which nonetheless insist on their imminent destruction announced by the wound. The queerness of the images — their difference from the rest of the poem and their own decentred meaning which deviates from their conventional meaning — acquires a dual force which adds to the general meaning of the poem but aims to subvert it, presenting the wounded Granada as the sign of the death drive, that which ceases to be. Spanish philosopher Paul B. Preciado defines writing as a subject-producing technology (2013), which, used as a queer artefact, can articulate bodies and subjectivities dissenting from gender and sexual norms. Reappropriating this normative technology to create a new queer subjectivity, the poetic voice in the gacela repurposes the folkloric material in an attempt to convey the unintelligible — invisible, unseeable — nature of the beloved. What cannot be seen, what cannot be perceived in the gacela is paradoxically what the poem strives to convey through its images: an amalgamation of borrowed folkloric songs and tales, impulses stuck between desire and death, and the poet's own rewriting of them as an attempt to 'write' his beloved.

The Granada in the choruses is aligned with the poet from the main stanzas, in that the images attributed to it are also enveloped in a halo of ambiguity and mystery. It is as if the city is transposed into the poet's body, so that his feelings are felt by Granada itself, in turn personified repeatedly. The couplets combined with the stanzas accentuate the poet's burning desire for his beloved and his desperation stemming from his/her uncertainty and unattainable nature: unseen but heard, disguised and unknown. The beloved has no identity but possesses the ability to physically harm the poet ('desgarré', 'me abrasaba'), who in turn merges with the city and embodies it, feeling a dual suffering. The lovers' relationship is indeed 'a love that cannot be seen', as difficult to identify as the voices and folkloric songs reused in the poem and as the chimes of the bell the poetic voice desperately wants to hear. Ultimately, the pain, suffering and death in the gacela, rewritten and repurposed, serve, somewhat perversely, as evidence that the poet has created something unprecedented out of what seemed unoriginal, unsatisfactory or unknown.

Among the casidas, the 'Casida primera del herido por el agua' is an apt example of the irregular versification through which Lorca subverts the original poetic form. Randomly alternating seven-, eleven- and nine-syllable lines, the poem's structure and syntax suggest the use of free verse more than a strict structural or rhyming pattern. Excluding the first and last stanzas, both formed of four almost identical lines, the body of the poem resembles poetic prose in its use of varying line lengths and dissimilar structures and tones. The poetic voice, whilst present all throughout the poem, speaks obsessively about the boy from the title, wounded by water, to the point that it becomes unclear where the boundaries between their identities lie. This boy may well be reminiscent of the boy from the 'Gacela del niño muerto', a connection Anderson notes (1990: 55, 94), in that it relates to three mutually dependent deaths: 'the figurative death of childhood occasioned by the passing of time, imaginatively envisioned here in the death of the child; the imminent actual physical death of the body which, on the passing of childhood, is ever-present in the consciousness of adult man; and the metaphorical "death" of love-making' (1990: 94).

As the poem begins, the poet situates the drowning boy as the other, a sympathetic character whose suffering he contemplates and laments:

> El niño herido gemía
> con una corona de escarcha.
> Estanques, aljibes y fuentes
> levantaban al aire sus espadas.
> ¡Ay qué furia de amor! ¡Qué hiriente filo!
> ¡Qué nocturno rumor! ¡Qué muerte blanca!
> ¡Qué desiertos de luz iban hundiendo
> los arenales de la madrugada! (*DT*: 159, ll. 5–12)

However, the tone of the poem blurs the distinction between pain and pleasure, superimposing ambivalent emotional connotations. 'Herido' is followed by 'gemía' and 'corona de escarcha', both of which make it unclear whether the scene connotes intense suffering and painful freezing or a pleasurable moaning with ecstasy and celebration. In addition, whilst the two following lines allude to the piercing swords emerging from every pond, well and fountain, the poet's exclamation further evokes the contrasting qualities of the boy's immersion in the water, intermixing love, fury and death; darkness and light; and wounding, piercing and the peacefulness of sleep.[23]

The structure of the casida situates the deathly scene of the wounded boy drowning in the centre of the poem, whilst the first and last stanzas seem to be the poet's assertions and reflections on it. The oneiric scene interweaving pain, pleasure and dreams is presented as an interruption, a memory or a flashback, an abrupt change of scenery and tone. Therefore, there is an ambiguity relating to the identity of the wounded boy, his feelings and his body. Whilst the water is presented as a deadly agent, causing him pain, the boy's physical responses connote both suffering and joy. In addition, the poet's sympathy and identification with him together with his desire to attain this ambivalent pleasurable death ('muerte blanca', 'quiero morir mi muerte a bocanadas') accentuate the mysterious qualities of this character. The boy's identity in the poem fluctuates between the poet's beloved and his own self, since the first and last stanzas and their more prominent first person poetic voice state a firm desire (evident in the anaphoric repetition of the verb 'quiero') to contemplate, empathise with, and ultimately merge with, the boy's state:

> Quiero bajar al pozo,
> quiero morir mi muerte a bocanadas
> quiero llenar mi corazón de musgo
> para ver al herido por el agua. (*DT*: 159, ll. 21–24)

The conclusion of the poem thus manifests the poet's desire to fully experience the boy's liminal state between life and death, equating his own demise with the most intense experience of simultaneous joy and pleasure. Only in the wound, representing his intense and overwhelming love (¡Ay qué furia de amor!) and his poignantly beautiful call for death ('quiero morir mi muerte a bocanadas') can the poet experience plenitude, but this is a plenitude that escapes signification and denies the possibility of fulfilment. This wound, as Lorca explains, 'se acerca a los sitios donde las formas se funden en un anhelo superior a sus expresiones visibles' (*OC* III: 310). Reaching for a place in which forms — that is, language and signification — wish to transcend and surpass their very capabilities of expression, they blur into one another and cease to signify. This fantasy place is a *jouissance* in the Lacanian sense, the promise of wholeness and completion which can never be fully achieved because it would imply succumbing to the death drive and the impossibility of moving beyond meaning and the symbolic order, beyond time and beyond mortality itself. This is a return to that place of liminality which Muñoz referred to as the utopia of queer time, the fantasy of escaping the finitude of life and death.

'Casida VII de la rosa', albeit short, is one of the most complex and idiosyncratic of Lorca's late poems.[24] With a very regular structure of three brief stanzas and a parallel line organisation and rhyme scheme conferring to it a repetitive and almost naïve or simplistic musicality, it explores and develops the idea of desire and its transgression of the limits between self and other. The rose motif is explored in depth in Lorca's contemporary play *Doña Rosita la soltera o El lenguaje de las flores* (1935), in which the image of the *rosa mutabilis* is used to mirror the burning but repressed desire of the protagonist, aptly named Doña Rosita.[25] The rose in the casida, in parallel with its theatrical counterpart but without changing colour, is characterised by its mutability. A traditional symbol of beauty and romantic love, it may stand for 'the transience of beauty, love and life itself' (Anderson 1990: 125) as well as evoke the 'rosa de los vientos', 'a compass-rose indicating the direction of the winds in the sky and of movement generally' (Anderson 1990: 127). As a protagonist in the casida, the rose is personified by the poetic voice. The rose's desire, anti-normative and subversive, is the *leitmotif* of the poem ('buscaba') and allows the poetic voice to challenge stabilising notions of essence, corporeality and self-identification:

> La rosa
> no buscaba la aurora.
> Casi eterna en su ramo buscaba otra cosa.
>
> La rosa
> no buscaba ni ciencia ni sombra,
> confín de carne y sueño, buscaba otra cosa.

> La rosa,
> no buscaba la rosa
> inmóvil por el cielo buscaba otra cosa. (*DT*: 166)

In the first stanza, the rose is dissociated from light and ascribed the capacity to desire. However, this desire is established as non-normative. Due to the conventions usually associated with plants and flowers, dawn connotes not only light but also the natural beginning of days and the sunlight necessary for plants to grow and survive. By contrast, the rose in the poem is seen as a creature of darkness/obscurity which does not search for the light of dawn and lives at night or in the shadows. This particular rose is almost eternal in its bunch, so expanding on its rejection of light and therefore of life as it is conventionally conceived, the rose also stands out from its flowery peers and transcends traditional ideas of mortality and time limitations, being 'both ephemeral and eternal' (Anderson 1990: 126). Its desire is just not containable within spatiotemporal boundaries, it remains other ('buscaba otra cosa') and therefore disembodied, limitless, unarticulated and unknown. This resonates with the suggested obscurity ascribed to the rose, although interestingly, obscurity itself is not articulated in the poem but is evoked by shadow and by opposition to dawn and to certainty of knowledge. What is unknown and unsaid, what lies in the shadows, gains more prominence and significance in the poem than what is actually articulated. As Gillett suggests, '[not] only the unfulfilment of the quest is the locus of the personification, but also the quest itself — and hence by implication the negations which define it' (2001: 136). The rose is positioned against articulation itself; it remains other to the system of signification, continually deferring meaning and differing from it, moving between what is expressed and what is silenced.

The rose further transcends epistemological boundaries in that it does not search for science or shadow, but remains on the edge of flesh and dream. This mix of bodily limits and materiality with immateriality, dream and the imaginary, complicate the nature of the rose. The poet denies the possibility of scientific knowledge of the rose and therefore its contention within corporeal limits. The rose eludes the rationalisation of science as it eludes the materiality of sensory perception: it cannot be seen in sunlight or shadow, and it cannot be perceived by the senses. Its corporeality is also questioned, such that it results in a mixture of body and the imaginary ('confín de carne y sueño'), an unlikely amalgamation of diverse fragments. This is confirmed in the final stanza, in which it is claimed that the rose's desire transcends its very being and searches for something other than itself ('buscaba otra cosa').

Through the casida's repetitive tone, which may recall the infamous dictum by Gertrude Stein that 'Rose is a rose is a rose' albeit with sharply different associations, the poet suggests a metamorphic vision of essence whereby the rose's unquenched desire makes it ontologically permeable and fluid, perpetually other to itself and to knowledge, never epistemologically fulfilled or articulated.[26] Lorca's rose breaks the boundaries that render identity stable and rationally understood, positivising mutability and multiplicity and their threat to signification. Things that defy the norms we are accustomed to may seem daunting or unintelligible at first, but in the rose's fantasy, a pervasive unquenched desire (a never-ending search for the unknown) bestows on the rose and on the poet infinite regenerating capabilities. As in Muñoz's idea of utopia, queerness points to a horizon which is not yet here; but which gives a sense of hope in what is to come, in that 'otra cosa'.

Much like the 'Casida de la rosa', the 'Casida IX de las palomas oscuras' explores the limits of identity and the permeability of self and other. It presents an allegorical tone in its running parable-like story and a rhyme scheme and naïve musicality reminiscent of nursery rhymes or folkloric songs, as well as some ballads in *Romancero gitano*.[27] In a game of opposites, a very recurrent trope in Lorca's later poetry, the two protagonist dark doves are identified with the sun and the moon.[28] This overarching poetic *chiaroscuro* establishes the poet's tone of existential enquiry and reveals a permeability and fluidity of bodies and identities. Throughout the poem, antithetical elements are sharply contrasted or merged — into one or into nothingness. As an agent of interrogation, the poetic voice initiates a dialogue with the two dark doves and their solar and lunar counterparts to enquire about his own existence and his death:

> Por las ramas del laurel
> vi dos palomas oscuras.
> La una era el sol
> la otra la luna.
> Vecinitas, les dije:
> ¿dónde está mi sepultura?
> En mi cola, dijo el sol,
> en mi garganta, dijo la luna. (*DT*: 169, ll. 1–8)

The poet's enquiries to the mysterious oracular characters seem to be thwarted by the ambiguity of the imagery, never resolving the polarisation between light and darkness, beginning and end, or life and death. The circularity of the two asters and that of their responses — they seem to 'go around in circles' but also to point to the cyclical nature of the asters' orbits — mirrors the repetitive tone of the casida. The initial question by the poetic voice and the protagonist's journey ('Y yo que estaba caminando | con la tierra por la cintura', ll. 9–10) both seem to circle back to the starting point when the casida ends: to the laurel and the same circular answer.

In the succession of antithetical elements, genders also playfully switch: the sun and the moon and day and night are masculine and feminine respectively, both grammatically and symbolically. In Spanish folklore and the popular imaginary, this usual gendering of the sun and the moon is found in children's songs, a connection which is not coincidental in the casida, as noted above.[29] The rhythm of the poem purposefully moves from one to the other as the pairs change and the rhyme repeats, transforming the doves first into the asters and then into eagles. In turn, distinctions between self and other are blurred as most pairs in the casida merge into each other and then into nothingness:

> Por las ramas del laurel
> vi dos palomas desnudas.

> La una era la otra
> y las dos eran ninguna. (*DT*: 169, ll. 19–22)

The allusion to a naked woman and the transposition of this image into the final lines connects corporeality with the doves, with the poetic voice and with his discussion about the limits of existence and identity. Anderson notes the connection between the imagery of the laurel bush or tree and the naked woman with the myth of Daphne and Apollo and its association with metamorphosis (1990: 137). In addition, the nakedness of the woman, later transferred to the doves, suggests the removal of all external signs of identity, such as gender and chromosomal sex. These are superseded in the casida by the power of desire merging self and other ('la una era la otra') and the imminent threat of mortality and non-existence ('la muchacha era ninguna', 'las dos eran ninguna'), suggesting that those signs have no meaning in the face of death. The final lines of the poem merge the identities of all the characters and the poetic voice witnessing them. Blurring the apparent distinctions among them in a fantasy vision of desire and mortality, the ending suggests both the complete disappearance into nothingness brought by temporality and the cyclical, never-ending creativity inherent in poetic transformation.

Both the 'Casida de la rosa' and the 'Casida de las palomas oscuras' hinge on an apparently simple and naïve structure to explore the poet's uncertain position between existence and non-existence, being and non-being. The linguistic and poetic transitional signs from self to other are simplified to acquire an almost playful and tautological quality ('la rosa no buscaba la rosa', 'la una era la otra | y las dos eran ninguna'), whilst actually proposing subversive images challenging the fixity of the body and identity and redefining the idea of death as an unequivocal end to existence. Lorca's poetic use of death is undoubtedly polysemic: it simultaneously points to the universality of the fear of mortality and the threat of loss and grief; to the artistic *pathos* achieved when a living being is faced with physical pain and suffering; to the negation of language and thought as reliable and univocal signifying systems; and, therefore, to the act of questioning faithful meaning and representation. The latter is evident in both poems' abundant use of indeterminate nouns and pronouns denoting uncertainty, otherness and non-existence ('otra cosa', 'la otra', 'ninguna'), creating a discourse which poses a threat to communication and interpretation. In doing so, the unreliability of these does nonetheless leave room for potentially infinite readings and possibilities, which ascribes a sense of freedom and a purposeful rejection of normativity to poetry far more liberating than nihilistic or pessimistic. Muñoz insists that queerness is a utopia, an 'ideality', but 'we can feel it as the warm illumination of a horizon imbued with potentiality' (2009: 1). While Lorca's casidas and gacelas create queer fantasies escaping temporality and threatening the certainty of life and death, their infinite potentialities as utopias shine through. The cyclical and recurrent performativity of *duende* thwarts any attempt to impose logical norms on or delimit existence, identity or desire. Transgressing straight time and futurity, self–other distinctions, and the stability of identities, the queer fantasy emerging from *duende*'s wound fittingly erases limits only to recreate them, refuting any hope of fulfilment but always promising new horizons that are yet to come. Together with the gacelas and the casidas of *Diván del Tamarit*, this kept promise is channelled through the love sonnet in Lorca's final poetic project. I will return to *Diván del Tamarit* in the final chapter in order to examine some of the gacelas and casidas in dialogue with Lorca's other creative practices.

Sonetos del amor oscuro

It is important to reiterate that within Lorca's later corpus, the sonnets are not a finalised collection intended for publication by the author. The group of eleven *Sonetos del amor oscuro*, as they have survived, were probably still drafts among a number of sonnets that might have featured in a hypothetical and unfinished collection entitled *Jardín de los sonetos* which Lorca was planning in the last months of his life. However, they are 'no arbitrary compilation of diverse texts' (Anderson 1990: 308) either. In tune with other late works, Lorca's thematic preferences and recurrent motifs — the confluence of *eros* and *thanatos*, the natural world, corporeal fragmentation and plays with pairs of opposites — find a prominent place in the sonnet cycle. The sonnets' intimate tone, 'above all about the tormented experience of love, passion, and suffering' (Anderson 1990: 307), is paired with innovative imagery that divests traditional tropes of their conventional associations, while adhering to the canons and long-standing tradition of this poetic form.[30] In so doing, the sonnets exhibit an exploration of the metamorphic nature of desire and death and point to a redefinition of the love sonnet to accommodate the questioning of normativity in relation to gender and sexual identities.

The titular image 'amor oscuro', translatable as 'dark' or 'obscure' love, announces a poetic voice wishing to subvert the conventional love sonnet and alludes to the duelling forces of desire and mortality by introducing a pair of antithetical images which is both typically Lorquian and universally recognised. As Leuci argues in her reading of 'oscuridad' in the sonnets:

> esta parece una entrada atractiva a un mundo atravesado por la oposición luz/sombra o claro/oscuro, una dicotomía que se desplegará en los textos lorquianos en un espectro de variadas gradaciones, en referencia, por ejemplo, a la oscuridad de lo no-dicho, lo secreto, lo velado, pero también, aludiendo a la noche como escenario e, incluso, llegando a la oscuridad abismal e intensa de la muerte o del alma y la carne del propio ser. (2008: 1)

Obscurity in *Sonetos* acquires a plurality of meanings, not only through the association with secrecy and the unknown, but also suggesting an addition to that meaning in its connotations of contrasting forces and opposed dichotomies within the bodies and objects in the poems. Among his friends and contemporaries, Lorca is said to have coined the term 'epéntico' to refer to the 'love that dare not speak its name', since those 'who create but cannot procreate' (Gibson 2009: 316–20) needed to resort to epenthetic devices to be able to express themselves. Epenthesis, in linguistic discourse, entails the insertion of an unetymological vowel or sound into a word, the addition or intrusion of something strange or foreign into the established grammatical normative system.[31] Lorca's use of the term speaks of a queering process, reinforcing the sense of covert expressiveness and subversive creativity that can be found in his poetics.[32] This, as will be seen, applies to stylistic, imagistic and thematic elements present in the sonnets particularly as well as to the reappropriation of poetic traditions in a hybrid process of homage and unique recreation.[33]

One of the sonnets which stands out for its prominent *chiaroscuro* imagery as an echo of the 'amor oscuro' title and which also links Lorca's antithetical games with spatiotemporal transgression is 'Noche del amor insomne'. In this sonnet, night and day are the scenarios in which the two lovers interrelate. However, spatiotemporal uncertainties abound, as do pairs of opposites which destabilise the meanings of images, adding new 'epenthetic' possibilities to them. The night in the poem is a sleepless night or a night of sleepless love (or lovers), which already suggests a plurality of meanings: the lovers are kept awake either by the enjoyment of erotic pleasures or by suffering in painful angst and desperation. The transition from night to day demarcates the lovers' sexual encounter, but boundaries between pain and joy become unstable and reversible, imitating the equally unstable flux between light and darkness:

> Noche arriba los dos con luna llena,
> yo me puse a llorar y tú reías.
> Tu desdén era un dios, las quejas mías
> momentos y palomas en cadena.
>
> Noche abajo los dos. Cristal de pena,
> llorabas tú por hondas lejanías.
> Mi dolor era un grupo de agonías
> sobre tu débil corazón de arena. (*PC*: 585, ll.1–8)

As the corporeal and emotional instability of the lovers transitions from desire to pain, so do the images in which they are inscribed, mutating from darkness to light and upwards to downwards through parallels in the two quatrains. The first quatrain is situated in an upwards movement, which is reinforced by the image of a full moon in the sky. In Anderson's view, this vertical movement might be a 'neologism calqued on the locative construction [...] in such phrases as "río/calle/cuesta arriba/ abajo"' (1990: 388), although it can also be seen as a synaesthetic transposition of the temporal progression of a night into a spatial journey upwards-downwards. As night goes on, its beacon — the moon — moves upwards and downwards in the sky in its orbit. This image later extends to the sun's movement in turn, since dawn and sunrise open the two tercets respectively. This combined spatiotemporal movement frames the fluctuation, emotional and corporeal, of the lovers. Through a chiasmic structure placing the poet and the beloved face to face, the 'I' cries while the 'you' laughs, their bodies moving in space and in time ('momentos y palomas en cadena'); gravitating towards each other and fluctuating between pleasure and pain, until the boundaries between these states become blurred and reversible during their erotic encounter.

In the second quatrain, the movement of the night downwards — again a form of spatiotemporal synaesthesia — presents the beloved crying this time, following the enjambement with the previous line in which there is a glass of sadness. The hard surface of glass and its reflective qualities are positioned against the emotional suffering of the beloved, mirroring the poet's agony in the next line and contrasting the weakness attributed to the beloved's heart of sand. The quatrain thus evokes the contrast between hard and soft objects and the intermittent feelings of the lovers across time and space ('momentos', 'arriba', 'abajo', 'hondas lejanías', 'grupo de agonías'). While the relationship in the sonnet seems to present the lovers, especially the poet, with more painful experiences than pleasurable ones, the constant spatiotemporal fluctuation suggests that the poetic voice may be trying to find some redemptive qualities to the affair. This may be his way of countering the perceived fickle nature of the beloved's emotions. Space and time are destabilised, as are the positions of the lovers in relation to each other: now close, now far, now upwards, now downwards, now laughing, now crying, now night, now day.

In the tercets, dawn loses its conventionally positive associations of light and rebirth; or rather, to these are added obscure overtones as the lovers drink each other's blood, which in turn becomes a jet stream that never ceases, an indissoluble union of pleasure and mortality:

> La aurora nos unió sobre la cama,
> las bocas puestas sobre el chorro helado
> de una sangre sin fin que se derrama.
>
> Y el sol entró por el balcón cerrado
> y el coral de la vida abrió su rama
> sobre mi corazón amortajado. (*PC*: 586, ll. 9–14)

In a similar vein to the 'Gacela del amor imprevisto', the appropriation of each other's bodies points to mutual pleasure but also to a mutual infliction of pain, with simultaneously erotic and Christological connotations.[34] The lovers feed off each other's blood like vampires, the immensity of the never-ending blood stream symbolising mutual nurturing and redemption; however, this unsettling image reinforces the pain this relationship imposes on the lovers. Even the temporal process of death is destabilised, since the continuous bleeding does not have an end and has therefore stopped the logical succession of events. The two tercets thus combine purposely ambiguous scenarios which fail to explicate the state of the lovers. Dawn, sunlight and coral attempt to counteract their bloody and deathly encounter, but the poet's enshrouded heart can be either redeemed or killed by them, as the end of the sonnet suspends the possibility of resolution to this conflict. Blood is here the principle by which life and death cease to be distinct processes, instead becoming a dual force that drives the desiring bodies of the lovers and blurs their sense of self and other as well as their state in the relationship.[35] As Blackman posits:

> bodies are not considered stable things or entities, but rather are processes which extend into and are immersed in worlds. That is, rather than talk of bodies, we might instead talk of brain-body-world entanglements, and where, how and whether we should attempt to draw boundaries between the human and non-human, self and other, material and immaterial. (2012: 1)

These entanglements are articulated in the sonnet to encompass the lovers' tumultuous physical and emotional communion as well as the more general ontological process of self-identification, which Lorca weaves as a multiplicity of aspects interrelating. In parallel, whether the lovers' bodies are male or female remains unclear: what seems crucial for the poetic voice is the excessive desire that drives them, and the capacity of the poem to convey the convoluted and unstable relationship between time and space, pleasure and pain, life and death and the lovers' bodily texture and composition. Their bodies offer an entrance into a world of reversibility, in which sex and gender are superseded — and therefore questioned — through the fluidity they can both acquire in their relationship. The lovers' communion occurs at the physical level, but the poet insists that their carnal encounter entails many entangled aspects relating also to their psyche and experience of reality (brain-body-world), such that their multi-layered identities merge. This holistic union, in interweaving *eros* and *thanatos*, body and soul, and self and other, serves to render other binaries (especially those normativising sex and gender) obsolete and irrelevant.

A similar exploration of the entanglement of self and other, pleasure and pain and life and death takes place in 'Soneto de la guirnalda de rosas', considered one of the richest and most complex among the sonnets.[36] The 'guirnalda de rosas', whose function in the poem is highly ambivalent, may mean both a garland and a funerary wreath. A garland of roses bears love associations, being an ornament of celebration of the passion evoked by the flower; whereas a wreath is used to commemorate death, in which case the roses would give a sense of danger and suffering, perhaps to do with their thorns that may cause pain and therefore suggesting an end to love or its painful consequences.[37] These opposed sentiments are explored throughout the poem, suggesting that 'the experience of love is a mingling, an interweaving of disparate emotions and states, just as love could here be seen as producing by turns singing and moaning' (Anderson 1990: 312):

> ¡Esa guirnalda! ¡pronto! ¡que me muero!
> ¡Teje deprisa! ¡canta! ¡gime! ¡canta!
> Que la sombra me enturbia la garganta
> y otra vez viene y mil la luz de Enero. (*PC*: 579, ll.1–4)

There is a confluence of lamentation and rejoicing simultaneous with the confluence of love (and life) with death, exposing the fluidity between loss or destruction and rebirth. The first quatrain produces an amalgam of opposing elements that coincides with the weaving of the garland/wreath. The poet urges the beloved or another addressee to weave it fast, as the garland seems to be able to bring both salvation and destruction and therefore urgency is required. The first two lines in the quatrain contain a series of exclamations which contribute to this sense of urgency and desperation. The end of l.1 ('¡que me muero!') suggests that the garland could be either the remedy to the poet's death or its very cause, placing the poet in a state of suffering or ecstasy derived from the beloved's presence. The second part of the quatrain further explains the poet's emotional state, making use of contrasting sensorial elements as is quite characteristic in the rest of the sonnet cycle and in *Diván del Tamarit*. 'Sombra', which inevitably suggests the idea of 'amor oscuro' associated with the sonnet group, is presented together with 'luz' to establish the interrelated emotions ailing the poet. This visual *chiaroscuro* is suggesting that the poet's state of simultaneous suffering and joy is linked to the passing of time and works in a cyclical fashion, as implied by the enjambement between lines three and four sequencing shadow and light and by the repetition expressed in the words 'y otra vez viene y mil'. The continuous cycle of light and obscurity hints at the site of spatiotemporal non-linearity and logical uncertainty which the lovers inhabit.

A further pair of elements converging in disparity are the first person poetic voice and the beloved, or rather, their distinct experiences of love. Anderson claims that 'enjoyment and violent destructiveness seem to go hand in hand' (1990: 318) but 'the poet still maintains a sort of desperate hope for 'communion' with the beloved despite or perhaps even thanks to all the suffering and the deathliness' (1990: 319). The second quatrain exemplifies the mutability of the lovers' relationship:

> Entre lo que me quieres y te quiero,
> aire de estrellas y temblor de planta,
> espesura de anémonas levanta
> con oscuro gemir un año entero. (*PC*: 579, ll. 5–8)

While both lovers are ironically interwoven like the ornament, and thus showing reciprocal love ('lo que me quieres y te quiero'), there seem to be a number of obstacles or factors which in the quatrain are literally positioned between them. These elements present a disparity of connotations related to the natural world especially. The visuality of the quatrain thus transposes the conflicting emotions of the lovers into spatial perils (air of stars, tremor of plant and thickness of anemones all convey a sense of unsurmountable difficulties facing the lovers) and also temporal obstacles (a whole year of dark moans has passed or will pass).[38] These confluences of opposing elements devolve into a new sense of urgency in the tercets, in which the poet again demands that the beloved give into carnal desire and joy, although this joy is, as usual, tinted with ambivalent tones:

> Goza el fresco paisaje de mi herida,
> quiebra juncos y arroyos delicados,
> bebe en muslo de miel sangre vertida.
>
> Pero ¡pronto! Que unidos, enlazados,
> boca rota de amor y alma mordida,
> el tiempo nos encuentre destrozados. (*PC*: 579, ll. 9–14)

The poet takes on a domineering role in this sonnet, in contrast with the subjugation often seen in the sonnet cycle and typical of Petrarchism and Courtly love. He is the one commanding the beloved in order to avoid the catastrophe he is expecting: both lovers' imminent death. However, the fear of death announced at the beginning of the poem gives way to an acknowledgement or acceptance of transience in the last tercet. The inevitable and imminent arrival of temporality in the last line seems to be countered by the poet's commands. The suggestion of *carpe diem* to the beloved, intertwining desire with the experience of pain, is an almost sadomasochistic depiction of their physical and emotional relationship. This is clearly reinforced by the imagery in the tercets: the beloved's joy in contemplating the poet's wounds, the destruction of the natural world and once more the drinking of blood off the poet's honey thigh. The lovers' corporeal communion ('unidos, enlazados') presents an ambivalence between pleasure and destructive pain ('boca rota de amor', 'alma mordida'), against an enemy well-known to the poet (temporality and transience). This battle is nonetheless left unresolved as usual, so the lovers remain crystallised at the end — fittingly, like the circular guirnalda being woven — in an indeterminate state of union and destructuration.

The sonnet as a whole thus suggests that the lovers' relationship is an ambivalent and metamorphic process, as able to save them and bring them joy as it is the cause of pain and death. In the face of the inevitable passing of time, the poetic voice realises it is better to pursue the experience of desire and revel in its immediacy as well as in its ephemerality and imminent finitude than to 'wait and passively let the passage of time take its inevitable toll' (Anderson 1990: 320). Furthermore, it is in the poetic task, in the creation of the poetic personae and their ambivalence that the poet finds the sole weapon fit to fight temporality, even though he knows this is a near-impossible task.

The title of the 'Soneto de la dulce queja' is in keeping with Lorca's recurrent antithetical games. The oxymoron foreshadows the ambivalent emotions experienced by the poet due to the paradoxical and masochistic nature of his relationship with the beloved:

> Tengo miedo a perder la maravilla
> de tus ojos de estatua y el acento
> que me pone de noche en la mejilla
> la solitaria rosa de tu aliento.
>
> Tengo pena de ser en esta orilla
> tronco sin ramas, y lo que más siento
> es no tener la flor, pulpa o arcilla,
> para el gusano de mi sufrimiento. (PC: 579–80, ll. 1–8)

The first quatrain presents the poet praising the beloved's features most precious to him: his/her eyes and breath, which he is terribly afraid of losing were their relationship to end. These corporeal elements simultaneously point to the nuanced relationship between the lovers: the beloved's eyes are those of a statue, suggesting their immense beauty comparable to an artistic object but also their inanimate or distant nature when looking back at the poet.[39] The beloved's breath, in addition, is transformed metaphorically into a solitary rose, which at night touches, by speaking, breathing or kissing, the poet's cheek. The image evokes, again ambivalently, the beauty and uniqueness of a rose in the beloved's words or his/her mere presence in close intimacy with the poet, whereas the epithet 'solitaria' adds a sense of solitude that may also be construed as the beloved's distant or aloof attitude. The lovers' relationship seems reciprocal, or at least it is suggested that it has had some duration, but their intimacy is tainted by a sense of unreachability or lack of complete closeness. The poet is troubled by the fear of loss that the beloved's inaccessibility causes, either by his/her distant behaviour or his/her overwhelming beauty, and, as the poem later suggests, the subjection of the lovers to the unstoppable passing of time and to the imminence of death.

The second quatrain delves deeper into the poet's psyche as he explains further the cause of his suffering. His transmutation into a branchless tree trunk and his lack of flowers, fruit pulp and clay are both stopping him from alleviating his pain, equated with a worm or maggot. This last image, a parasite and a sign of decay, also has significant metamorphic connotations, since 'gusano' evokes both the transformation of living organisms into inorganic matter and the metamorphosis of caterpillars into butterflies.[40] These antithetical transformations, combined with the natural imagery, point to the process of metamorphosis that temporal transience brings about in nature and its inherent creative and destructive powers. A tree's growth is evident in its expansion into branches and roots, as well as in its cyclical production of flowers and fruits, a process similar to the moulding of clay into different forms — which relates to the artistic creative process introduced earlier by the statue reference and to the Christian myth of human creation in which God created humans out of clay — in its generation of a new being by transformation. As seen in other sonnets, this reference also has aesthetic resonances in that the poetic task itself may well be the tool the poet is using to tackle his anxieties about the love affair.[41] In parallel, 'pena', 'siento' and 'sufrimiento' connect the second quatrain with the fears and sorrows expressed earlier, placing the poet in a position of perceived inferiority in the face of the beloved.

The tercets, while establishing a more intimate connection between the lovers, imply that the love affair is or has been reciprocated, but is nonetheless fragile or perhaps clandestine:

> Si tú eres el tesoro oculto mío,
> si eres mi cruz y mi dolor mojado,
> si soy el perro de tu señorío,
>
> no me dejes perder lo que he ganado
> y decora las aguas de tu río
> con hojas de mi Otoño enajenado. (*PC*: 580, ll. 9–14)

The poet adopts a submissive yet masochistic role in the first tercet, but the anaphoric conditional structure of the three lines serves him to retaliate in the second, introducing the crux of the sonnet: his request or command that the beloved let him keep being intimate with him/her and that they attain a union or fusion both physical and emotional. The adjective 'oculto' in line nine and the 'master-dog' relationship in line eleven corroborate the secrecy and lack of reciprocity evoked earlier. The beloved is then a secret or clandestine source of pain or agony ('cruz' in the martyrdom sense) as well as of pleasure and wonder ('tesoro') and the poet, in turn, is a dog to the beloved as a master or mistress.[42] Due to the usual gender indeterminacy of the beloved (and that of the poet for that matter), the masochistic imagery here links the Petrarchan echoes with marked gender-blurring associations.[43] These are, furthermore, reinforced by the reversibility of the poet, who in the final lines adopts a more demanding, persuasive role. More fluidity and gender ambiguity are added through the images related to water flowing ('orilla', 'las aguas de tu río'), which may be read as erotic but also may symbolise tears of sadness or pain ('dolor mojado'). Anderson points out the usual association in Lorca's work between rivers and (male) desire and sexuality, especially in its qualities of 'powerful, elemental, deep, surging, forceful, wet and fertile' (1990: 327); so the riverbanks and flowing water connecting the lovers in the sonnet are apt images representing their indeterminate and permeable identities.

The end of the sonnet implies, on the one hand, the beloved's 'indifference, impassiveness, and narcissistic self-absorption as well as the desperation of the poet' (Anderson 1990: 328); and, on the other hand, 'the use of the verb *decorar* for the action that might possibly signal [the lovers'] reconnection [...] brings aesthetic considerations into play' (Bonaddio 2010: 190). Furthermore, embracing fluidity and metamorphosis seems to be the overall conclusion of the sonnet. Recalling the paradoxical oxymoron from the title, it is clear that the poet wants the affair to continue despite its ambiguities and is also conscious of the powers — aesthetic, creative and persuasive — of the 'sweet complaint' that is the poem itself. The poetic voice urges the beloved to be transformed ('decora las aguas de tu río') by the lovers' entanglement, which is itself defined as cyclical, transient and ever-changing ('Otoño enajenado'). The decaying and metamorphic qualities evoked by autumn and, moreover, by its ambivalent quality of 'enajenado' — which can mean 'crazed' and 'insane' but also 'ecstatic' and 'fascinated', as well as refer to a process of alienation from oneself or others — suggest that the union proposed by the poet is neither stable nor Platonic and ideal. Far from offering a definitive conclusion, the sonnet ends on an ambivalent note evoked precisely by the abundance of paradoxes, oxymora and indeterminacies throughout. Performing the role of a Petrarchan lover, the poetic subject opens up a possibility unforeseen by the 'convention and artifice' (Bonaddio 2010: 190) borrowed from tradition: that the lovers' union might supersede in more ways than one the normative system of binaries from which it emerged.

Possibly one of the best-known sonnets by Lorca is the untitled '[¡Ay voz secreta del amor oscuro!]', which contains the only explicit use of the phrase that became the title of the sonnet cycle. This sonnet's formal particularities, its vehement tone and its nuanced imagery can be taken as an encapsulation of *Sonetos del amor oscuro*'s poetics and an appropriate ending to this chapter. Many thematic and structural elements examined in the sonnets can be found here: antithetical images, paradoxes and plays of opposites, allusions to darkness and obscure love, the natural world of flora and fauna, the union of *eros* and *thanatos*, parallel structures and spatiotemporal uncertainty:

> ¡Ay voz secreta del amor oscuro!
> ¡ay balido sin lanas! ¡ay herida!
> ¡ay aguja de hiel, camelia hundida!
> ¡ay corriente sin mar, ciudad sin muro!
>
> ¡Ay noche inmensa de perfil seguro,
> montaña celestial de angustia erguida!
> ¡ay perro en corazón, voz perseguida,
> silencio sin confín, lirio maduro! (*OC* I: 947, ll. 1–8)

The quatrains present a parallel syntax organised as a series of juxtaposed apostrophes preceded by the interjection 'ay' in anaphoric repetition and enclosed within exclamation marks. This symmetry is reinforced in the repeated use of a noun followed by qualitative adjectives or prepositional phrases modifying it and adding an antithetical, disconcerting, or unusual connotation to it. Following this systematic fashion, then, the first item highlighted by the poet is the 'secret voice of obscure love', which articulates succinctly but ambivalently the nature of a desire which is unknown or clandestine, difficult to voice because it is either too complex, inadequate or painful to tackle.

As discussed in the opening paragraphs of this section, 'amor oscuro' has been taken to signify the secret nature of homosexuality in Lorca's time, despite *and* due to the profound ambiguity and vagueness that characterises the entire sonnet cycle and the lack of overt allusions to same-sex desire in it. Returning to the introductory discussion of the title of the sonnet cycle and to the concept of epenthesis used by Lorca, it seems that the intrusive addition of a strange element reappropriating the norm but challenging it is one of the processes at play in the sonnet. As is usual in Lorca's poetics, indeterminacy and ambivalence serve to convey the complex and at times contradictory or paradoxical experiences of the poetic subject.

What is clearer to see is that the vehement and intimate tone evident in the exclamations inscribes this secret voice of obscure love in a series of unusual images, which may be paralleled to it or consequences of it. 'Balido sin lanas' suggests the image of a sheep which lacks one of its defining features and is here a disembodied, spectral lament without agency or a lost animal 'devoid of all connotations of warmth and softness' (Anderson 1990: 373). A wound and a needle of bile, both evoking corporeal pain and physical destructuration, point to the recurrent experience of love as bitter suffering with which the poetic subject is coming to grips. A drowned or sunken camellia in line three suggests 'coldness and death' (Anderson 1990: 374), but simultaneously, its red or white colour and the allusion to water may evoke passion and change as well. In parallel, 'corriente sin mar' and 'ciudad sin muro' both resonate as transgressive images insofar as they are incomplete or lacking what seem like defining or essential features: a current unable to reach the liberating sea and a city without walls to protect it or delimit it. All these exclamations invoke a sense of dissatisfaction and fittingly they appear next to the evocative '¡ay!', a word as fluid and rich in potential meanings in the Spanish language as it is disconcerting and polysemic. 'Ay' can refer to the 'quejío' present in flamenco songs; to the immense *pathos* evoked in tragedies (similar to the English 'alas!'); or it can be an idiomatic sign of commiseration and recognition expressing pain, surprise, happiness, endearment and even pleasure and celebration. This multiplicity of connotations are at work in the sonnet and add a disorienting and ambivalent signification to the images. If 'ay' is the sound of pain but can also be a cry of celebration or even desire, the position of the poetic voice is thus as unclear and ambiguous (a 'voz secreta') as the images presented. Is the poetic subject complaining, lamenting, suffering, admiring, acknowledging, or wondering about all these images? It seems that all these options could be possible and simultaneous.

The second quatrain continues the list of lamented or contemplated realities, adding an immense night with a clear-cut profile, a celestial mountain of erected angst, a metonymical dog within a heart, a persecuted voice, a limitless silence and a mature lily. The ideas in this quatrain are even more detached from logic and clearly hinge on their contradictory or paradoxical nature. The first two lines play with the visual contrast between darkness, focus and size. The immensity of night and the mountain and the latter's celestial quality situate the images in a natural setting, but the human qualities attributed to both ('perfil seguro', 'angustia erguida') personify them, so their resonance affects the poet who is here an observer in awe of their proportions and the angst they produce in him. The poet is conflicted and his resentment and suffering get mixed with the realisation and acceptance of his unstable position. The final lines of the quatrain expose this conflict in the contrast between verbal and acoustic elements ('voz', 'balido') and the allusions to silence and repression ('secreta', 'perseguida', 'silencio', 'confín', 'muro').

Following this array of elements brought together by their dissimilarities and particularities, the two tercets seem to contradict each other and thus reinforce the poetic subject's conflicted position:

> Huye de mí, caliente voz de hielo,
> no me quieras perder en la maleza
> donde sin fruto gimen carne y cielo.
>
> Deja el duro marfil de mi cabeza,
> apiádate de mí, ¡rompe mi duelo!
> ¡que soy amor, que soy naturaleza! (OC I: 947, ll. 9–14)

The first one sees the poet ask this voice to leave him lest he be lost or fall into the dangerous place where his desire would be realised; while the final one presents the poet's self-conviction that his initial thoughts were too limiting and that his desire deserves redemption as his love is, after all, natural and pervades different aspects of reality. As Bonaddio posits, 'if the unspoken is to be spoken, then the voice will have to emerge from the limbo that is conveyed by its qualification in the first tercet as both hot and icy' (2010: 195). This indeterminate limbo is the spatiotemporal realm the poet strives to create in the sonnet by presenting a multitude of impossible, unexpected, obscure objects. Whilst the conflict is, as usual, never resolved, the very act of exposing and embracing queerness by articulating it and simultaneously silencing it is the poet's rejection of binarism, his contestation of (hetero)normativity. The vehemence and directness in the final lines of the sonnet show the poet's acknowledgment of the multiplicity of aspects that separate him from the norm, which are in no way avoidable or rejected. His pairing of love and nature is presented as the possible — and preferable — resolution of his conflict, suggesting that his desire is far too powerful and immense to ignore despite the suffering it may likely bring and the subjection to death which it necessarily announces. This desire is both lamented and celebrated, spoken and unspoken; it is neither homosexual nor heterosexual, neither carnal nor spiritual.[44] Queerness allows us to not have to choose between one or the other; to explore, in Sara Ahmed's view, 'the strange and perverse mixtures of hope and despair, of optimism and pessimism, within forms of politics that take as a starting point a critique of the world as it is and a belief that the world can be different' (2011: 161). Thus the ending of '[¡Ay voz secreta del amor oscuro!]' situates the poet in that indeterminate epistemological realm in which contradictions can be transcended, with desire and nature seen as a continuum rather than as a reductive linear development.

Mirroring the mimetic process of re-appropriation seen in *Diván del Tamarit*, Lorca borrows and reconfigures a set of traditional conventions, only to perform an unexpected queering representation, a novel poetic artefact. The pairing of antithetical elements reveals the concern with the limits of desire and its inextricable link with mortality; while the reappropriation of traditional tropes points to a performative process both imitative and subversive, moving in the interstices between expression and silence/disguise. In *Sonetos del amor oscuro*, he 'rewrites' the sonnet in order to articulate the obscurity of the beloved and of his desire, bestowing 'nuevos paisajes y acentos ignorados' (*OC* III: 318) on the poetic images he (re)creates. In so doing, his poetic discourse acquires the unprecedented aesthetic substance he seeks: the (endless) redefinition of preconceived and restrictive norms, and the transgressive *pathos* that *duende* playfully performs.

Notes to Chapter 1

1. Lorca said to his parents in a letter: 'I've become a fashionable little boy [...] after my useful and advantageous trip to America' (Stainton 1998: 268; cited in Bonaddio 2010: 170), also mentioning the many editors intent on publishing his work at the time (García Lorca 1997a: 695). Although *Poeta en Nueva York* (1929–30) was also written during his American trip and Lorca organised recitals and lectures about the collection and planned its publication very keenly, it was, like the other two poetic works discussed in this book, published posthumously in 1940.

2. This study will not examine *Lamento por Ignacio Sánchez Mejías* and *Seis poemas galegos* in detail, because the specific nature of both works is outside its main scope. Textual analyses of both works can be found in Anderson (1990) and Bonaddio (2010). However, there is room for further research relating mainly to the elegiac aspect of the former long poem and its awareness of the inevitability and imminence of death, as well as its connection with temporality ('A las cinco de la tarde' is obsessively repeated in the first part of the poem) and the process of sensory apprehension of death in the form of mourning and the sense of loss. For an insightful examination of the imagery of the *Llanto*, see Domínguez Gil (2008). Lorca's linguistic exploration of Galician and its literary tradition (especially his homage to Rosalía de Castro) in *Seis poemas galegos* is also worth studying further, as this brief cycle constitutes the only work by Lorca written entirely in a language other than Spanish.

3. The 'Gacela del mercado matutino', despite carrying the gacela title, was excluded from the collection as it was going to be published by Lorca in 1934–36 for reasons still unknown (Anderson 1990: 141–42), and it has intermittently been included or excluded from subsequent editions of the *Obras completas*. Cátedra's latest edition of *Diván del Tamarit* (2018) restores this poem as the last of the gacelas, trying to offer readers the *Diván* exactly as the poet envisioned the project (*DT*: 105–06). It is noteworthy as well that some poems in *Diván* were originally conceived as part of other poetic projects (the never realised *Tierra y luna*, for example) and that during the planning stages Lorca changed some of the poem titles from gacela to casida and viceversa (*DT*: 18–19).

4. The only exceptions are 'El poeta habla por teléfono con el amor', which presents the slightly different rhyming pattern ABBA/ABBA/CDC/CDC and 'Soneto de la dulce queja', which uses the alternative ABAB/ABAB rhyme scheme in the quatrains.

5. Talens (2000) hypothesises Lorca's intention of including these and other late sonnets in a larger project entitled *El jardín de los sonetos* never realised. In Maurer's view, this truncated endeavour 'would have brought together some of the many [sonnets] he had written over the course of his lifetime', an example of the return to the sonnet as a 'trend in Spanish poetry' (2007: 37).

6. The edition of *Diván* published was part of a section of 'Poemas inéditos' in a special number of the *Revista* (Anderson 1990: 16), while several poems in *Diván* were printed in a number of other publications during Lorca's lifetime (*DT*: 142; 146; 149; 152; 153; 154; 160; 161; 163; 164; 166; 169).

7. The clandestine edition, postmarked 14 December 1983 in Granada, was sent anonymously to various literary figures and magazines in Spain and abroad and is believed to have originated from one of the copies or manuscripts given by Lorca to friends before his death, although the identity of the publisher(s) is still unknown. In March 1984, the authorised edition was published in the Madrid newspaper *ABC* (Eisenberg 1988: 261–62). For a detailed account of the long and irregular publication process and of the various editions and manuscripts of the *Sonetos*, see Moreno Jiménez (2019).

8. Anderson cites Vicente Aleixandre as one of Lorca's contemporaries to have referred to the sonnets under this title, but of course the only untitled extant sonnet, '[Ay voz secreta del amor oscuro]', is an important reference (1990: 305). On the controversies surrounding the title and the publication of the sonnets, see Mario Hernández (1984). The title was a cause for some debate around the time the *Sonetos* were published in the 1980s: 'The length at which the title was discussed suggests that it has been to some extent responsible for the delay in publication of these sonnets; the title in question would seem to imply that Federico had written a book of homosexual love sonnets, or even worse in its impact, first-person sonnets which envisioned homosexual love as an equally valid type of love' (Eisenberg 1988: 263). Francisco García Lorca insisted that the sonnets be published as *Sonetos* or *Sonetos de amor*, whereas Eisenberg sustains the validity of the current title judging from first-hand accounts by friends of Lorca's and contemporary artists.

9. For a full account of the Arabic background of *Diván del Tamarit*, see Anderson (1990: 17–28). See also the 'Introducción' to the Cátedra edition of *Diván* by Pepa Merlo for details of the edition of the collection projected by Lorca with the Universidad de Granada which never came to fruition. Lorca gave the original manuscript to Antonio Gallego Burín, who went ahead with the publication process, but there were a number of delays for causes still unknown. Many believe it was the start of the Civil War which prevented the publication, but there may have been other circumstances at play (*DT*: 92–103).

10. The 'Gacela I del amor imprevisto' correlates the beloved's forehead with a moonlit square in which 'Mil caballitos persas se dormían', an Orientalist reference which may be added to the less evident but recurrent images of gardens ('Gacela del amor que no se deja ver', 'Casida de los ramos'). The latter image has been associated with the garden of Gethsemane (Maurer 2007: 35) at the foot of the Mount of Olives in Jerusalem, but the reference obviously resonates more directly with Andalusian landscapes and folklore (Pedrosa 2012: 335).

11. The marked Orientalist exoticism of Modernist poets, especially in the Latin American context, has been considered elitist, Eurocentric and, therefore, in opposition to ideas about Latin American identity. However, there have been attempts to consider 'el orientalismo de los modernistas en un contexto que incluyera la emergencia del discurso latinoamericanista — dentro del propio modernismo, — los discursos racista, médico-higienista, antropológico, criminalista, y sobre la sexualidad que alcanzaron un particular auge en Occidente a fines del siglo XIX, así como la importancia del estilo en las imposturas y mascaras del modernismo' (Morán 2005: 385). For critical approaches to Orientalism in the poetry of Hispanic Modernismo, see Morán (2005), Tinajero (2004) and Román Lagunas (2017).

12. In Anderson's view, 'although we know from Lorca's biography that if these poems, or at least some of them, were directed at or originally inspired by "real people" from his private life, then they are likely to be male, nevertheless many of the poems, and much of the imagery in the poems, work equally well if the beloved is imagined as male or female' (1990: 29). One of the most prominent queering values of the poems in the *Diván*, as well as in the *Sonetos*, is this ambiguity, which is made explicit as an integral part of the poetic artifice.

13. For a fuller treatment of classical Arabic-Andalusian poetry, see Rubiera Mata (1982, 1992).

14. Anderson notes that the 'moon suggests night-time and a lovers' tryst, but more specifically, in terms of Lorca's habitual use of symbols, some impending fatality or ill-omen' (1990: 32).

15. Shakespeare's very well-known 'Sonnet 18' points to this idea: 'So long as men can breathe, or eyes can see, | So long lives this, and this gives life to thee' (1997: 18, ll. 13–14). It has been documented that Lorca knew Shakespeare's sonnets quite well (Fernández Montesinos 1988: 13–23), and he makes multiple references to works by the Bard throughout his entire production, from the juvenilia poetry to *El público*.

16. In the 2018 edition by Merlo, 'no me enseñes' replaces 'no ilumines', following the published version in *Quaderns de Poesía* (1935) and thus creating an exact replica of the imperative structure in the final line 'no me enseñes tu cintura fresca' and making the beloved's body even more carnally tempting for the poet and the beloved's agency in the (sexual) relationship more explicit (*DT:* 142).

17. The most widespread version of this line is 'Déjame en un ansia de oscuros planetas' (*PC:* 544), while Merlo's 2018 edition reproduces the version published in *Quaderns de Poesía* (1935), in which 'oscuros' is absent. It seems logical that the former version has been continuously adopted in past editions by analogy with Lorca's preference for the use of 'oscuro/a', which will be discussed in light of the *Sonetos*. See also Domínguez Gil (2008) for an examination of 'la muerte oscura' in Lorca's poetry.

18. It is very relevant to read this desire for unfulfilment in light of an existentialist vision of mankind. As Anderson notes: 'ningún cuerpo y ninguna conciencia pueden fundirse — unirse — con otro, y de allí se deriva la fundamental separación, soledad y enajenación del hombre. Al mismo tiempo esa conciencia que tiene conciencia de sí misma quiere superar su aislamiento, su «otredad», pero precisamente por el hecho y las condiciones de su propia existencia — los términos de su autodefinición — nunca podrá hacerlo. De allí ese apuro humano básico de ansiar juntarse, penetrar, fusionarse en el otro, y la inevitable imposibilidad de tal anhelo' (1986: 499). Miguel de Unamuno's thought and, especially, his *Del sentimiento trágico de la vida* (1983 [1912]) is a useful backdrop to these ideas.

19. Anderson suggests the 'grutas del vino' might allude to the bars in the caves on the Sacromonte in Granada (1990: 56), although wine may also symbolise here, as in other poems examined, the image of blood linking the lovers through both erotic and deadly associations.

20. This date marked the anniversary of the reconquest of Granada from its Arabic rule by the Catholic Monarchs in 1492, when Cardinal Mendoza raised his flag on the Vela tower (Anderson 1990: 49).

21. The syntax of the first line can be construed in two different ways: Anderson chooses to read this retrospectively, meaning 'Simply/solely through having heard the bell of the Vela' (1990: 50), although there is the alternative use of the preposition 'por' as conveying finality ('Solely *in order to* hear'), which I prefer in this case. This implies the poetic voice longs to hear the bell toll in the same way as he desires the beloved as well as for the prophecy to be fulfilled, a reading which seems to be supported by one of the original songs from which the line is borrowed and reused: 'Quiero vivir en Granada | solamente por oír | la campana de la Vela | cuando me voy a dormir' (Anderson 1990: 49).

22. In Lorca's early *Libro de poemas* (1921), 'Balada triste. Pequeño poema' includes the lines: 'Pasé por el jardín de Cartagena | la verbena invocando'; and his play *Mariana Pineda* (1925) contains the reference 'Soñar en la verbena y el jardín | de Cartagena, luminoso y fresco', both of which echo lines extracted from the oral tradition and nursery rhymes from Fuentevaqueros: 'Pasimisí, Pasimisá, | por la Puerta de Alcalá, | la de adelante corre mucho, | la de detrás se quedará. | Verbena, verbena, | jardín de Cartagena' (Pedrosa 2012: 335).

23. Anderson notes the phallic symbols and erotic associations embedded in the images relating to fountains and water reservoirs (tanks, pools, ponds, cisterns, etc.), typical of the urban configuration of Granada (1990: 95). In parallel, Barón Palma (1990) posits that the poet's feelings for the boy in this casida and the multiple references to drowning in the *Diván* allude to the idea of loss and the mourning of the beloved, which he identifies as male, after his death by water.

24. Anderson mentions its resemblance to Juan Ramón Jiménez's 'poesía pura' in its minimalist composition (1990: 125). For two important studies of this poem, see Laffranque (1986) and Gillett (2001).

25. Cate-Arries (1992) draws on Freud's *The Interpretation of Dreams* to examine the language of desire and repression that underscores Lorca's play and its use of flower symbolism to express the characters' psyche.

26. While Stein's tautological image has often been said to symbolise the immutable nature of essence, it is also plausible to relate her fragmentary and syntactically incongruous and abstract prose style to the flouting of normativity, 'in ways that break laws (of grammar) and challenge conventions, often with sexual connotations' (Reed 2011: 126–27), similarly to Lorca's rose in the casida.

27. 'La luna vino a la Fragua | con su polisón de nardos. | El niño la mira, mira. | El niño la está mirando.' ('Romance de la luna, luna', *Romancero Gitano, OC* I: 393). 'Pero yo ya no soy yo. | Ni mi casa es ya mi casa.' ('Romance sonámbulo', *Romancero Gitano, OC* I: 402). Anderson suggests that the dedication to Jorge Guillén's son Claudio reinforces the childish tone and flavour of the casida (1990: 137).

28. Anderson ascribes this to an illustrated manuscript that Lorca examined in Granada in 1923 in which one miniature illumination represented the trees of the sun and the moon as Alexander the Great's oracular trees (1990: 138).

29. In popular Spanish children's songs, the sun is often called Lorenzo and the moon, Catalina; and in children's books and illustrations, they are usually personified as male and female respectively. Anderson notes Lorca's use of the sun and the moon as symbols of heterosexual and homosexual love (1990: 137), citing the two '[Normas]' as an example. See also Climent (2004) for an insightful analysis of Lorca's use of popular culture, especially the folklore and popular imaginary related to childhood (lullabies and popular songs, nursery rhymes, 'refranes', etc.), in which symbology of the moon and the sun feature prominently.

30. Anderson (1986), Matas Caballero (1999) and Bonaddio (2010: 188) notice the many references to the sonnet tradition (Quevedo, Góngora and, especially, San Juan de la Cruz) scattered around the *Sonetos*, while pointing out Lorca's awareness of these references and therefore, his wish to counter, comment on or add to them through his work.

31. According to the *Dictionary of Linguistics and Phonetics*, epenthesis is 'a term used in Phonetics and Phonology to refer to a type of intrusion, where an extra sound has been inserted in a word; often subclassified into Prothesis and Anaptyxis. Epenthetic sounds are common both in historical change and in connected speech' (Crystal 2008).

32. Both Cleminson and Vazquez García (2007: 229–30) and Martínez (2017: 52) have provided evidence of Lorca's inclusion in a more or less self-aware homosexual community or subculture in his time, but there is not much historical evidence, beyond Ian Gibson's (1999, 2009) and Alberto Mira's (2004) work, that corroborates the existence of an 'epenthetic movement' *per se* in Spain, which is a clear example of its clandestine nature and, paradoxically, both its marginality and elitism.

33. In looking at Lorca as a Petrarchan poet, Anderson speaks of 'rasgos que tienen historia y resonancia milenarias pero que al mismo tiempo reciben un tratamiento singular, original y único en sus manos' (1986: 497).

34. In his article 'García Lorca como poeta petrarquista', Anderson cites Nicolas J. Perella, who traces the history of kissing and situates the correlation between kissing and eating as a ubiquitous trope in literature (Anderson 1986: 502).

35. This is obviously an overarching motif in the late play *Bodas de sangre*. The eponymous blood relates throughout the play to the bloodlines of the protagonist families and, by extension, to their honour, reputation and offspring; but also, to the blood that will be spilled through violence and death. In parallel, see Chapter 3 for a discussion of the treatment of blood motifs in the drawings.

36. In his reading of this sonnet, Anderson establishes the classical myth of Venus and Adonis as an important backdrop to the imagery developed in the poem, especially in relation to images linking the yearly cycle to vegetation (1990: 310–21).

37. For a thorough and insightful reading of the garland/wreath motif among others as erotic/deadly symbols in Lorca's oeuvre and their inscription within Western and Spanish cultural history, see Salazar Rincón (1999).

38. The phrase 'espesura de anémonas levanta' appears *verbatim* in Act III, Scene 1 of *Así que pasen cinco años*. Anderson links the images in the sonnet with the play, in which temporality and dream are crucial elements interacting with desire and fulfilment (1990: 315–16). See Chapter 2 for my analysis of the play in terms of delayed heterodox desires and reproductive futurism.

39. In Acts II and III of *El público*, the beauty of a marble statue carries associations with classical antiquity but especially with the idea of unity and fixity, which is seen as impossible and lethal for the main characters (see Chapter 2); and in *Viaje a la luna*, the image of the statue evokes the myth of Pygmalion and the idea of an obsessive desire for the sculpted body, again an epitome of classical harmonious beauty, with violent and deadly connotations (see Chapter 4).

40. Anderson suggests the images juxtaposed to the worm can also be taken as the three phases of life: 'the initial flowering, maturity and death' (1990: 325), mirroring respectively 'the relationship and the concomitant suffering in its different manifestations or stages' (1990: 325).

41. Bonaddio indeed suggests that 'the fear of loss conveyed in the first quatrain might equally convey anxieties about the inability to capture the true effect of the loved one's features and presence in verse' (2010: 190).

42. Anderson notes the Christological analogy, with the implication that the beloved 'is a "cross to bear" because of the pain [the poet] receives', yet 'the beloved is what gives life any sense, just as Christ's life and death do for a Christian' (1990: 326).

43. Shakespeare's sonnets to the 'Fair Youth' come to mind in this respect, especially those in which the poetic voice subscribes, laments or subverts gender conventions of the time. Sonnet 20 is especially indicative of this, as the male beloved is described in terms of combined male and female traits which the poet picks apart throughout the sonnet. The beloved is 'master-mistress of my passion' to the poet (Shakespeare 1997: 20), an image which is clearly evoked in Lorca's sonnet. Anderson notes the use of a similar image in Act III of *Bodas de sangre*, in which the Bride wishes to be 'una perra' in service of Leonardo as a master (Anderson 1990: 326).

44. Domínguez Gil posits that the Lorquian *eros* goes beyond binary distinctions: 'la poesía lorquiana "deconstruye", entre otras, la antítesis heterosexualidad/homosexualidad, trascendiéndola en un concepto de erotismo que engloba y supera las dos tendencias, aunque la diferencia se siga manteniendo' (2008: 19).

CHAPTER 2

❖

Fluid Times, Spaces, and Theatres in the 'Impossible Plays': *Así que pasen cinco años* and *El público*

El teatro es la poesía que se levanta del libro y se hace humana.
Y al hacerse, habla y grita, llora y se desespera.
El teatro necesita que los personajes que aparezcan en la escena
lleven un traje de poesía y al mismo tiempo
que se les vean los huesos, la sangre.

(*OC* III: 673)

The Impossible Theatre

If temporality and space were queered by the poetic voice in Lorca's late poems, in the New York theatrical works — the so-called 'impossible plays' — this is manifested through characters, scenarios and plots, moving decidedly across temporal as well as spatial boundaries in unexpected ways. This chapter explores the staging of spatiotemporal and sexual instabilities in Lorca's most modernist plays, *Así que pasen cinco años* and *El público*. Written against the backdrop of an attempted renovation of the Spanish stage, these two works deal boldly with heterodox sexualities, presenting in shocking and innovative ways characters whose desires challenge binary identifications and stable or normative sexualities and instead embrace fluidity and reversibility. Meta-theatrical devices are used profusely so as to inscribe these queer identities within aesthetic debates considering the unstable interrelation of life and theatre and the latter's ability to reveal, disguise or tap into the inner desires and identities of those involved in the theatrical experience. In *Así que pasen cinco años*, I argue, temporality is disrupted and manipulated to show the characters' efforts to delay and eschew the fulfilment of their desires, in order to escape the linearity of heteronormative time and thus the imminent advent of reproductive futurism and mortality. I then suggest that *El público* represents a conflicted view of theatre and reality, mirroring the conflict brought about by the performative nature of gender and sexual identity. Queer visibility serves in the play to challenge a unitary vision of identity, be it sexual or ontological, proposing instead that multiplicity and fragmentation are more suitable principles to approach human existence and how this is represented through the theatrical medium.

Lorca's New York plays find an antecedent in the plans for a renovation of the Spanish stage during the 1920s and 1930s, when attempts were made by dramatists, stage directors, actors and intellectuals to create a new kind of 'Art Theatre' inspired by avant-garde European models which would raise the bar from contemporary practices, more mainstream and commercially oriented and therefore retaining nineteenth-century approaches and methods of organisation. These tended to '[appease] the lowest tastes of the bourgeois audience with post-Romantic melodramas like those of Echegaray, comic novelties or *costumbrista* works (Comedies of manners) like those of Carlos Arniches or the Álvarez Quintero Brothers [*sic*], or at best, the elegant but empty 'well-made' plays of Benavente' (Sánchez 1998: 8). According to De Ros, playwrights and critics 'coincided in blaming the bourgeois mentality of Spanish audiences for the theatre's decadence' (1996: 110) and Lorca himself was fiercely critical in this respect.[1] However, the renovation some wanted at this time was largely thwarted by a series of factors: the imbalance between the new ideas that influential figures such as Cipriano Rivas Cherif, Ramón del Valle-Inclán, Margarita Xirgu or Lorca himself tried to put into practice and the problems stemming from existing production mechanisms, economic limitations and the tastes of contemporary Spanish audiences meant that some of these new and radical ideas had to be abandoned or were poorly received.

Both sociopolitical and economic reasons can account for the perception that Lorca himself and his circle of friends had of his avant-garde New York plays as 'irrepresentables'. As Dougherty and Anderson suggest:

> issues such as social justice, political corruption or sexual inequalities were pushed to the margins of mainstream theatre. Censorship was governed by the regulation established in 1913 which prohibited works that might disturb public order or endanger morality and good manners, and somewhat stricter norms were enforced during the dictatorship of Primo de Rivera. (2012: 290–91)

Processes of censorship were responsible for a significant delay in the first staging of *Amor de don Perlimplín con Belisa en su jardín*, whose text was confiscated by the police before its planned premiere and could not be staged until 1933, thanks to the help of Club Anfistora's founder and Lorca's friend Pura Maortua Ucelay. Furthermore:

> the conservative inertia of mainstream Spanish theatre was related to its commercial base. Impresarios and company directors were in business and had to turn a profit if the theatre were to perform its well-established social and aesthetic functions. Heavily taxed and devoid of state subventions until the late 1920s, the industry could not afford the luxury of prolonging an unconventional play's run if it proved unpopular: thus the paradoxical practice of a market constantly in search of new material but averse to innovation. (Dougherty and Anderson 2012: 294)

Despite the difficulties that avant-garde, unconventional or experimental plays experienced and the struggles of authors like Valle-Inclán or Lorca to stage them, 'impossible' remains too strong a term to describe them. Anderson suggests that a series of attempts were made to stage *El público* in the early 1930s (1992: 345–46), and *Así que pasen cinco años*, finished in 1931, was expressly written to be performed by the Club Anfistora, with rehearsals taking place in 1936 (Fernández Cifuentes 1978: 190).[2] The tensions and innovations in Spanish theatre thus have a dual importance when considering Lorca's more avant-garde plays. Firstly, the very innovations that he and his contemporaries perceived as 'unstageable' were a crucial part of both plays discussed in this chapter, insofar as theatre itself and meta-theatrical elements become part and parcel of the plays' plots and aesthetics. This can also be seen in Valle-Inclán's plays, whose 'esperpentos' show meta-theatrical elements used in similar ways in order to make audiences reflect upon the theatrical experience.[3] Furthermore, Lorca's plays focus on what Cordero Sánchez calls his 'meta-autores' (*El público*'s Director and the Joven in *Así que pasen cinco años*), not only because these characters resemble Lorca himself as playwright, stage director and poet/theatrical creator (2012: 145) as well as the emerging director figures in the early twentieth century, such as Martínez Sierra, Gual or Rivas Cherif; but also because in dealing with a meta-author whose concerns relate to time, desire, truth and theatre and the norms and rules that govern them, he effectively repositions his norm-transgressing aesthetics as centrefold in the drama. As De Ros puts it, a 'crisis in human relations reflects the crisis between author and audience in modern theatre' (1996: 110). This theatrical crisis was evidently one of Lorca's main concerns around this time, and he found ways to explore it in some of his plays as a dual reflection on theatre and reality. *Dragón*, one of his unfinished plays, opens with one such meta-author, a Director mirroring that of *El público*:

> DIRECTOR. [...] Yo, como Director de escena, estoy cansado del teatro, y quiero que la vida, tal como se presenta en todos sus aspectos, sueño y vigilia, día y noche, irrumpa en la escena para que la marquesa que toma el té, Pepe Luis el galán, y el criado eterno que dice: 'Sí, señorita, sí, señorito', puedan entrar en el jardín de sorpresas y gracia a que tienen derecho después de su largo servicio. (*TC*: 730)

Similarly, in *Comedia sin título*, also known as *El sueño de la vida*, the Autor takes on the same critical approach to theatre's social functions: 'AUTOR. [...] hoy el poeta os hace una encerrona porque quiere y aspira a conmover vuestros corazones enseñando las cosas que no queréis ver, gritando las simplísimas verdades que no queréis oír' (*TC*: 737). Lorca thus insists on the necessity of creating theatre that will, paradoxically, destroy the pillars on which theatre has been standing: mere artificial and evasive entertainment hiding away from uncomfortable, unseen or unheard realities. His purpose, instead, is to show how realities not easily categorisable or reducible to simple and univocal principles and norms are in fact worth staging, in order to show the audience 'un pequeño rincón de realidad' (*TC*: 737).

Así que pasen cinco años and *El público* both revel in the transgression of conventional dramatic structure and aesthetics, seeking to appeal to audiences who will have to question the limits of theatre as well as those imposed by preconceived notions about desire, identity and what constitutes reality. In portraying characters whose queerness invades the entirety of the play, shattering the firm basis that elements like spatiotemporal certainty, realism, identity or unity of action provide, Lorca proposes a kind of dramatic space in which the very act of questioning established norms acquires a poetic/theatrical substance powerful enough to call for and produce change.

Así que pasen cinco años

In Lorca's 'Leyenda del Tiempo' — the subtitle to *Así que pasen cinco años* — waiting and the dynamics of temporality are brutally opposed to desire and fulfilment. Time is a prominent thematic element that characters constantly conjure in the dialogue and that shapes the central action of the play. Many critics have also noticed the importance of oneiric elements, such that the entire play could be seen as a dream of the protagonist, or as a space in which dream and reality are perpetually intertwined.[4] The main character, el Joven, is engaged to a woman, la Novia, who has agreed to marry him upon her return from a long five-year journey. When this time has passed, the Joven visits her only to be rejected, as she has decided to break off their engagement and elope with her lover, a Jugador de rugby, because she no longer wishes to be with the Joven. In despair, the Joven seeks his previous employee, the Mecanógrafa, who was originally in love with him but who finally rejects him as well, asking in turn for another five-year postponement before they can marry. At the end of the play, the Joven returns to his library and dies at a peculiar game of cards from an arrow to the 'ace of hearts' he has played, magically transposed into his actual heart, while being told by his fellow poker players that living means seizing the moment instead of endlessly waiting for what may come. Throughout the play, a series of characters (some of them human and some imagined, fantastical, or symbolical) interact with the Joven and among themselves, often enacting scenes that relate to the Joven's concerns about time and mortality.

The temporal progression of the three acts in the play, however, is difficult to establish, since time seems to have stopped at the beginning (the first act starts at six o'clock and at the very end the Criado tells the Joven it is six o'clock again), but it rapidly goes by between the second and third acts (the eponymous five years from the title have passed at the beginning of the second act and it is assumed that no more time elapses in the third as concrete references are scarce). In the cuadro último, the clock strikes twelve at the very end of the play, signalling that, despite any efforts made throughout, time inscrutably and irrevocably passes.[5] In Act one, the conversation between the Joven and the Viejo focuses on the metamorphic nature of reality, such that knowledge of the world is necessarily bound up with change and mutability. Discernible reality cannot be immutable, the Viejo reminds the Joven, and thus the idea of fixity and stability the Joven is desperately seeking is only achievable by suspending time, by making it stop in order to 'exist in a state of perpetual limbo' (Wright 2000: 63). Antonio F. Cao observes that the Heraclitean vision of mutability prompts the Joven to find a way towards oblivion, so as to escape the pain and anxiety of uncertainty: 'el Viejo niega la esencia inmutable del mundo objetivo, expresándolo mediante la fórmula heraclitiana, es decir, en función del cambio continuo, única realidad discernible' (1984: 88). In using imagery of rivers flowing towards the sea to symbolise the incessant and mutable flow of time, the Joven ascribes to the sea the soothing abilities of forgetting: 'Basta [...] mirar al mar una tarde poniendo atención en la forma de cada ola para que el rostro o llaga que llevamos en el pecho se deshaga en burbujas' (*TC*: 302).

Rivers, however, and the imagery of water ('escarcha', 'nieve', 'manantial') are in the play also a clear allusion to *eros*, carnal desires which, as unstoppable life forces, lead inevitably towards death. The structure of the play and the Joven himself attempt to disrupt this flowing movement, to shut it down. The Joven's reticence to marry and consummate the heterosexual imperative has been identified with sexual heterodoxy: 'JOVEN. La he conocido poco. Pero no importa. Yo creo que me quiere. [...] Se fueron a un largo viaje. Casi me alegré... [...] Por causas que no son de explicar, yo no me casaré con ella... hasta que pasen cinco años' (*TC*: 301). Like the old man Perlimplín in *Amor de don Perlimplín con Belisa en su jardín*, the Joven is inexperienced in matters of love, but seems to assert his knowledge of the necessary fulfilment of social norms relating to marriage and procreation.[6] The thought of realising what is to come makes him afraid, so he insists on exacerbating his isolation: 'JOVEN. (*En alta voz.*) Juan. Cierra las ventanas. [...] ¡Pues no quiero enterarme! (*En alta voz.*) Todo bien cerrado. [...] No me importa lo que pase fuera. Esta casa es mía y aquí no entra nadie' (*TC*: 307). In Wright's view, the Joven 'has retreated into the inner world of illusion' and 'of the psyche, rather than having to cope with the pressures of action in the world' (2000: 64). Compulsive heterosexuality and its emphasis on reproduction are what lies outside his home, the necessity to fulfil the male roles of husband and procreator of children. As Smith suggests, the play effects 'a rupture between desire and reproduction, between sexual instinct and its "natural" (heterosexual) object' (1998a: 88). The linear temporality implied by the fulfilment of these roles is what the Joven attempts to alter and manipulate, firstly by creating an ideal unchanging image of the Novia and then by imposing temporal hurdles on their prospective union: 'Pero es que yo estoy enamorado y quiero estar enamorado, tan enamorado como ella lo está de mí, y por eso puedo aguardar cinco años, en espera de poder liarme de noche, con todo el mundo a oscuras, sus trenzas de luz alrededor de mi cuello' (*TC*: 302). The Joven wants to be in love as much as the Novia is in love with him, or in other words, to be able to equate his desire with hers while keeping desire alive, intact, in waiting. His expectation of consummation, after five years have passed, will bring about his access to her corporeality, her braids around his neck a potent erotic but ambivalent symbol. In this delayed and imagined encounter, the simultaneity of darkness and light — a nightly scene in the darkness illuminated by 'trenzas de luz' — and of pleasure and pain — the metonymical carnal union with the Novia through her hair evokes a scene of suffocation — suggest the Joven's embrace of both the positive and negative aspects of sexual fulfilment. The crucial conundrum he faces is thus inevitably temporal, for desire's temporal progression towards fulfilment automatically denies stasis and announces the irruption of potential pain, loss and death. In the Joven's view, *eros* and *thanatos* cohabit in such a close union and operate in such an urgent temporal consequence that he must face the linearity of heterosexual time, or as Freeman suggests, 'the dominant arrangement of time [...] into consequential sequence' (2010: xi). In her discussion of the critical potential of temporality for queer theory, Freeman posits that queer aesthetics prefers:

> to elaborate ways of living aslant to dominant forms of object-choice, coupledom, family, marriage, sociability, and self-presentations and thus out of synch with state-sponsored narratives of belonging and becoming. Even so, their project is less to negate than to prevaricate, inventing possibilities for moving through and with time, encountering pasts, speculating futures, and interpenetrating the two in ways that counter the common sense of the present tense. (2010: xv)

Thinking against 'straight time', Lorca's play allows the Joven and other characters — be it through dream, hallucination or simply through the oneiric quality of the Joven's projections — to create a spatiotemporal alternative in which the performative and the theatrical are able to invent new possibilities in the face of the Joven's conundrum.

Time is therefore disrupted and purposely confused by the characters. Ruiz Ramón observes the play's lack of 'una verdadera unidad dramática, diseminada en varios "momentos" no siempre motivados interiormente en su enlace ni realmente integrados' (1986: 188), something characteristic of Surrealist and Expressionist theatre. As I will discuss further in relation to *El público, Así que pasen cinco años* can be read as a series of moments or tableaux, purposely lacking integration with one another to reinforce the temporal disruptions at work.[7] The Viejo, who could be read as the Joven's projection of his future self, tells the Joven it is important to 'recordar hacia mañana' (*TC*: 301), while the Amigo 2°, a younger character who could be the Joven's child alter ego or an incarnation of his past, insists that: 'Quiero morirme siendo | ayer' (*TC*: 320). Constant use of future clauses ('hasta que pasen cinco años', *TC*: 301; 'lo que ha de llegar', *TC*: 30; 'en estos cinco años las volverá a tener', *TC*: 302;, 'serán unas trenzas...', *TC*: 302; 'volveré por aquí', *TC*: 304, '¡Ya se abrirá!', *TC*: 30; 'subiré la escalera', *TC*: 306; '¡Los truenos tendrás que oírlos!', *TC*: 307); juxtaposed or mismatched verb tenses ('VIEJO. 'Se me olvidará el sombrero [...] es decir, se me ha olvidado el sombrero', *TC*: 307; 'MUCHACHA. [...] ¿Quién lo dice? | ¿Quién lo dirá?', *TC*: 342; 'MECANÓGRAFA. ¡Te he querido tanto! JOVEN. ¡Te quiero tanto! MECANÓGRAFA. ¡Te querré tanto!', *TC*: 350); and marked temporal adverbs and phrases ('JOVEN. Ahora... MECANÓGRAFA. ¿Por qué dices ahora?', *TC*: 351; 'Nunca es enseguida', *TC*: 345; 'VIEJO. ¿Qué haría usted mañana? ¿Eh? Piense. ¡Mañana!', *TC*: 305) evidence the effort to make language transgress and confuse time.

The Joven, who remembers always 'saving his sweets to eat them later' as a child, is reluctant to let time progress, delaying fulfilment of his desire in order to savour, idealise or sublimate that desire: 'VIEJO. [...] porque hay que recordar, pero... JOVEN. Pero las cosas vivas, ardiendo en su sangre, con todos sus perfiles intactos' (*TC*: 300). Memories for the Joven and the Viejo distill 'hilitos de agua fría' (*TC*: 300), that is, the Joven can only preserve his desires intact by keeping them crystallised and unchanged, for bringing those memories to the present implies letting them be altered by time. Acting on his desire, actualising it in the here and now, has for the Joven terrible and ominous connotations: 'JOVEN. Novia... ya lo sabe usted; si digo novia la veo sin querer amortajada en un cielo sujeto por enormes trenzas de nieve. No, no es mi novia (*Hace un gesto como si alejara la imagen que quiere captarlo.*), es mi niña, mi muchachita' (*TC*: 303). By bringing his image of the Novia preserved in the past to the present, she becomes a living entity and is consequently subjected to change, transience and death. Her actualisation makes her a painful reminder of the Joven's unwanted urgency to fulfil his performative role, both sexual and as a living being prone to die:

> VIEJO. [...] Están las cosas más vivas dentro que ahí fuera, expuestas al aire o la muerte. Por eso vamos a... a no ir... o a esperar. Porque lo otro es morirse ahora mismo y es más hermoso pensar que todavía mañana veremos los cien cuernos de oro con que levanta a las nubes el sol. (*TC*: 304)

Hope and expectation are construed in the play as poetic agents of creation and transformation. By eschewing temporal linearity and actualisation, they allow the characters to step out of the here and now and inhabit an alternative, queer space positioned against the dominant structures of heteronormative time. As we saw in the previous chapter, in *Cruising Utopia* José Esteban Muñoz makes use of Bloch's approach to hope as a critical methodology, describing hope as 'a backward glance that enacts a future vision' (2009: 4), a remembrance towards tomorrow. In Muñoz's view, hope and utopia bring about a queer(ing) mode of thinking outside the linearity of straight time, outside of the sequential framework of heteronormativity. In this 'autonaturalizing temporality', Muñoz argues, 'straight time tells us that there is no future but the here and now of our everyday life. The only futurity promised is that of reproductive majoritarian heterosexuality' (2009: 23). In his insistence to stay in the potentiality of his memories and that of his future projections yet to come, the Joven in Lorca's play can articulate his queer desire, defying mortality, reproductive futurism and compulsive heterosexuality.

A study by Joaquín Roses-Lozano posits that the play is structured around a triple discourse: in Marxian interpretative terms, one discourse would be the thesis, associated with a conservative attitude of waiting or expectation; the antithesis would be the *carpe diem* attitude (represented by the Amigo 1° and the Novia and later in the play by the Joven), which evokes immediacy, pragmatism and hedonistic fulfilment of desires (1989: 117–28). Roses-Lozano proposes that the third, synthesising discourse is that representing the realm of literature and poetic creation: 'la solución lorquiana, su propuesta de interpretación de la realidad, es un proyecto poético, teatral, en el que los elementos imaginativos y ficticios configuran la dimensión cultural, pero culturalmente viva, de la sociedad' (1989: 129). Against the inevitability of temporal progression and mortality and the conflicting attitudes towards desire and normativity's power, the play alludes to an alternative spatiotemporal realm which is associated with the poetic and the theatrical. The passages in which non-naturalistic characters appear and theatricality and poetic discourse are heightened suggest this utopic realm of crystallised temporality and logic-defying possibilities:

[sus] actuaciones son claramente teatrales, refuerzan los sentidos de irra-
cionalidad, sensibilidad e imaginación propios del discurso C' [the third
discursive level], comprendidos en la actividad teatral y literaria. Un discurso
que, desde la producción dramática, propugna la producción creativa frente a
la transformación alocada o la conservación reaccionaria características de los
anteriores. (Roses-Lozano 1989: 129)

The Joven is thus not the only character to disengage from temporal linearity. The
Amigo 2° epitomises the utopia of queer time, followed by the series of mythical
or non-naturalistic characters in the subsequent acts. The Niño muerto and the
Gato/Gata muerto/a problematise the linear division between life and death and
between past and future, also associating closely with the poetic and the theatrical.
Both characters appear in Act one as already dead. However, the moment of their
death takes place later in the play: the death of the Niño is mentioned as his body
is taken to be buried towards the end of Act one, while the Gato dies as the Joven
goes to his fiancée's house in Act two, although it has previously been killed by
some children at the end of Act one. Furthermore, the dead child reappears as the
Joven talks to the Maniquí in Act two and as the Mecanógrafa talks to the Mask in
Act three, supposedly all (dead) reincarnations of the caretaker's (Portera) deceased
child, mentioned again at the start of the final act. These characters, together with
the Amigo 2°, also introduce the theme of gender indeterminacy and fluidity in the
play, which will recur in the subsequent acts.

The Gato/Gata changes sex and gender halfway through its dialogue with the
child: 'GATO. No me digas más gato. NIÑO. ¿No? GATO. Soy gata. | NIÑO.
¿Eres gata? GATO. (*Mimosa*) Debiste conocerlo. | NIÑO. ¿Por qué? GATO. Por mi
voz de plata' (*TC*: 309). The alternating gender markers (GATO. (*Mimosa*); *El Gato,
sentado*; GATO. (*Enfática*), *TC*: 309–10) emphasise the cat's gender-bending abilities,
as does the location of its gender identity not according to biological expectations
('Yo no tengo cuca') but in its poetic discourse, its 'voz de plata'. Poetic discourse,
in a combination of free verse and consonant rhymes, punctuates the characters'
dialogue, which creates a scission from the initial scene in the Joven's library.
The two characters' interaction suggests both their return from death as well as a
temporal regressive motion towards childhood ('¡Yo quiero ser niño, un niño!', *TC*:
312). Juxtaposed to the Joven's dilemma, they propose a spatiotemporal realm in
which time moves backwards and escapes mortality. This will be emphasised by the
Amigo 2°, who also sings the joys of crystallised childhood and reversed temporality:
'AMIGO 2°. Cuando yo tenía cinco años...no, cuando yo tenía dos...¡miento!, uno,
un año tan sólo, es hermoso, ¿verdad? [...] Se hizo cada vez más pequeña, más niña,
como debe ser, como es lo justo' (*TC*: 317).

As has been noted by several critics, childhood is a motif ripe with connotations
in the play and throughout Lorca's oeuvre.[8] The return to childhood can be read as
both a regression to a state prior to sexuality as well as an allusion to reproduction
and its futurity: the perpetuation of oneself through offspring. The Joven laments
the child he will not have, as does the mannequin once the engagement has been
broken in the second act. The dead child(ren) in the play would thus figure the
Joven's unborn children and his lost infant life. The ambivalence of childhood in this

sense is, I argue, precisely in keeping with the play's utopic spatiotemporal realm. The Joven's temporal conundrum is related to the linearity of time, a linearity which implies both the necessity to fulfil his desire as well as the realisation that this fulfilment entails transience, reproduction and death. The refusal to succumb to sexual fulfilment is the refusal to acknowledge the temporal linearity imposed by 'straight time' and reproductive futurism, and the impossibility of escaping it, thus returning to a non-sexual child state. Wishing to remain a child unaware of desire or wishing to not fulfil his role as procreator to avoid growing old and dying are both impossible options for the Joven, which is why they remain in the play's utopic realm, the realm of poetic creation. Only in this realm do the possibilities of 'remembering towards tomorrow' or 'dying being yesterday' and of changing and reversing gender roles and differences become actualised. In addition to the Amigo 2°'s gender indeterminacy — the stage directions specify that this role be played by a very young actor or, failing that, a young woman — the Amigo 1°'s sexual ambiguity and disregard for gender difference — his initially exacerbated heterosexual desire later suggests he may find men attractive too — and the cat's gender fluidity, there are the gender role reversals of the Novia and the Mecanógrafa in contrast with the Joven.[9] As Plaza Agudo notes:

> frente a la imagen tradicional de 'la mujer que espera', ellas manifiestan reiteradamente su necesidad de poner distancia y de alejarse de un amor que intuyen poco saludable y satisfactorio. El Joven es, en cambio, el 'hombre que espera', el hombre que se encierra en su casa, donde finalmente acabará encontrando la muerte. (2019: 221)

Heteronormative roles of gender and sexuality and their temporal linearity are shown in the play to oppress characters other than the Joven. The Mecanógrafa, in the final plot twist in which she imposes her own five-year delay on the Joven, makes it evident that their initial attitudes have been interchanged. Despite the Joven's sudden urge to attend to his present desires and stop waiting, she in turn realises the impossibility of escaping the temporal progression that disintegrates desire: 'JOVEN. Yo esperaba y moría. MECANÓGRAFA. Yo moría por esperar' (*TC*: 351). She decides that the only way to keep desire alive is to keep waiting, making time stand still again for the Joven. Conversely, in his new role as the 'expecting man', the Joven fittingly adopts the role of child-bearer: 'JOVEN. ¡Sí, mi hijo! Corre por dentro de mí, como una hormiguita sola dentro de una caja cerrada' (*TC*: 351).

The Harlequin (Arlequín), the Clown (Payaso), the Mask (Máscara) and the Young Woman (Muchacha) appear as projections on stage before the final encounter between the Joven and the Mecanógrafa. While the Harlequin brings our attention to the relationship between dreaming and temporality (the former creating illusions as the latter exerts its unstoppable power), the Muchacha appears as a victim of the inevitability of death. Her beloved is dead, drowned at the bottom of the sea, a further projection of a delayed union which will never be fulfilled. The Harlequin and Clown, as theatrical and comedic characters, try to confuse and entice the Young Woman, sardonically evidencing the inescapability of time and death. They offer her the possibility of recovering her dead lover by using a long ladder down to the bottom of the sea, but their attempt is interspersed with cruel allusions to farcically theatrical and circus elements. The Harlequin feigns the lover's voice and then plays the violin, while the Clown addresses the audience, shattering the woman's illusion and making it abundantly clear that they are only performing tricks and mockeries on stage: 'PAYASO. A representar' (*TC*: 343). It is through these performative tricks that an alternative temporality is suggested, a reality in which the dead lover can come back from among the dead, escaping the inevitable routes imposed by time: 'A la media vuelta | del viento y el mar' (*TC*: 342). This possibility is, however, questioned repeatedly by the characters themselves:

> ARLEQUÍN. (*Gracioso.*)
>> Mentira.
> MUCHACHA.
>> Verdad. [...]
>> ¡Abajo está!
>> Banderas de agua verde
>> lo nombran capitán.
> ARLEQUÍN. (*En alta voz y gracioso.*)
>> ¡Mentira!
> MUCHACHA. (*En alta voz.*)
>> ¡Verdad![...]
> ARLEQUÍN.
>> Tu amante verás
>> a la media vuelta
>> del viento y el mar.
> MUCHACHA. (*Asustada.*)
>> ¡Mentira!
> ARLEQUÍN.
>> ¡Verdad!
>> Yo te lo daré.
> MUCHACHA. (*Inquieta.*)
>> No me lo darás.
>> No se llega nunca
>> al fondo del mar. (*TC*: 340–41)

These *commedia dell'arte* personae corroborate the inevitability of temporal transience, however intently they seem to collaborate with the Joven's attempt to stop and freeze time, delaying the action and thus trying to delay death: 'PAYASO. Una música. ARLEQUÍN. De años. | PAYASO. Lunas y mares sin abrir. | Queda atrás… ARLEQUÍN. La mortaja del aire. | PAYASO. Y la música de tu violín.' (*TC*: 353–54). They point, however, to the utopic possibilities afforded through the poetic-theatrical medium: the chance to escape death or return from it ('a la media vuelta | del viento y el mar'), the exposure of the futility of gender roles or differences and of the mutability of identity.

The queer time-space in the play is anchored in the realm of literary creation and imagination. It is only at this level that the impossible battle against time is feasible. By suggesting an alternative epistemology of temporality in which stepping out of the here and now leads to 'remembering towards tomorrow' and hoping for 'death to come yesterday' or to not come at all, the characters in the play manage to disintegrate time, creating through the poetic-theatrical, through the realm of imagination and literary creation, a utopia in which alternatives to mortality, gender difference and orthodox sexualities become possible.

El público

The epigraph to this chapter recalls Lorca's conviction that 'los personajes que aparezcan en la escena lleven un traje de poesía y al mismo tiempo que se les vean los huesos, la sangre' (OC III: 673). These words allude to the central tension at the core of El público: the unstable interrelation of life and representation and how theatre can articulate or destabilise the identities of those involved in the theatrical experience. The play combines 'the terms of its reflection on theatre [...] with the portrayal of an emotional conflict with homosexual overtones' (De Ros 1996: 110), often through a variety of meta-theatrical elements. Made up of six 'cuadros', the length and order of which have survived in seemingly incomplete form, the play introduces the main conflict — emotional, sexual and meta-theatrical — through the character of the Director and his visitors in Cuadro primero, and then it is reworked through different scenarios in the subsequent acts, with the main characters reappearing as different theatrical incarnations, a play-within-the-play unravelling off-stage followed by the audience rioting and then trying to escape the theatre. After the brief 'Solo del pastor bobo', the play reaches an ambiguous *dénouement* in Cuadro sexto, which ends exactly as the play started, with the Director beckoning the audience into the theatre.[10] In this section, I will assess how these main ideas are developed in the play in light of Lorca's queer poetics of destructuration, challenging the fixity and closed individuality of bodies and (sexual) identities while proclaiming the advent of a much-needed new aesthetic mode. The play suggests that the medium of theatre and its performative exchange with the audience can serve to alter the preconceived notions of those watching the spectacle by exposing the inauthenticity and mutability of the personae and events developing on stage. The tension between truth and artificiality hinges on images of the body as open and metamorphic, leading to a discussion of desire and mortality as necessary elements of the new kind of theatre offered to the audience.

The Cuadro primero unfolds in the Director's room, seemingly part of a theatre or adjacent to a stage. However, the space in this act is made deliberately nondescript, bare of much furniture or decor around the Director. In the introductory stage directions, the room is seen in objective detail: the windows are made of x-ray photographs, a giant hand is printed on the wall and the space acquires blue tones. The evocation of the intra-corporeal vision that an x-ray photograph provides — linked to the corporeality of the big hand on the wall — suggests that the play will look inside the Director's body at his inner desires and thoughts, while also claiming to show a clinical, objective and detached view of his world. His theatre — both the space where the play unfolds around him as well as his own theatrical production as author — is depicted as a space paradoxically devoid of ornaments and artificiality. However, during the first act, this room becomes a stage as characters and audience members join him. The *dramatis personae* themselves play ambivalent roles as actors and spectators, so it is never clarified who is part of the spectacle to be watched and who is the audience watching. The question of whether theatrical representation reflects a true, objective reality or whether it is always necessarily false and artificial is thus posed, both to the intra-diegetic (the play's eponymous *público*) and the extra-diegetic audiences (the readers or spectators of the play):

CRIADO.	Señor
DIRECTOR.	¿Qué?
CRIADO.	Ahí está el público.
DIRECTOR.	Que pase. (*TC*: 250)

The Director's invitation suggests that the audience (and readership) of the play will witness the fine lines about to be drawn between theatre's simultaneous roles as representation of reality and artificial mask.

The first act thus delves into the tensions between what is inside and outside theatre, what can be seen and what is hidden, and who are the participants in the play. The discussion throughout Cuadro primero of the 'teatro al aire libre' and the 'teatro bajo la arena' evidently relates to the renovation of the Spanish stage Lorca sought, a renovation that points not only to the subject-matter, style and aesthetics that should characterise the theatre, but also to the audiences fit to attend that new kind of theatre. As Anderson observes, if the 'teatro al aire libre':

> represents conventional drama, untroubled and untroubling, designed to engage the spectators' easier sentiments and to enable them to spend two or three hours of diversion in the theatre, then clearly the 'teatro bajo la arena' points to innovation and experimentation, a concept of drama that will tackle more serious themes and challenge the intellect of the audience. (1992: 341)

In this first act, the Director is afraid of challenging the audience, because 'showing the mask on stage' would have dire consequences. However, from the very beginning Lorca 'undoes the safe distance between spectator and spectacle, blurring the lines between the action on stage and the spectator's fantasies and associations, such that audience members may feel so exposed and ashamed that they want to intervene' (De Witte 2017: 27). The play has already managed to pose a troubling question to the audience: if the limits between the spectacle and the spectators have been blurred, there may be no other alternative than to be involved in the play to find answers.

While the space of the entire Cuadro primero seems to remain the Director's quarters, the indeterminacy of the room and its dual value as private space and public stage reinforce the play's general concerns about the nature of theatre. The time in which the characters operate is also far from stable, as conversations fluctuate between the present moment in the play, an alluded past time all the characters share and multiple references to a play-within-the-play already staged and another one about to be staged. Both in relation to theatre and to his existence as an artistic creator, the Director acts as a fluid mediator who exposes and espouses artificiality, not as false or untrue but precisely as the poetic substance needed to challenge the falsity of norms and conventions. Pleased with the success his 'teatro al aire libre' enjoys with audiences, he nonetheless belies his theatrical output and himself. Throughout the first act, the emotions he and the other characters express never stay fixed: laughter or sarcasm turn into rage and anger, which quickly change into sadness or melancholy. None of these emotions ever seems genuine, which evidences the inauthenticity characteristic of the 'teatro al aire libre'. In turn, the 'teatro bajo la arena', which at first sight would evoke the hidden and the mysterious, acquires a sense of truth and authenticity. Monegal notes that 'the motion towards truth is associated with the opposite of what it would be in colloquial expression, in which openness signifies authenticity and sincerity' (1994b: 206–07). Thus, in this inverted structure, the '"teatro al aire libre", instead of disclosing the truth and bringing it into the open, is presented as deceptive, while the "teatro bajo la arena" is presented as the revealing enterprise' (Monegal 1994b: 207). The visit of the four white horses provokes a violent reaction in the Director, who abruptly and threateningly tells them to leave. They make him reflect upon his own theatrical career and the hypocrisy of his 'open air theatre', reminding him of his childhood and of a past relationship they all share. Their exchange fluctuates between emotional or sexual attachment and violent recrimination: 'DIRECTOR. [...] ¡Fuera de aquí! ¡Fuera de mi casa, caballos! Ya se ha inventado la cama para dormir con los caballos. (*Llorando*.) Caballitos míos.' (*TC*: 250). The insistence on reminiscing about past encounters (sexual or otherwise) will be picked up by the Hombre 1 moments later. After the horses leave, the three men dressed in tuxedos enter.[11] The same dynamic continues, with the Hombres taking turns critiquing the Director's vision of theatre as well as bringing up past interactions they share with him. The unresolved debate among the four men is intensely ambivalent, referring simultaneously to strong desires bursting forth in a more or less veiled manner and meta-theatrically to the play itself and to the openness or lack thereof of the various ways of making theatre. This openness or closure of truths and emotions also affects the openness of corporeal boundaries.

Anderson (1992) and Wright (2000) note the importance of imagery relating to the body in *El público*. References to external appearance, clothing, cosmetics or hair lead to a progressive journey inside the human body, with lexicon ranging from flesh, orifices and bodily issue to skeletons, bones and blood. Crucially, the fears of the Director in the face of the 'teatro bajo la arena' and un-masking the artifice on stage relate especially to the body in pain, a body that, as in the Bakhtinian carnivalesque, is not fixed, closed and individuated. Rather, it is in a constant state of destructuration: open, fragmented, broken and pierced by the outside world. What the characters realise throughout *El público* is that bringing this porous and unstable body onto the stage entails a grave danger: showing corporeality — and mortality — in its authenticity demands that the audience be aware of the constructed and easily destructible nature of human existence. As De Ros suggests, 'the blurring of bodily boundaries, whose extreme and pervasive expression is death, is articulated in the repeated references to the body's orifices, as well as to cutting implements, and also in the emphasis on bodily excretions' (1996: 113). Thus, what is sought in *El público* is 'que se sepa la verdad de las sepulturas' (*TC*: 252), that is, an awareness of mortality and of the multi-layered configuration of existence, evidently subjected to destructuration and restructuring.

The two opposing attitudes towards theatre also present opposing connotations associated with light and darkness. However, it is the obscurity and chthonic qualities of the theatre beneath the sand that Hombre 1/Gonzalo values. The Director/Enrique is convinced that it is dangerous to carry out this kind of underground theatre and is thus recriminated by the men. Julieta's sepulchre is the most obvious underground space where the feared new theatre is taking place, but there are several examples of dark hidden places beneath the ground throughout the play:

DIRECTOR.	Es en un pantano podrido donde debemos estar y no aquí. Bajo el légamo donde se consumen las ranas muertas. (264)
HOMBRE 3.	Podemos empujarlos y caerán al pozo. Así tú y yo quedaremos libres. [...] Es mucho mejor para ellos y para nosotros. ¡Vamos! El pozo es profundo. (266)
CABALLO BLANCO 1.	A lo oscuro. En lo oscuro hay ramas suaves. El cementerio de alas tiene mil superficies de espesor.
JULIETA. (*Temblando*.)	¿Y qué me darás allí?
CABALLO BLANCO 1.	Te daré lo más callado de lo oscuro.
JULIETA.	¿El día?
CABALLO BLANCO 1.	El musgo sin luz. El tacto que devora pequeños mundos con las yemas de los dedos. (267–68)

Since surfaces — especially faces, costumes and, crucially, theatre stages — are revealed as deceptive and inauthentic, it is beneath the ground, in swamps, wells and cemeteries, where darkness and obscurity will paradoxically shed light on the mysterious and the unknown. The initial inversion of values between 'aire libre' and 'bajo la arena' or between truth and deception is mirrored by another inversion: that which associates light with objective knowledge and certainty and darkness with mystery and secrets. It is clear that 'la verdad de las sepulturas' will not be found in the open air, but in the dark recesses of the human body and the mysterious hidden places not shown usually on stage.

If this new theatre is that which shows the blood of those involved and which opens bodies to show what is beneath — even though it is still clothed in poetry and artifice — then it is no surprise that the mask is an inherent part of it. Masks will show the multi-layered nature of the characters, but, as Wright posits, the search to find the centre or core of the human body 'seems to show that the more one attempts to arrive at the truth, the more it recedes' (2000: 109). If these masks reveal other masks underneath, making the self 'like an onion, a sum of the parts, an accretion of layers, but with no hidden core or centre' (Anderson 1992: 344), the metamorphic becomes the best way to represent the hidden truths and mysteries of the characters. One element to achieve this in *El público* is the biombo from Cuadro primero. When the folding screen is brought out, it initiates a series of transformations that will recur throughout the play, starting with the Director and the Men but reappearing through the two Figures in Cuadro segundo, the masks in 'Solo del pastor bobo' and the Ballerina and Harlequin costumes towards the end. In this crucial element, the meta-theatrical tricks the play performs find its cornerstone. Not only will character transformations, costume changes and disguises be prominent within each cuadro; more generally, the entire structure of the play will undergo a transformation of its own. On the one hand, the theatre that the main characters discuss suffers an important metamorphosis: from the 'teatro al aire libre', it mutates into 'teatro bajo la arena', as the Director and the characters around him gradually descend into the profundity of the drama — metaphorically, Julieta's underground sepulchre. On the other hand, each cuadro presents similarities with the previous and subsequent cuadros, which suggests that the play itself is 'trying on different masks' to create similar effects, all artificial but equally powerful: from the Director's room to a Roman Ruin, back to the stage, down to Julieta's tomb and around the theatre building, only to end up back on the stage. The 'Solo del pastor bobo', whether it is thought of as a prologue, an epilogue or an interlude, reinforces the idea that the play has shown nothing but a succession of masks, different guises or props to adorn similar artifices. If Lorca's aim was to call attention to the necessity for new attitudes towards theatre — theatre-making as well as theatre-going — by presenting a meta-play about all those involved in the theatrical experience and the inevitable changes to which they are all subjected, he was literally making a new *theatrum mundi* where everybody is allowed: 'tenéis sitio en el drama. Todo el mundo' (*TC*: 254).

The Cuadro segundo, subtitled *Ruina romana*, is one of the most enlightening in this respect, because transformation leads to the argument for the inevitable multiplicity of human identity. The Figura de pámpanos and the Figura de cascabeles embody in their encounter a passionate and violent metamorphic process, based on a playful and performative dialogue which resembles both a dance and a bloody fight. They represent two lovers who dance in a transformative repartee, creating alternating fantasies through language. The dialogue confounds desire and death, it is a sexual interaction with violent overtones based on the figures' capacities to adopt multiple guises. This is the crucial episode in the play in which Lorca theorises about the complex nature of desire and identity. On the one hand, the lovers demonstrate that identity is not fixed and stable, it changes inevitably and the desire the lovers feel for each other fluctuates in a game of domination and submission. This evidences power relations but also how reversible and fickle emotions can be. It also evidences the creative and destructive power of desire and how death is inextricably linked to the experience of love through artistic discourse. Performativity is a key element of this interaction, since the figures manage to deconstruct the edifice of their identities, showing how the many layers they put on can be easily discarded and their roles reversed. Therefore, 'beneath the versatility of their roles, the characters reveal a nature which is portrayed as fragmented, vulnerable and susceptible to expansion into new forms which supersede their own individual status' (De Ros 1996: 113).

Towards the end of the cuadro, the threat of the Centurión and the Emperador in an avid search for 'el uno', interrupts their dialogue. Given that theatre and desire are inextricably linked in the play, this reference to the classical world entails a vision of tradition in theatre and in human relationships. The idea of unity is then emphasised. The Emperor is looking for 'the one', and in the association of the Emperor with the law as well as tradition and power, his desire for unity can apply to both theatre but also to a heteronormative view of sexuality. Paradoxically, the act finishes with an embrace between the Emperor and the figure of bells. Nonetheless, what the Emperor does is interrupt the *pas à deux* in which the two figures were rehearsing multiplicity by proclaiming the importance of unity. Both here and in the next act, the Emperor appears as a threatening force against the main characters.

Pedrosa suggests that the Figure of Vine Leaves is, according to multiple sources of cultural symbology, associated with the feminine or the effeminate, while the Figure of Bells is associated with the masculine or the virile.[12] This contrast, however, is made explicit in Cuadro segundo but is also shown as reversible and fluid. I suggest that precisely the archetypal nature of their distinctive personae emphasises the figures' transgressions. Both claim to be 'un hombre, más hombre que Adán', and both also recriminate each other for not being enough of a man:

> FIGURA DE PÁMPANOS. Si tú te convirtieras en pez luna, yo te abriría con un cuchillo, porque soy un hombre, porque no soy nada más que eso, un hombre, más hombre que Adán, y quiero que tú seas aún más hombre que yo. [...] Pero tú no eres un hombre. [...]
> FIGURA DE CASCABELES. Ciego, porque no eres hombre. Yo sí soy un hombre. Un hombre, tan hombre, que me desmayo cuando se despiertan los cazadores. (*TC*: 257–59)

During the erotic/violent fight, both characters assume domineering or submissive positions alternately, negating the principle of unity to which they both seem to aspire. It is this unity which the Emperador is seeking, but it is made abundantly clear in the cuadro that assuming unity would lead to one's demise or dissolution into non-existence:

> FIGURA DE PÁMPANOS. Tú me conoces. Tú sabes quién soy. (*Se despoja de los pámpanos y aparece un desnudo blanco de yeso.*)
> EMPERADOR. (*Abrazándolo.*) Uno es uno.
> FIGURA DE PÁMPANOS. Y siempre uno. Si me besas, yo abriré mi boca para clavarme, después, tu espada en el cuello.
> EMPERADOR. Así lo haré.
> FIGURA DE PÁMPANOS. Y deja mi cabeza de amor en la ruina. La cabeza de uno que fue siempre uno.
> EMPERADOR. (*Suspirando.*) Uno.
> CENTURIÓN. (*Al EMPERADOR.*) Difícil es, pero ahí lo tienes.
> FIGURA DE PÁMPANOS. Lo tiene porque nunca lo podrá tener. (*TC*: 262)

This final transformation for the Figura de pámpanos implies his abandonment of the metamorphic game and his assumption of unity symbolised by the classical marble statue. Embracing the Emperor is synonymous with being stabbed in the neck and decapitated, perhaps by assuming a corporeal/existential unity which is false and impossible. The Figura de pámpanos commits a self-sacrifice to give the Emperor 'uno' 'y siempre uno', he becomes a body which is immutable and everlasting, an unachievable ideal ('nunca lo podrá tener'). In the next cuadro, when the Director and the men discuss the two figures' desires and masculinities, the opposition is drawn between a classical statuesque appearance — an Apollonian ideal beauty with perfect proportions — and its incompatibility with the anus, that is, with those corporeal orifices which evidence the porousness of the human body and open up its boundaries to accommodate carnal desires. Paradoxically, Lorca claims here that denying the intricate and ambivalent connection between human desire and mortality and seeking an impossible purity and fixity while ignoring the multiplicity of contradictory identities one can adopt is nothing but self-immolation. The Emperor in the Roman Ruin, a potent symbol for official powers inherited from antiquity, can be read as the mighty effects of normativity, the ubiquitous forces regulating the validity of bodies and identities. As Butler suggests, heteronormativity, considered a set of rules regulating sex, gender and sexuality, makes biological sex 'not what one has or a static description of what one is: it will be one of the norms by which the "one" becomes viable at all, that which qualifies a body for life within the domain of cultural intelligibility' (1993: xii). The Emperador's search for 'the one' mirrors that highly rigid regulatory system in which the illusory constructs of gender and sexual identity 'congeal over time to produce the appearance of substance, of a natural sort of being' (Butler 1990: 33). *El público* tries to show that those constructs operate like theatrical masks or costumes, and that pretending that one is 'one and always one' is futile and harmful.

In Cuadro quinto, the audience become literally and symbolically trapped in the theatre. In true Pirandellian fashion, the conversations among members of the audience, the Estudiantes and the Damas, are interspersed with the action between the Enfermero and the Desnudo Rojo, while the Traspunte intervenes as a stage crew member. The fusion between reality and theatre is thus intensified. The transgressive theatrical space that the Director and the men have been alluding to throughout the play, a space which includes all of them as *dramatis personae*, has now been extended to the audience members themselves. Being confronted with the 'theatre beneath the sand' production of *Romeo and Juliet* and the artifices that enveloped it — Romeo was played by a thirty-year-old man and Juliet by a fifteen-year-old boy while an actress who also played Juliet was kidnapped, gagged and hidden under the theatre stalls — they have no choice but to be involved in the drama as well. As Jerez-Farrán notes, 'the members of the audience manifest their defensiveness by lynching the sexual dissidents as soon as they discover that two men demonstrate a mutual attraction in defiance of the common rules and, what is more serious, they truly love one another. This the public cannot tolerate' (2000: 731). The shock at discovering the gender illusion performed by the two main actors is combined with that of discovering that performance itself can simultaneously be artificial and authentic: 'DAMA 2. Las voces estaban vivas y sus apariencias también' (*TC*: 281). The Director's production of *Romeo and Juliet* has tapped into the multiple libidinal possibilities afforded the bodies on stage, by showing that two men can desire each other. Furthermore, the performance has shown the audience that theatre, as artificial and constructed as it is, can mirror life's own inauthenticities and artifices, a prominent one being the illusion that is gender and the arbitrary norms that govern and sanction its performance:

> ESTUDIANTE 4. La gente se olvida de los trajes en las representaciones, y la revolución estalló cuando se encontraron a la verdadera Julieta amordazada debajo de las sillas y cubierta de algodones para que no gritase.
> ESTUDIANTE 1. Ahí está la gran equivocación de todos y por eso el teatro agoniza: el público no debe atravesar las sedas y los cartones que el poeta levanta en su dormitorio. Romeo puede ser un ave y Julieta puede ser una piedra. Romeo puede ser un grano de sal y Julieta puede ser un mapa. ¿Qué le importa esto al público? (*TC*: 282)

The usual ambivalence and polysemy in relation to heterodox desires and theatre that pervades the play is here expressed by one of the students in the audience: while theatrical performance is arbitrary and can deal with a host of multifarious ideas while maintaining the illusion of reality and authenticity, so can gender and sexuality pass for authentic realities. The drama successfully presents these performative constructions to the audience, who have a choice to enter the illusion and suspend their disbelief but are nonetheless prompted to reflect upon it critically in order for theatre to fulfil its social function. Lorca shows that both his play and the play-within-the-play are emotionally touching as well as socially conscious and critical:

> ESTUDIANTE 4. La repetición del acto ha sido maravillosa, porque indudablemente se amaban con un amor incalculable, aunque yo no lo justifique. Cuando cantó el ruiseñor yo no pude contener mis lágrimas.
> ESTUDIANTE 3. Y toda la gente. Pero después enarbolaron los cuchillos y los bastones porque la letra era más fuerte que ellos, y la doctrina cuando desata su cabellera puede atropellar sin miedo las verdades más inocentes. (*TC*: 285)

Some of these 'innocent truths' relate to the genuine desire felt by the protagonists of the play-within-the-play, but also to the difficulty in distinguishing fiction from reality and in discerning the social dogmas that are being imposed on people. The unjust rivalry between the Montagues and the Capulets that prevented Romeo and Juliet from loving each other is no different from the heteronormative convention that impedes same-sex relationships or condemns cross-dressing or gender transgressions — the irony that in Elizabethan times the role of Juliet would have been played by a young man was probably not lost on Lorca when referencing this particular play.

El público thus claims that all identities are illusory, that theatre and art resemble life in that we can play with the idea of truth by 'changing costumes', by performing or questioning the roles and rules which have been imposed on us. In carnivalesque fashion, the characters expose how artificial desire is, but how aggressive and deadly the consequences can be if the carnival is exposed, looked at from a different perspective. The mirroring process rehearsed in the play between desire and theatre leads to the realisation that there is no fixity in identity, much like there is no attaining the one which is always one. Multiplicity characterises desire, selfhood and theatre — there are multiple masks being shown, revealed, broken and reconstructed — but there is no 'getting to the core', because masks reveal a multiplicity of further masks underneath. The Pastor Bobo shows this idea clearly to the audience, but the rest of successive cuadros, disconnected, fragmented and troubling the already complex plot linearity, also reinforce it. The queerness discussed within the play inevitably mirrors the queerness of *El público*'s play-text. In turn, the Director reveals himself as not only 'one' either: his transformations and reincarnations and those of the men evidence there is no hidden inner truth of the self, while their fluid desires reveal a multifaceted identity in all the characters, including the 'crew' and the actors in the play-within-the-play.

The tragic death suffered by Romeo and Juliet is present in both incarnations or versions of the play-within-the-play: both the 'teatro al aire libre' and the 'teatro bajo la arena' performances must end in tragedy. While they reveal distinctive styles of artificiality, the tragic elements remain in both. It is not the 'truth' or verisimilitude of either version that Lorca favours, but the capacity they have to move the audience or effectively produce a valuable dramatic substance. This implies that one type of love or identity is not being favoured over another, but that it is the way the artifice is created that matters, since at the end of the day, all of it is artifice.

Similarly, the play does not favour masculine homosexuality over a feminised one, nor does it seek 'universal love'. Instead, Lorca suggests that the theatre should aim to show the value of disruption and fluidity, since that is what will make the audience react and engage with the theatrical experience. As Jerez-Farrán suggests, by revealing sexual heterodoxy on stage, *El público* manages to 'infuriate the audience, in part because the efficacy of their homophobic discourse depends primarily on the invisibility of this human reality they want to treat as nonexistent' (2000: 730). Queer visibility and the exposition of the multiple levels of artificiality shaping existence imply the inclusion of the mysterious and the inexplicable into the drama, the inclusion of death into life itself, which is what the aesthetics of *duende* ultimately seeks. The final cuadro sees the Director discuss the events of the play with the Prestidigitador, and there is a brief appearance of Hombre 1/ Gonzalo's mother, who enquires about her son's corpse to no avail, accompanied by the Harlequin costume (which the Director was previously wearing). The Director has repeatedly suggested throughout the play that the 'theatre beneath the sand' entails tangible and real consequences: the performance of 'serious' and authentic topics will necessarily lead to actual change in the audience, who will question their moral and ideological assumptions. As Anderson posits, the 'teatro bajo la arena' 'will be a theatre that does not close itself off from life (and death), but rather one open to what is going on in the outside world, and one that takes a leading — even revolutionary — role in advances and changes. It will oppose the easy acceptance of the *status quo* and challenge the *bien-pensant* bourgeois morality' (1992:

342). Gonzalo's death is thus redemptive in that it has aimed to provoke a strong reaction in the audience, who are inevitably summoned to engage in what has been discussed and shown on stage ('DIRECTOR. Yo hice el túnel para apoderarme de los trajes y, a través de ellos, enseñar el perfil de una fuerza oculta cuando ya el público no tuviera más remedio que atender, lleno de espíritu y subyugado por la acción', *TC*: 291). The Director insists that those involved in the performance have poured their own blood and been willing to sacrifice their own lives in defence of their artistic discourse ('Aquí está usted pisando un teatro donde se han dado dramas auténticos y donde se ha sostenido un verdadero combate que ha costado la vida a todos los intérpretes', *TC*: 293). It is now up to the audience to take a better-informed approach to those issues and to engage with them in a more just and less judgmental manner.

This 'dificilísimo juego poético' thus resonates with what *duende* meant for Lorca. The necessity of showing how the dark and mysterious aspects of mortality relate to desire and life experiences is what the poet deemed worthy of expressing through art forms, aiming to provoke a substantial reaction in the spectator/reader ('DIRECTOR. Es rompiendo todas las puertas el único modo que tiene el drama de justificarse, viendo, por sus propios ojos, que la ley es un muro que se disuelve en la más pequeña gota de sangre', *TC*: 293). In *El público*, breaking the limits of what constitutes theatre and, crucially, how theatrical performance relates to human experience is the characters' main objective. Showing the audience how multiplicity is a more appropriate category to represent human desire and identity and questioning norms which differentiate truth from artifice have contributed to the creation of a new kind of drama which will call for epistemological change, once the audience dares to enter it.

Notes to Chapter 2

1. In a 1933 interview about his work with *La Barraca*, Lorca was questioned about the state of contemporary Spanish theatre, to which he responded: 'Right now, generally speaking, [Spanish theatre] is theatre for pigs, by pigs. It's theatre made by pigs, aimed at pigs.' (Francisco Perez Herrero, 'Nuevo Carro de Tespis', *La Mañana*, León, August 1933, cited in Sánchez 1998: 7).
2. Anderson mentions 'three or four separate initiatives to stage the play [*El público*] within [Lorca's] lifetime. In early 1931, it was read by the actress Irene Lopez Heredia, and if she did not accept it (which she obviously did not), "un grupo de amigos y poetas jóvenes quieren representar mi drama"; in May 1932 Cipriano Rivas Cherif and the Teatro Español announced a summer season to include *El público*; in late 1933 there were plans to create a Teatro-Escuela de Arte Experimental at the Teatro Español during the 1933–34 season, with the Teatro-Escuela to premiere the play' (1992: 345–46). Fernández Cifuentes traces the staging process of *Así que pasen cinco años*: 'Pura Ucelay ensayaba la obra en los días que precedieron al 18 de julio de 1936. Se representó una escena en la sala Yena de París el 13 de septiembre de 1937. [...] Entre las varias representaciones que se han arrogado la "premier mundial" parece la más antigua la del Jane Street Group en el Provincetown Playhouse de Nueva York en 1945' (1978: 190). The play was first staged in Spain in September 1978 (Vilches de Frutos 2008: 79–80).
3. Valle-Inclán's 'esperpentos' are a clear example of the dissatisfied reaction of playwrights and stage directors to popular and commercial types of theatre, highly successful on the Spanish stage. The idea of 'esperpento', linked to innovations coming from European trends, was born as a means to provoke strong reactions and deep reflections among audiences, who were prompted

to look at characters and plots as puppets or farcical grotesque figures completely detached from reality or naturalism. Many of Valle-Inclán's plays were not conceived to be staged or failed to do so precisely because of their anti-naturalistic elements, too avant-garde to be appreciated by mainstream audiences: 'Valle-Inclán had more or less given up on getting his plays staged, and these new texts are meant, at least in the first instance, for reading, as the lyrical and highly detailed stage directions would suggest' (Dougherty and Anderson 2012: 300–01).

4. Hardison Londré (1983), Cao (1984), Huélamo Kosma (1992), Soufas (1996), Smith (1998a), and Wright (2000), amongst others, interpret the play as a dream or reverie, either by the Joven or, in Soufas's case, by the Viejo as a dreamer who imagines the Joven, in the manner of Don Perlimplín (1996: 69–70). In Smith's overview of the critical approaches to dream in the play, he mentions that 'the lyrically oneiric atmosphere of the play is derived from García Lorca's knowledge of Freud's *Interpretation of Dreams*. That familiarity is thought to make itself manifest either in a literalist vein (the action of the play is simply the dream of the character within it) or in a more subtle, structural mode (the composition of the play exhibits patterns characteristic of the dream-work' (1998a: 71–72).

5. Luis Fernández Cifuentes (1978: 180) and Farris Anderson (1979: 274) see this final temporal reference to twelve o'clock as a doubling or duplication of the two previous references to six o'clock, as a result of the presence of the echo as a character (Eco).

6. Klein (1975), Smith (1998a), Cordero Sánchez (2012), Wright (2007b) and Plaza Agudo (2019) read the reticence of the Joven to fulfil any physical relationship with the women in the play as a sign of his sexual heterodoxy.

7. In Farris Anderson's view, the play is made up of 'countless fragments of inner plays, analogues of the Joven's own fragmented drama' (1979: 252). Sarah Wright reads the 'frozen progression' of the characters in the play as a succession of photographs, in which 'characters appear often limited to hollow visual images' (2000: 82). She mentions Marie Laffranque's discovery of a theatrical project about which Lorca told Melchor Fernández Almagro and which consisted of three plays conceived as 'ampliaciones fotográficas' (Laffranque 1987: 20). The motif of the photograph, often favoured by Lorca, is closely analogous to that of the tableau as the basis for poetic and dramatic creation, both of them bringing together an aesthetic consideration of visuality and temporality.

8. See Binding (1985), Smith (1998a), Wright (2000), Cordero Sánchez (2012), Jerez-Farrán (2015), and Plaza Agudo (2019). The usual interpretations link the dead child motif to a lament for the loss of childhood innocence as well as to a coded lament by Lorca for the children he would never beget due to his heterodox sexuality. Also, see Chapter 1 for the treatment of this motif in *Diván del Tamarit*.

9. 'AMIGO. [...] Iba con una mujer feísima, ¿lo oyes? Ja, ja, ja, ja, feísima pero adorable. Una morena de esas que se echan de menos al mediodía de verano. Y me gusta (*Tira un cojín por alto*) porque parece un domador. JOVEN. ¡Basta! AMIGO. Sí, hombre, no te indignes, pero una mujer puede ser feísima y un domador de caballos puede ser hermoso y al revés y...¿qué sabemos?' (*TC*: 306).

10. The division of the play into 'cuadros', an element often used in expressionist theatre, relates to Lorca's graphic works and, especially, to *Viaje a la luna* and its tableau structure (see Chapters 4 and 5). Lorca finished writing *El público* on 22 August 1930 and, before his final trip to Granada in 1936, gave the manuscript to Rafael Martínez Nadal. In that manuscript, the basis for the edition we have today, there was no 'cuadro cuarto', and the numbering of the acts preserved was inconsistent, so the order of the cuadros in the play as Lorca conceived it is not entirely clear. There are reasons to believe, for example, that the 'Solo del pastor bobo' was meant to be a prologue to the play (Anderson 1992: 343) instead of appearing between the fifth and sixth cuadros. In her introduction to the Cátedra edition of *El público*, María Clementa Millán also notes that there is evidence suggesting Lorca might have rearranged the play into five cuadros in its definitive version (lost today), which would mean that no cuadro cuarto is actually missing and that the play is indeed complete in the way it has survived (García Lorca 2016: 99–102).

11. This typically elegant attire is revisited in Lorca's *Viaje a la luna* to explore a similar type of character involved in a masquerade of repressed desire in the bar sequences (see Chapter 4).

12. See Pedrosa (1998) for an account of the multiple sources (from ancient mythology, early modern folklore and multiple cultural ideologies) in which vine leaves and bells present erotic connotations related to male and female symbology.

CHAPTER 3

❖

The Lorquian Grotesque in the Late Drawings: Plastic Poems, Wounds and Boundaries

Regalo al alma, tiros al sentido. (Soria Olmedo 2009: 3)

Lorca created a rich visual universe not only through his literary poetics, evidenced in the poems and plays, but also through the pictorial imagery developed in his drawings. Lorca's graphic oeuvre spans roughly from 1923 until his death in 1936, although there are drawings dating as far back as 1917. In the major catalogue available to date, compiled by Mario Hernández with the assistance of the Fundación Federico García Lorca and the Spanish Ministerio de Cultura (1990) and translated into English by Christopher Maurer (1991), there are around 380 catalogued pieces organised chronologically.[1] Of all these drawings, there are some which stand on their own, that is, which were drawn or conceived as independent pieces; and some which were designed to serve another purpose, such as to accompany an artefact like a book of poems (by Lorca or by another author) or for the stage of a play or puppet play; as a dedication or gift to one of the poet's friends; as costume designs for the theatre; or even as autographs or illustrations of documents. The two only major exhibitions of Lorca's drawings during his lifetime were an individual one in Barcelona in 1927 at the Galerías Dalmau, aided by the poet's friends Sebastián Gasch and the owners of the gallery themselves, and a section in a collective exhibition at the Ateneo Popular in Huelva, as part of the *Semana del Arte Nuevo* in 1932.[2]

Due to the high volume of graphic works in existence and their varied nature and purpose, a selection is necessary for the scope and purpose of this study. Since this book concentrates on Lorca's later works following his stay in New York and showing his negotiation with the avant-garde and his innovative efforts, I will focus on the drawings produced in his later years (1930–36) and primarily on the ones designed as independent works, although occasionally I will have recourse to earlier drawings or illustrative works as points of reference or contextualisation. Another selecting principle must relate to Lorca's treatment in his later years of the confluence of desire and death and of the search for *lo insólito* and the transgression of norms and boundaries in the creative process. I will therefore examine in this chapter those drawings which explore the intertwining of *eros* and *thanatos*; those which blur spatiotemporal or corporeal limits; and those which aim to represent deviant, transgressive or ambiguous identities.

In the period from 1929 to 1930, Lorca's sojourn in New York proved to be the beginning of a new and important chapter in his life and his work. This change of scenery, which has often been described as the result of a 'severe personal crisis' for the poet (Harris 1998: 83), meant the opening of new horizons and an opportunity to renew his creative confidence. From his New York years onwards, his conception of himself as a multimedia artist became more prominent and the influence of avant-garde movements more palpable. The interests of contemporary artists were varied and often aimed to experiment with new modes of expression, perhaps a reason for Lorca's incursion into film and other creative practices, although his earlier years at the Residencia de Estudiantes in Madrid and particularly his friendship and collaboration with Salvador Dalí and Luis Buñuel also set this in motion.[3] Furthermore, his wish for innovation started to take shape at a more profound level as he tried his hand at Cubism, Expressionism and Surrealism in his *Poemas en prosa* and his New York works. After completing *Poeta en Nueva York*, Lorca was determined to include photography, photomontage and drawings in the published version of the poems, a wish which unfortunately never became a reality due to his abrupt death and which only came to fruition partially with the inclusion of some drawings and photographs in its posthumous editions. Lorca's insistence on gathering and publishing his graphic works after his 1927 exhibition and his prolific graphic production from then onwards attest to his sense of pride and determination as a pictorial artist, contradicting the beliefs that his drawings were just a passing fad in his career.[4]

Lorca's drawings from 1930–36 reveal themes, motifs and processes which recur across his post-New York works: chief among them are the confluence of *eros* and *thanatos*, the wounded body and the transgression of corporeal limits and boundaries. Depictions of fragmented body parts, bodily issue and physical destructuration abound, which on the whole contributes to create a sense of shock and morbid attraction, whilst prompting unsettling and disconcerting reactions in the viewer. Ultimately, these wounded bodies aim to transgress expectations related to idealised beauty and to explore and destabilise the limits of life and death. Some works present the enlivening function of wounding on presumably dead bodies, while others veil or blur the identification of characters or figures as fixed and finite — both corporeally and in terms of sex and gender.

The late drawings also reveal a preference for the grotesque. Originally referred to mural art usually depicting floral or animal motifs which tended to be fused with human forms, the word 'grotesque' comes from the Latin *grotto*, meaning a small cave or hollow. Its original meaning was applied to an extravagant style of Ancient Roman decorative art rediscovered and then copied in Rome at the end of the fifteenth century which proliferated in the underground caves and corridors of the city. Spreading from Italian to other European languages, the term was long used largely interchangeably with 'arabesque' and 'moresque' for types of decorative patterns using curving foliage elements. Since at least the eighteenth century, 'grotesque' has come to be used as a general adjective for the strange, fantastic, ugly, incongruous, unpleasant, or disgusting, and thus is often used to describe weird shapes and distorted forms. In art, performance, and literature, grotesque may also refer to something that simultaneously invokes in an audience a feeling of uncomfortable bizarreness as well as empathetic pity. Although there are several motifs associated with the grotesque and different typologies identified by scholars, many agree that its three main tropes are doubleness, hybridity and metamorphosis. The representation of human/animal/plant fusions and coalescences have often been studied as the artistic exploration of alterity and change affecting human existence and experience while challenging ideated canons of beauty in art.[5]

Some pervasive elements in Lorca's drawings bear significance in relation to the introduction and development of the grotesque in modern art. The romantic period marked the entrance of the grotesque into the mainstream of modern expression, as a means to explore alternative modes of experience and expression and to challenge the presumed universals of classical beauty, especially the neoclassical foundations of art history and aesthetics, with their emphasis on ideated beauty and rational inquiry. In *Modern Art and the Grotesque*, Connelly (2003) outlines three actions or processes at work in the grotesque image, actions that are both destructive and constructive. Images gathered under the grotesque rubric include 'those that combine unlike things in order to challenge established realities or construct new ones; those that deform or decompose things; and those that are metamorphic' (Connelly 2003: 2). The metamorphic grotesque can combine and deform in the same way as its static counterparts, but the metamorphic 'exists in the process, the "morphing" from one thing or form to another. It also seems much more reliant on mimesis and illusion, transgressing them for its impact' (Connelly 2003: 3). Grotesques are typically characterised by what they lack: fixity, stability, order. Mikhail Bakhtin emphasised the creative dimensions of this flux, describing the grotesque as 'a body in the act of becoming [...] never finished, never completed; it is continually built, created, and builds and creates another body' (Bakhtin 1984: 317). Bakhtin's description of the grotesque finds its roots in its particular depiction of body-world and life-death coalescences:

> the body swallows the world and is itself swallowed by the world [...] Eating, drinking, defecation and other elimination (sweating, blowing of the nose, sneezing), as well as copulation, pregnancy, dismemberment, swallowing up by another body — all of these acts are performed on the confines of the body and the outer world, or on the confines of the old and new body. In all these events the beginning and end of life are closely linked and interwoven. (1984: 317)

The grotesque is thus 'a boundary creature and does not exist except in relation to a boundary, convention, or expectation' (Connelly 2003: 3). These boundaries mark the sites in which the body relates to the world surrounding it and in which the limits between life and death become blurred. Lorca's drawings offer the viewer shocking images of dismembered bodies, monstrous creatures in the process of being created and overlapping corporeal boundaries that defy expectations and interpretations. Mirroring the unexpected metaphors and image associations from his poems, the multiplicity of identities in his modernist plays and the incongruity explored in his film script, Lorca's graphic works question and distort the limits of corporeality, erotic desire and temporality, mixing human, animal and floral motifs in unprecedented and shocking ways. The grotesque image allows Lorca to articulate in visual terms his idea of human experience as unstable and metamorphic and his notion of *poiesis* as a rule-breaking and anti-normative creative process.

Lorca's knowledge of modern art and his negotiation with avant-garde artistic movements show signs of the influence of the grotesque tradition, especially in relation to Spanish artists like Francisco de Goya or El Greco (both cited in *Juego y teoría del duende*). *Duende* is keen to play with edges and boundaries, crossing and breaking them so they can be redefined and recreated in the process of art making. It is perhaps quite apt to refer to *duende* as a chthonic force, as Maurer does (2007: 35), in that its connection with the earth and what is under its surface, like the subterranean grottoes used to be, constantly mixes and distorts limits between differentiated realms. Thus Lorca's drawings in the 1930s will aim to transgress bodily forms and contours, confounding and mutating the characters depicted. Some late graphic works will also experiment with lines and abstract images departing altogether from logical expectations and human forms, relying however on similar processes of movement, change and distortion. They may be considered Lorca's version of Valle-Inclán's 'esperpentos', insofar as they often combine tragic and comic elements; they depict duality, circularity, transformation and metamorphosis; and they tend to distort and transgress human figures, usually adding elements of the supernatural or the macabre.[6]

Apart from the exploration of urban settings in his many depictions of the metropolis — very likely inspired by his visit to the United States — Lorca's drawings of the late period focus especially on male figures: sailors, young men and dead or wounded male bodies. The unconventional bust portrait 'Busto de hombre muerto' (ca.1932) depicts a sombre interaction between the wounded human figure or corpse dominating the drawing and its earthy surroundings. Even though the eponymous dead man is portrayed as a corpse — his vacant eyes and his pale colour contrasting with the white, brown and blue more lively background — he is not completely devoid of movement and activity. His eyes are animated by green and brown leaves and roots emanating from them, as if they were tears. His ears have little boxes attached to spiralling lines of thread or wire coming out of them and falling on the ground in the drawing, where they create a sense of weight by leaving marks spreading around them. In the far background, a pale blue sky overlooks disparate groups of plants springing into life as well as further actual metal springs like the ones coming out of the man's ears. Thus, the living natural background surrounding the man ironises the assertion of death in the drawing's title and the man's corpse-like demeanour, while connecting the growth of plants with the cyclical transience of nature, which inevitably announces temporality and death. The pale white canvas of the man's body is animated by the colourful objects springing from it and merging with it.

Towards the centre-right of the man's chest there is a unique red/orange mark (these colours are not used in any of the other motifs in the drawing), consisting of a sinuous irregular line describing a semicircle but bifurcating along its trajectory and ending in thick dots. The singularity of this mark, simulating a wound or a trail of blood around the man's heart area, and its position towards the bottom of the drawing convey a sense of movement downwards and an acute perspective foregrounding the man and distancing the background at the top. This effect makes all the objects in the drawing point down towards the wound mark — the plants on the man's shoulders, the springy boxes on both sides of his head, the leaves of the plants growing in the background — which acquires a central position and becomes the epicentre of the entire scene. Moreover, the curved angle of the wound accentuates the triangular direction the composition follows, starting from the wider background (formed by the horizontal line created by the blue fringe of sky at the very top and the more disparate objects at the back) and narrowing down in the foreground with the man's shoulder line and the leaves growing closer together and pointing towards the corpse's chest mark.

Because the wound is given such a prominent position, it becomes a sign of alert to the convergence of life and death in the drawing. The blood secretion from the wound sets the scene in motion, alerting the viewer to the multiple interactions between the man's body and the world around him, the coalescences and mutations which disturb his supposed lifeless state. The drawing ultimately suggests that the dead man from the title is not clearly dead after all. Instead, life envelops him and penetrates his body, whose transformation fills the scene with colour, movement and desire to grow and create. What would seem at first a sombre image of decay and decomposition actually foregrounds change and creation, transforming the corpse's body into a source of life and grotesque beauty. With blood as the nexus between destruction and creation, this plastic poem elaborates on the idea of the natural cycle of death in life and life in death, including the incongruous, the unsettling and the metamorphic, taken from the grotesque tradition but made uniquely Lorquian.[7]

Lorca's six-month sojourn in Argentina in 1933–34 exemplified his renewed self-confidence and maturity as an artist: he gave several lectures (*Juego y teoría del duende* took place at this time), came in contact with well-known artists and received international acclaim for his work.[8] He was sought after as an illustrator as well at this time, which shows the acceptance of the value of his graphic works in their own right. A group of ten India ink drawings, all produced in 1934 in Argentina, were the result of a unique collaborative edition of Pablo Neruda's book of poems *Paloma por dentro, o sea, la mano de vidrio*, a one-copy edition with typewritten poems by the Chilean poet and drawings by Lorca intended as a gift to a mutual Argentinian friend, Sara Tornú de Rojas Paz 'La Rubia' (Olivares 2001: 41; Gibson 1990: 371). This multimedia collaboration was one amongst the three collector's editions to which Lorca contributed his drawings, and serves as a starting point to analyse the close relationship between multiple media in the poet's later years.[9]

The Argentinian drawings were conceived as an intermedial project, since they were designed as part of a literary-illustrative collection. Each drawing presents a typewritten title at the top, which invites an addition of the title's meaning to the visual meaning of the pictorial elements. Bearing in mind that drawings are 'by their very nature much more immediate than paintings and so can give us greater insight into the process of making a work of art' (Acton 2009: 175), it is important to examine how these drawings hinge on the immediacy of visuality and the connections established with linguistic and further sensory elements. These meaning combinations will shed an interesting light on Lorca's graphic exploration of fragmented bodies as a way to disrupt and play with preconceived notions and norms on the representation of desire, mortality and gender.

One of the most intriguing drawings in this group is 'Labios', also bearing the title 'Walking around', in which the minimal representation of isolated body parts precludes the better-known 'Manos' drawings. 'Labios' evidences the influence of 'vibracionismo', with which Lorca came into contact through the Uruguayan artist Rafael Pérez Barradas (Plaza Chillón 2014: 218–19), in the sharp contrast established between the individual and the world around them.[10] Formed of seven sets of lips all closed in a pout and connected to one another by elongated lines, the composition suggests an upwards movement, from the biggest pair of lips at the bottom right corner to a dark spot surrounded by a bigger circle towards the upper left section. This double circle resembles an eye's pupil or a bullseye, prominent and intense in contrast with the more stylised and delicate thinness of the lines connecting the sinuous shapes of the closed mouths. The drawing has at the very top the English words 'walking around' typed in a plain typewriter's font, which could be considered a title or heading to the drawing in isolation, apart from its function as title to the subsequent Neruda poem. This spatial reference to the act of going for a walk serves to reinforce the movement evoked by the numerous mouths around the drawing, all connected to the focal circular shape, the starting point or destination of the alluded walk. In addition, the different sizes of the lips, diminishing as we move upwards from right to left and then right again from the circle upwards, also reinforce the sense of distance and perspective, simulating a bigger distance between the viewer and the smaller lips at the top. The fact that the three smaller mouths at the top right are directly in contact with the circle suggests a gradual movement from the bottom upwards, situating the middle part of the drawing as a middle stage between the beginning and the end of the 'walk around'.

A multiplicity of meanings coalesces in the drawing. From a general perspective, there is a combination of the fictive movement implied by the lines and composition and the propositional movement signified in the linguistic element. To this combination must be added the sensory movement evoked by the multiple mouths and the eye-like dot whose potential sensory functions (i.e. the tactility of kissing, the sound of talking, the act of looking) are graphically interconnected by linking lines. The broader composite meaning of all these elements may suggest that 'our bodily experiences motivate conceptualisation and are, therefore, expressed in all of our meaning systems' (Borkent 2010: 148). If visual and verbal cues are blended to form a wider meaning, Lorca's drawing offers a vision which moves past the barriers separating these diverse elements, conveying a multilayered journey both poetically meaningful and visually vivid.[11]

The multiplicity of mouths in 'Labios (Walking around)' can also be contrasted with the uniqueness of the central circle or dot, perhaps a representation of a single subject or object as opposed to other entities. If the circle is taken to be the 'I' in the drawing, the poetic voice if this were a poem, then the mouths would be the others, external individuals surrounding the 'I' with whom this entity communicates or interacts. The singularity of the circle makes it 'other' to the homogeneous mouths, but the walk enables the 'I' to interact with them, to travel from one to the next. In the drawing's symbology, this walk around can be seen as the artist's expression, the means by which communication is achieved, or at least aimed at. The lines connecting the elements in the drawing evoke the desire for human interaction as well, in the act of talking or kissing, or even emotional intimacy, sexual intercourse or friendship. However, the difference or otherness of the circular object in opposition to the mouths is palpable, so the movement or communication may be frustrated or impossible, something which is reinforced by the use of an English sequence of words in the drawing. Despite it being taken from the title of a poem by Neruda and the fact that Lorca studied English during his time in New York, the use of a different language from his mother tongue suggests a break in communication or at least an added difficulty in understanding an interlocutor. It also resonates with the multiple mouths, talking agents whose interactions and communications paradoxically depend on language, whichever that may be.

Whether communication is achieved or not, the drawing indeed possesses a circular sense — evoked by the round composition, the homogeneity of the peripheral elements, the black dot surrounded by a circle and the implications of walking 'around' — that leaves this question open-ended, since there is no starting or ending point, but rather a flowing motion mouth-circle-mouth implying a return to the beginning. The configuration may also resemble a plant or a system of branches or roots, which would evoke Lorca's exploration of plants and flowers and their symbology in his poetry, as well as the many instances of roots present in his drawings. Both these connections may in turn be linked to the natural cycle of the four seasons, also circular and repetitive. 'Labios', as its depiction of bodily communication — whether spoken, visual, tactile or spatial — suggests, remains circular and therefore indeterminate and uncertain, transgressing logical and spatiotemporal norms and leaving the viewer with an unsettling sense of disorientation, precisely the effect that walking around (in circles or without a sense of direction) usually has.

Corporeal transgression, this time through a more concrete depiction of the human body, is exemplified in 'Material nupcial'. The drawing depicts a male figure that can be associated with the recurrent 'sailor' figures of other drawings and poems, but is also reminiscent of Jean Cocteau's graphic works, especially those from *Le livre blanc* (Cocteau 1969 [1928]).[12] The sailor's eyes are expressionless, vacant empty ovals, like those of a corpse, and his lips are closed in a neutral gesture, neither smiling nor pouting. He is wearing a typical sailor's cap with a wider circular top and a long ribbon or tally tied around its base, with the long ends hanging loosely in opposite directions, one flying upwards and the other one falling down in a straight line touching the man's neck area. The other distinctive feature of the man's attire is the big triangular collar on his shirt with irregular ends on both sides, the right one extending diagonally to the upper right corner of the drawing, its tip touching the upper edge. The lower angle in the triangular collar goes down to his chest area, and the position of his elevated right hand, the only one visible in the drawing, makes it converge with the end of the collar. This accentuates the geometrical nature of the composition and also the disproportion between the man's broad shoulders, arms and chest and his smaller head, slightly tilted to the left and thus creating a perpendicular angle with the slanted horizontal line of the shoulders. The man's body is traversed diagonally from left to right by a flower with an elongated stem, positioned in such a way that the flower itself is coming out of one of his eyes, whilst the stem line goes through the eye cavity and re-emerges at the back of his head, travelling all the way down his body through his open right hand and ending in one of the two groups of words in the drawing (the other one being the typewritten title at the top). The sentence at the bottom, resembling three lines of verse or a short message, is formed by the same discontinued line that formed the flower and its long stem, although this line is also split into two. This compositional feature serves to physically blend the handwritten lines — the linguistic element — with the visual element of the drawing, which indicates the intended combination of both meanings to create a broader one. The lines at the bottom read 'Solo el misterio | nos hace vivir | solo el misterio'. The other linguistic element in the drawing is placed at the top of the drawing, a title with the typed words 'Material nupcial', which in turn refers the drawing to Neruda's corresponding poem. Finally, a series of short dark vertical lines are arranged in a group around the man's neck area, on top of the bigger collar flap on the right side, almost below his face. The short lines are slightly curved, which gives them a sense of movement, similar to droplets or raindrops, although they are unusually long. Their arrangement in a more or less homogeneous group but not too close to each other reinforces their vertical movement downwards and also conveys some texture. They are also thicker than the other lines in the drawing, which highlights their presence in contrast with the sailor's body.

The composition emphasises the contrast between geometrical figures made of sharp, finite and straight lines and the curved, sinewy lines which form the piercing flower and the handwritten words. In turn, these words resembling a dedication or caption are opposed to the typed words at the top, regular and symmetrical. The triangular sailor's collar, the circular sailor's cap top and the slanted straight line of the man's shoulders similarly clash with the curved shape of the hanging cap ribbon and the lines forming the curvy contour of the man's arms and upper body. The triangle's left side is interrupted at the bottom near the man's hand by a sinewy line superimposed on the original straight line, which suggests a tear or scratch in the fabric and also mirrors the handwritten lines. All these compositional contrasts evoke the existence of two opposing sentiments or poles in the drawing: proportion and rupture, symmetry and asymmetry, firm geometrical lines and sinuous, vibrating, handwritten lines. The disrupted harmony gives the drawing a more unsettling look which accentuates the puzzling 'quiet movement' evoked. The scission produced by the flower's long stem takes place on the man's body, pierced by the plant and thus cut in half, highlighting the asymmetry of the two halves on either side of the stem. This positions the sailor's body in a middle stage between the background and the foreground of the drawing and between his contact with the flower and his separation from it. The flower becomes part of his body but is also a separate entity conveying movement against it, altering, dividing and wounding it. The idea of the wound thus becomes central to the drawing in that it is the site in which the sailor's corporeality is threatened, prompting an interrogation into his emotional, psychological and even ontological state, all of them mysterious and vague. The handwritten lines insist that it is that mystery which makes us (and the sailor) alive, although his vacant demeanour, his wounded body and his asymmetrical position point to death and decomposition instead. On the other hand, the words created by the stem of the plant at the bottom of the composition play with this multiplicity of meanings as well. Mystery can signify that which is unknown or cannot be known, but the poet insists that it is mystery, in other words the desire to know or comprehend, that makes us live. It is the middle stage between knowledge and the unknown that the drawing strives to represent, a boundary space like the scission on the sailor's body.

The figure of the sailor has often been connected to Lorca's 'Ode to Walt Whitman' and other poems from *Poeta en Nueva York*, especially in reference to images of homoeroticism and homosexual culture during the years when Lorca visited the Big Apple. To this must be added the also contemporary erotic drawings of sailors by Cocteau and the early paintings by Dalí which Lorca witnessed at Madrid's Residencia de Estudiantes.[13] In this context, sailors have frequently been a symbol of marginality and promiscuity: prostitution, seedy taverns, underground culture, ports and borders; but they have ultimately represented a sense of freedom, not least the transgressive freedom of expression associated with the historical avant-garde (Plaza Chillón 2016: 533). Threshold locations, freedom, movement and indeterminacy are indeed apt features of Lorca's mysterious sailor. Furthermore, the stylised depiction of his sculptured body in 'Material Nupcial' creates a figure who is unavoidably the object of an eroticised gaze and which suggests a dialogue with the corresponding poem by Neruda.

The Chilean poet explores a lustful and oneiric scene in which the poetic voice sees the image of a young girl in a photograph or a magazine ('miro una niña de papel y luna') (Neruda 2000: 80) and he then describes his brutal physical and psychological response verging on sexual violence. In Lorca's drawing, the also voyeuristic representation of the handsome young sailor situates the artist's gaze in an ambiguous position, either looking lasciviously at a dead body or inflicting physical pain on a living one. The sailor flaunts his muscular arms and broad shoulders — accentuated by the contorted position of his upper body and tilted head — and his delicate handsome face and sinuous lips. However, his vacant eyes and the foregrounding of the long flower stem piercing his eye and cutting his body signal a darker meaning. The 'niña de papel y luna' and the sailor's body are eroticised, but both visions combine harmonious stylised lines and details with ominous allusions to violence and death. The title of the drawing and the poem adds to this disconcerting sense in its double evocation of sexual desire and gender roles. The nuptial material refers to a young woman and a young man respectively, so the erotic and penetrating gaze crosses gender boundaries as it crosses media ones, but disturbingly it also swings from sex to violence, from love to rape, from desire to death. The use of the word 'nupcial' thus carries an ironic sense: neither the poet nor the artist seem to have traditional marriage in mind while admiring their respective love objects and their beguiling bodies being penetrated and destructured, rather they are revelling in their heterodox and unsettling carnal desires. The fact that the same title serves its purpose about both male and female objects (and therefore about homosexual and heterosexual subjects) situates 'Material nupcial' in an ambiguous and queer terrain, mirroring the mystery that envelops the sailor and that Lorca verbally and visually inscribes in the drawing. The complexities of the drawing's gaze are accentuated by the indeterminate psychological and ontological state of the sailor and the presence of death alluded by the piercing flower — which is in turn reminiscent of the drawing 'Busto de hombre muerto' in which plants grow from the eponymous dead man's body (who has identical empty eyes). The group of short lines below the sailor's face also resemble the well-known drops of other drawings evoking blood pouring out. Even though they are displaced from the supposed centre of the wound in this drawing, they are parallel to the flower itself, which also appears to be expelling liquid, possibly bleeding too. Through the lines 'Solo el misterio | nos hace vivir | solo el misterio', the mysterious middle stage between knowledge and the unknown can then be read as an intermediate stage between life and death, the state in which the sailor has been immortalised and which the wound has opened.

A further transgression of corporeality occurs in a free-standing drawing not paired with any of Neruda's poems. 'Cabezas cortadas de Federico García Lorca y Pablo Neruda' is, as the title explains, a depiction of two severed heads resembling those of Lorca and Neruda but with barely any facial features except Lorca's eyes and nose and Neruda's eyebrows and small eyes. The two heads are bleeding small drops of blood at the bottom as they rest on a table. At the very top, on the right hand corner, a waning moon with an open eye in its centre overlooks the scene. The explanatory words at the bottom of the drawing also give some details about its creation: 'este patético dibujo fue realizado la tarde del martes 13 de 1934 en la ciudad de Santa María de los Buenos Aires, así como todos los demás dibujos', which makes the drawing act as an introduction to the whole collection.

The description of the drawing as 'patético' — presumably in its sense of inspiring pity — plays out the idea of Lorca as a self-critic, but also aptly implies a sense of pathos in that extreme emotions are being explored in the drawings and are meant to be inspired in the viewer. The two authors' heads introducing the book are seen as graphic instances of the process involved in its creation, a symbol of the embodiment of artistic expression in the two poets' work. As Acton suggests, the spontaneity inherent in a drawing always alludes to the artist's craftsmanship, their hand-eye coordination and the immediacy of the drawing as opposed to a painting. This translates into the viewer 'witnessing the many layers, the twists and turns and ultimately the mysteries of the creative process' (2009: 201). The more immediate and spontaneous nature of drawing reveals a faster creative process than painting, involving the hand-eye-brain coordination and the craftsmanship of the author all combined and syncretised. The book of poems would be Neruda's life and blood poured into his work, as would the drawings be Lorca's.

Lorca's final drawings show that he was gradually moving towards an aesthetics of corporeal fragments steeped in forms of abstraction. Within the Argentina group of drawings there are some signs of this preference, but the depiction of female bodies is nonetheless rare, which makes the next drawing all the more fascinating. 'Venus', preceding the poem 'Agua sexual', depicts a female figure whose sex explodes into a multitude of little hands extending in all directions through thin sinewy lines. Her body is drawn in two separate blocks: her head and long, flowing hair occupy the top left part of the drawing, insinuating movement downwards to the bottom right part. Her upper body down to her pubic area consists only of her breasts, handless arms, hips and upper thighs, a gap opening around her absent neck area (which disconnects her head from the rest of her body) and her absent legs. Her pubic hair, which is formed of a series of darker line strokes and sinewy lines which then extend outwards, constitutes the focal point in the composition of the drawing and is situated in the central section of the page. Lines coming out of her mouth traverse her body to the right edges of the drawing, creating the words 'amor' (twice on the right top part) and 'luna' (on the right bottom part).

The sketched body of the Venus, because of its contour and its construction as three basic circular shapes (her head, her breast and waist, and her hips and thighs) suggests an emphasis on female sexuality, evoking on the one hand the famous handless sculpture of Venus by Milo and on the other a classic nude painting in which the sexual features of the female body are foregrounded and eroticised.[14] However, the contrast of this conventional subject-matter with the unusual little hands coming out of the woman's genitalia strikes the viewer's attention and challenges expectations. The woman's face presents a vacant expression, with two empty ovals as eyes and thick closed lips, and her fragmented body seems to be immobile and passive, incapable of any action. This passivity accentuates the frantic movement evoked by the multiple little hands extending in all directions and the sexual connotations of the hands, the woman's sex and the twin instances of the word 'amor'. Her desire is overpowering, exerting force and control over her still body. However, the drawing hinges on the horror this desire provokes, on its aggressiveness imposed on the woman's body. Her facial expression and posture are a mixture of void and horror, suspended between two poles which become signified in the drawing by the words on opposite sides. Whilst 'amor' suggests the woman's emotions and her agency in the erotic meaning evoked, the word 'luna' is also leaving her lips to invoke the darkness and mysteriousness of the moon's femininity and deathly overtones.

In Neruda's poem, images of liquids flowing become multiplied and transform into objects forcing themselves upon the human body, penetrating and harming it but also stirring it from its idle, observant and passive state:

> Rodando a goterones solos,
> a gotas como dientes,
> a espesos goterones de mermelada y sangre,
> rodando a goterones,
> cae el agua,
> como una espada en gotas,
> como un desgarrador río de vidrio,
> cae mordiendo,
> golpeando el eje de la simetría, pegando en las costuras
> del alma,
> rompiendo cosas abandonadas, empapando lo oscuro.
>
> (Neruda 2000: 82)

The water in the title may well be affecting the body of the woman in the drawing both as a piercing agent and as a revitalising one. Her desire seems awakened but her destructuration is evoked by bodily issue. The depiction of her genital area is purposely exaggerated through darker and violent lines, excessively flying in all directions and ambiguously representing exuberant pubic hair or gushing streams of blood (both epitomes of her sexual and reproductive capabilities). Carnal desire and corporeal pain are fused, which conversely problematises the agency of the group of hands: are these meant to represent her desire flowing out to embrace her carnality or are they a sign that her body is unavoidably subjected to others as a sexual object? In a suggestive play of opposites, Lorca veils the resolution of this conundrum, instead offering a vision of the Venus which incorporates eroticism, female empowerment and motherhood but simultaneously evokes unsettling images of passivity, objectification, rape and horror. The viewer is left to adopt these visions as fluid components of an uncertain whole, flowing like water to reach, in Neruda's words, inside one's bones ('Veo pasar sus aguas a través de los huesos') (2000: 84).

Within the Argentina collection, 'Imagen de la muerte' or 'Solo la muerte' can be considered a climactic piece owing to its condensed exploration of the desire/death dichotomy under Lorca's particular pictorial rubric. The drawing contains an amalgam of Lorca's recurrent motifs in what could be described as a multi-perspectival depiction of a human body. In a collage-like fashion, the artist portrays a disproportionate and asymmetrical creature with a combination of human features and non-figurative elements in an irregular juxtaposition. In addition, the setting of the drawing brings together concrete, recognisable objects and abstract shapes and forms, merged seamlessly into a quasi-ordinary background scene, depicting a human character going for a walk in a domestic outdoor space, perhaps a patio or back garden. Multiple little hands come out of various parts of the figure's body: from one of the figure's heads, with long sinewy lines simulating its hair; from its central part, reaching towards the top and bottom of the drawing; and from the contours of its bottom part signalling the movement of its human legs wide apart, caught in the moment of stepping forward onto a semi-circular patio with two plant pots on its sides. The creature's second head is shaped like a face with its eyes closed, encircled by a longer pair of lines coming out of the figure's ribcage and floating towards the upper left corner of the drawing, like a balloon. A further series of long thin lines ending in small hands emerges from the same central point in the ribcage, situated in the central section of the drawing. Two of the small hands, each on either side of the body, are holding long-stemmed flowers, one of which has what seems like an open eye in one of its stem leaves. The most unusual motif is situated at the centre of the drawing and becomes the focal point of the composition. It is a group of dark curved lines forming a dark symbol which resembles a scar or a birth mark and which gives a strong sense of depth due to the width of its lines and its uniqueness in the drawing (it is very similar to that of the corpse figure in 'Busto de hombre muerto'). Situated at the 'heart' of the creature (and also as a heart of sorts), its central position accentuates the contorted pose of the figure, its top part extending left and creating a diagonal line across the drawing towards the right leg, elevated behind its other leg and reaching the lower part of the picture. Another diagonal line in the opposite direction is created through two additional elongated lines coming out of the figure's scar and its middle section, these ending in shorter lines with dotted tips mirroring small roots or branches. This complicated asymmetry gives the drawing an energetic dynamism in which the straight geometrical lines forming the creature's skeleton and upper body contrast with the extending curved lines that explode outwards in all directions. It also highlights the constructedness of the creature's body, which surpasses logical limits and appears as de-centred and deformed. Lorca's use of the line elegantly establishes a marked distinction between contrasting shapes superimposed and combined, whilst also conveying a sense of chaos and randomness in the drawing's unusual and excessive juxtapositions.

The drawing hinges on the figure's metamorphic state, in that the non-matching incongruous elements superimposed on its body present the figure's corporeality as an unfinished entity being recreated. Gender and sex marks have been eliminated and are practically non-existent, considering that the figure's long hair and one of its faces are not specific or determinate enough to be defined as male or female. Sensory transgression is another remarkable element. The creature's sight is decentred in that its human elements (its two faces) are both blinded, whilst the open eye on the flower's stem becomes its sighted counterpart staring at it from the edge of the composition. Also, the creature's body lacks arms per se, so the multitude of extending hands serve as its tactile tools, together with its obvious spatial movement represented in its walking legs. The creature's speaking abilities are also transgressed, for while one of the heads has a closed mouth, the other one lacks a mouth altogether and instead has two horizontal lines formed of shorter lines or dots which extend from its mouth area towards the hand on the right side holding the flower. This head's 'impaired' senses are thus substituted by other sensory connotations in a sort of synaesthesia: the non-existent mouth does however 'communicate' through the lines coming out of it which reach its hand and the flower. Conversely, the flower's position facing the creature's head suggests both these lines reaching it as 'visual sound' and the flower's fragrance travelling back to the creature's non-existent nose as 'visual smell'.

All of these instances hinge on the purposeful confusion and disruption of representation. As Plaza Chillón suggests, the drawing performs an attack on the classical image of a harmonious, mythical and flawless body, dismembering and disembodying an organism in an attempt to liberate it (2006: 838). The creature's human senses are, like its constructed body, repositioned in a weird and unusual space within the drawing, transgressing the viewer's logical expectations and preconceived ideas and thus resisting the norms that would make it intelligible. This can be read as Lorca's queer treatment of the senses, for the drawing replaces the creature's bodily and sensory abilities by non-normative sensory agents, while also questioning the very system of binaries from which the creature in the drawing strives to escape. Queer is here not a matter of specific sexual identities, which are made decidedly elusive in Lorca's drawing. As Weinberg posits, it may be that 'the world is queer, because it is known only through representations that are fragmentary and in themselves queer. Their meanings are always relative, a matter of relationships and constructions' (1996: 12).

The relationships in 'Solo la muerte' are so incongruous that attempts to draw from them consistent and faithful representations seem futile if not impossible, precisely because they expose the creature's constructions (its body, its life/death, its gender, its senses, even its humanity) as relative, fluid and in constant (trans) formation. Hence, only death (as expressed in the title) is the way to experience the creature's resistance to being identified with certainty, for it announces the death of meaning, of the assumed distinction between being and non-being and even of the reliability of the drawing itself. Death inevitably invades the scene, alerting the viewer to the creature's fragile existence and its position invoking both (re-)creation and destruction. The figure's sensory elements (sight, tactility, smell, sound) and its spatial movement hinge on life energies, thus proving it is indeed alive despite its ominous and grotesque appearance. Conversely, though, its imminent fragmentation and constructed quality announce this death as an unwonted and unsettling creature which resembles a Grim Reaper incarnation. Unresolved, unfinished, alive yet dying, queer in its form and corporeality as well as in its movement and relation to its environment, 'Solo la muerte''s unsettling character is undoubtedly one of Lorca's pictorial masterpieces, despite (and probably because of) its unconventional and seemingly random and unpolished appearance.

Lorca's treatment of corporeality was at this time becoming more sharply directed towards issues of human connection or the lack thereof. The human senses are used to signify this connectivity graphically, starting from sight and image and moving to tactility and sound. Also, the boundaries between bodies and their surrounding realities and their finitude and fixity are challenged and displaced, favouring visions of blood as the palpable sign of destructuration and decomposition. The wounds that have been announced so far in his drawings will become recurrent signs of infinite potentialities when depicted closely and in abstract isolation. The drawings from 1935–36 are quite varied in style and imagery, although as Lorca's final graphic

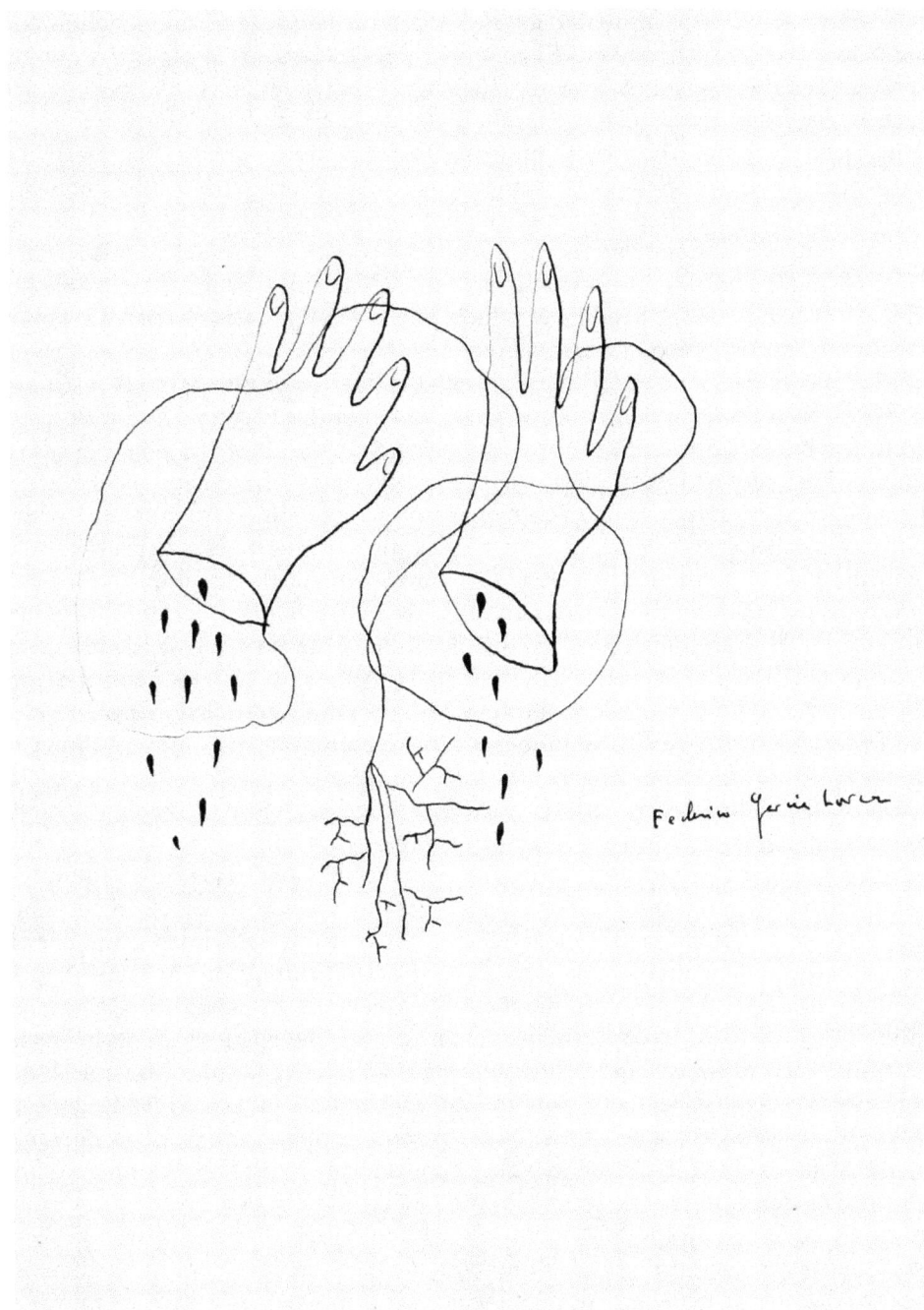

FIG. 3.1. 'Manos cortadas' (ca. 1935–36)

works these are perhaps his best-known. Back in the late 1920s, Lorca's friends Dalí and Sebastián Gasch already talked about the poetic plasticity of his first exhibited drawings and the pure intuition with which he attempted his graphic works, praising the way that inspiration drove the author's hand.[15] The higher level of abstraction of Lorca's later drawings, their focus on smaller details and decontextualised fragments and their shocking and unusual themes make them more opaque and polysemic while confirming the importance of the poetic meaning synthesised in them and of the intuitive abandonment and independence that these abstract details acquire. They all share a preoccupation with processes of deconstruction, fracturing and physical disintegration, phenomena which will ascribe restorative and life-giving qualities to images of wounds and blood.

'Manos cortadas' is one of Lorca's last graphic works and one of the best-known to date.[16] The drawing depicts two hands that have been cut off, with drops of blood dripping out of them towards the bottom of the drawing. There is also a squiggly but uninterrupted line that goes from the wrist of the hand on the left to the bottom of the drawing and in turn ends into an extending system of lines which split into smaller ones, resembling the ramification of the roots of a plant or tree. This line follows a circular trajectory that travels around the hand on the left side and across the drawing to the hand on the right side, circling around it in a zigzag movement. The line connecting both hands creates a curved parabola around them, but does not actually reach the hand on the right; it only touches upon it before ending in the dividing roots at the bottom of the drawing. Both hands are extended and facing upwards, giving the impression of reaching for something, wanting to touch.

The drawing focuses on empty space and absence almost as much as on the presence of the pair of hands. It makes the viewer wonder what is outside the drawing's frame and what preceded it. The elements in the drawing, albeit figurative and identifiable, interact unusually, which creates a sense of shock. The hands clearly allude to human tactility and agency, but they are free-floating and cut off from a body, as suggested by the title. The droplets coming out of them suggest bleeding, although because it is a monochrome drawing, they could also be tears or raindrops, motifs used in other drawings. Either way, the relationship between the hands and their dripping liquid particles evokes a moment in time which is absent from the drawing. If the hands were indeed severed, this violent scene has already happened, it belongs to a past time. Not only would this image point to immense pain, it would also suggest barbaric violence, possibly murder. The movement in the drawing, however, suggests a different kind of aftermath to this event, as the hands are stretched out, reaching for something, while the line that circles around them evokes movement, the growth of living roots.[17] The visual metaphor in the drawing suggests that life/growing and death/violence are interwoven. As parts of a missing whole, the status and purpose of the hands remain unresolved and uncertain. If they belonged to a body, they would now be dismembered, disembodied fragments. However, as free-standing entities without a body, they invite the viewer into an imagined reality where hands are self-moving agents signifying the creative powers of physicality. Hands can touch, they can hit, they can break, but they can also write, they can draw, they can paint, they can play a musical instrument or mould a sculpture, to name only a few activities. Lacking other parts attached to the hands, they can attain infinite powers without accounting for any other governing entity, such as the intellect or language. If this was the artist's intention, then these hands could be conveying a sense of automatic creation, art in its purest form disembodied from any logical restraints. 'El poeta', Lorca said in one of his letters, 'tiene la sensación vaga de que va a una cacería nocturna en un bosque lejanísimo' (Cavanaugh 1995: 21), implying a haphazard violent act in which creation needs to be hunted down by the artist and appropriated into their hands.

In tune with this, the roots clearly allude to the idea of connection, of entities searching for a state of contact with other entities (perhaps like the isolated lips in 'Labios'). The sense of touch is prominent, but the drawing focuses on the lack of tactility: two free-floating open hands not touching anything or anyone. They are expectant, reaching for something, perhaps desiring to touch. The moment depicted in the drawing lacks closure or completion, the movement implied is crystallised in the reaching out moment. In parallel, the contact of plants with the earth through their roots returns to the idea of the life cycles in nature, but also points to the organic search for nutrition and survival. The resemblance of roots to human veins is also evoked by the blood drops. If the tactility of the hands is read as an allusion to human contact, this erotic connection would imply violence and pain, an image of castration (Plaza Chillón 2006: 835) or a break-up. *Eros*, the human drive towards life preservation is graphically juxtaposed in the drawing to the imminence of the death drive, signalling the inevitable coexistence of both processes. In Bakhtinian terms, conversely, the grotesque depiction of the boundaries connecting the body with the outside world hinges on the coalescence of existence and mortality.

The drawing also explores issues of authorship and craftsmanship in art. The artist's hands are free, cut off from the intellect or any rules or norms governing his or her technique. There is freedom and a sense of infinite creativity in this disconnection, in the fact that the will of the artist dominates their creation and the value of the work of art lies in the physical act of producing it single-handedly. However, Lorca seemed to avoid ascribing his art to well-known Surrealist creative modes or techniques like automatisation or unconsciousness, instead defending the value of hard work and 'rootedness' in reason and logic. This could account for the connecting lines that 'root' the hands in the drawing to a source (perhaps the artist's spirit, his *duende*, his blood) which, concrete or abstract and stable or not, guides the artist's hand in their 'hunt-like' process of creation.

There are thus two main arguments that may be derived from this and other representations of hands in Lorca's drawings. Firstly, the coalescence of violence, mutilation, and physical pain and the erotic impulse to touch, interact and possess is syncretised in the dismembered but open hands. The cyclical interrelation of *eros* and *thanatos* is signified through the allusions to natural growth emerging from destruction. The severed hands may refer to the end of physical contact, to the ominous presence of death in sexuality (in extreme terms, to castration), or to the inevitable pain inherent in human relationships. In parallel, the relationship of human hands with the artistic process is also evident, since ideas of craftsmanship and physical creation lie at the root of every artwork. The hand creates the drawing, it is the single most important tool for artistic creation. The immediacy of drawing as opposed to the process of creating a painting gives us a greater insight into the artist's development of an idea. In the drawing there is a translation of what the eye sees into the movements of the hand. Time is a factor too: a drawing is created in a shorter period of time, so its immediacy speaks to the impending threat of time passing and the capacity of the drawing to capture a still moment in time. Subsequently, giving the hand itself a leading role in the act of creation ties in with the idea of automatism associated with Surrealism. It may be argued that the centrality of the hand's role implies the Surrealist tendency towards automatic creation, abandoning reason and logic to let the hand lead the artist. It is known that Lorca was reluctant to ascribe this tendency to his work (Plaza Chillón 2008: 15). Nonetheless, the tactile connotations of hands do allow him to explore intuitive and sensory aspects of artistic creation, like its immediacy, craftsmanship, embodiment and materiality. Much like the severed heads from his Argentinian collection wished to present the two artists' work laid bare humbly before the viewer, Lorca here presents the work of his hands as an offering of sorts, his craftsmanship and his 'handiwork' as the medium and result of his aesthetic theory.

The series of faces with arrows, featured in many of Lorca's autographs, were exercised as independent drawings on various occasions, especially in his final years. 'Rostro de las dos flechas' and 'Rostro con flechas' (1935–36) are two well-known examples. Their graphic brevity and immediacy and their small size tie in with the inclusion of a verbal component, the author's signature. Issues of selfhood and authorship are mixed in with the visual-verbal interactions in them, suggesting a playful coalescence between Lorca the author and the faces, although their resemblance to Lorca is vague. Are they self-portraits, masks or *commedia dell'arte* figures? Their clownish appearance incorporates the ludic and the grotesque: smiling and crying at the same time like a Pierrot would, but also destructured, decapitated, unfinished bodies whose flesh is being pierced. The artificiality derived from both traditions envelops the faces so that it becomes, ironically, unclear whether they are meant to be autographs or stand-alone pieces, private self-portraits intended as gifts or artworks to be deciphered. As usual, this doubleness is unresolved, which makes the drawings even more intriguing.

'Rostro de las dos flechas' consists of a half-oval describing the contour of a human face and pointing upwards via the two arrows in which the extremes end. These two arrows in turn present three dark points each, one on each end of the arrow's triangular shape. The only element constituting the facial expression in the image is a human mouth, with thick, sinuous lips closed in a half-smile which moves upwards to the right side, thus accentuating the movement of the right arrow, proportionally longer and extending further upwards in the drawing. Dark drops fall downwards across the featureless face and the mouth, dripping towards the bottom of the drawing like tears or drops of blood. The apparent simplicity of

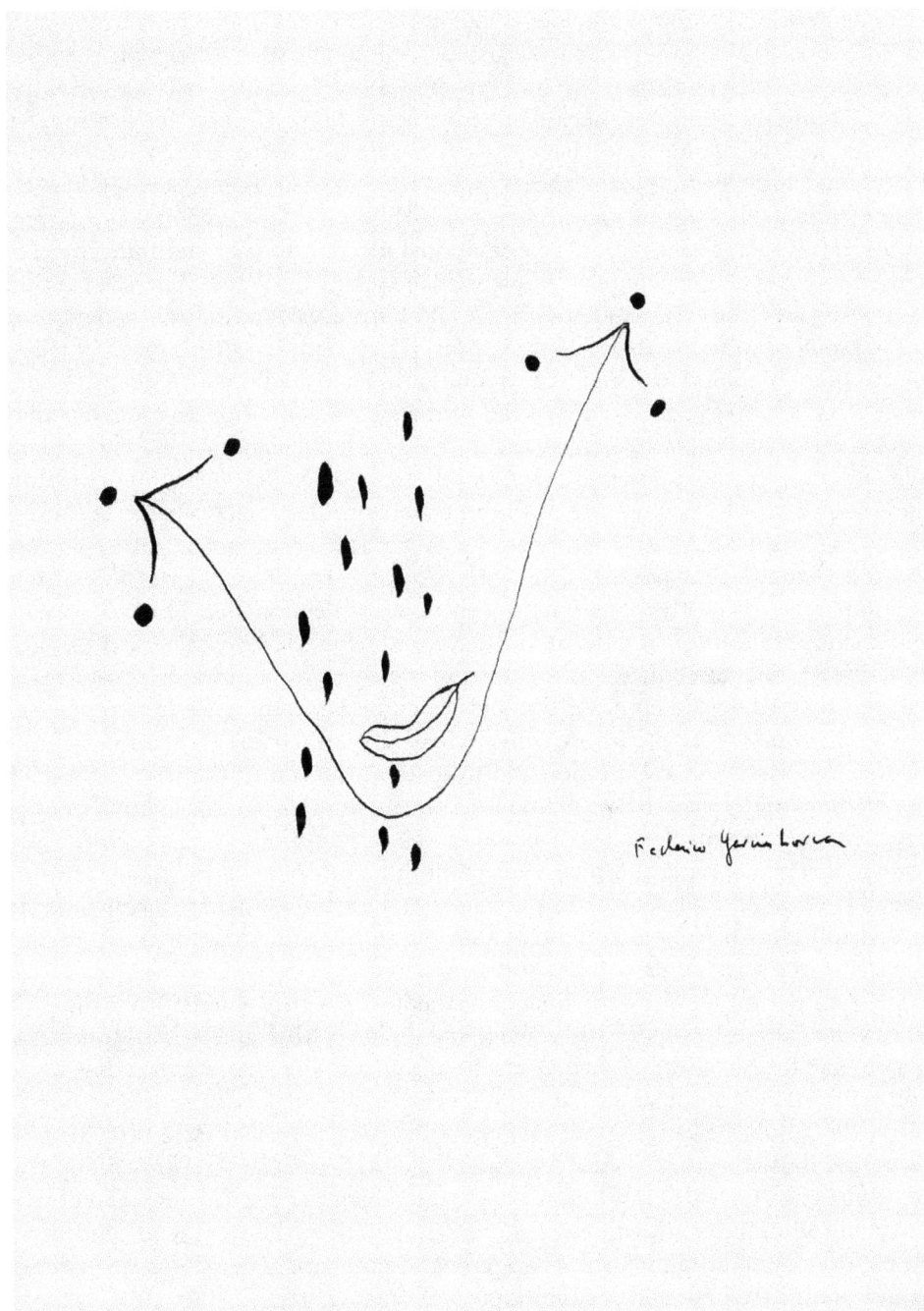

FIG. 3.2. 'Rostro de las dos flechas' (ca. 1935–36).

the composition combines figurative and abstract elements. The tears can be read as an expression of anguish and melancholia, although their ambiguous darkness might be connected to the wounding capabilities of a figurative arrow, a motif that evokes Lorca's earlier 'San Sebastián' drawings.[18] Plaza Chillón further suggests that the face is ambiguously shaped like a heart, which the arrows symbolically pierce, causing bleeding and/or tears (2014: 232–33). The points surrounding the arrows might be marking their entry points into the flesh, evoking the pierced body and its subsequent bleeding or emotional reaction to pain and suffering. The static nature of the dark circles emphasises the artificiality and abstraction of the wounding moment, thus suggesting a separation from the logic of time and space, as if the moment were frozen in time. Very much like 'San Sebastián' (1927), in which martyrdom is sublimated and the wound abstracted and stylised geometrically, 'Rostro de las dos flechas' combines the abstracted concentration on the moment of wounding — devoid of time, space and form — with the emotional and melancholy state evoked by the figurative tears/blood, signs of embodiment, humanisation and mortality. This, in addition to the ambiguous smile, creates a sense of fluidity between pleasure and pain and between creation and destruction.

'Rostro con flechas' presents a similar level of abstraction and a series of recurrent motifs but seems slightly more figurative than the former drawing. This face presents more complete features: a nose, an open eye with elongated eyelashes and a similar mouth with full closed lips. The contours of the face end in upwards arrows again, but this time so do the nose, the eye and the chin. The latter ends in two opposite arrows surrounded by dark dots, which create a symmetrical axis contrasting the slanted and asymmetrical position and features of the rest of the face. At the top of the drawing, black droplets fall down from the figure's forehead above its open eye. Again, these may be tears, blood drops or raindrops. The multiple facial arrows also intermingle and their ends point to a multitude of directions, creating a further sense of displacement and asymmetry. The figure's head is incomplete but sufficiently drawn to be identified as human, yet the superimposition of abstract lines creates a sense of destructuration and therefore of constructedness. Its vacant expression is contrasted by the long and sinuous lines that emerge from the eye's side, which add expressivity and further ambiguity — this time related to sex and gender distinctions. Both 'Rostros' may be alluding to the mask, to the constructed and artificial face disguising what lies underneath, although as suggested in Lorca's plays, this might be nothing but further and further masks ad infinitum. If these faces are indeed masks, they may also be pointing to the transformations that performance allows (Plaza Chillón 2014: 232), which the circular lines and arrows travelling in multiple directions connote.[19] In addition, the faces tend towards an ambiguity of expression which, while failing to emote or reflect intimate passions, represents the strength and stoicism typical of drama (Plaza Chillón 2014: 232).

Considering the connections with Saint Sebastian's martyrdom and its much-debated homoerotic gaze, the two 'Rostros con flechas' similarly explore the aesthetics of the wound but move past sex and gender binary distinctions. The faces in both drawings problematise the erotic/deadly qualities of the phallic object

FIG. 3.3. 'Rostro con flechas' (ca. 1935–36).

piercing the flesh, but by depicting indeterminate sex and gender markers, they open up the coalescence of desire and mortality to a queer arena. The viewer is prompted to wonder whether the notion of gender itself is at all relevant to interpret the drawings; whether the faces are smiling, suffering, or simply pretending; and whether these are human faces or mere artificial masks. Lastly, it remains unclear whether the signatures in both face-arrow drawings play with ideas of authorship and selfhood by introducing an intermedial interaction between word and image. Lorca becomes present in the drawing through the inclusion of his name, but is Lorca the man or Lorca the artist who inhabits the work? Are the faces meant to be self-portraits or are they clowns (or even *duendes*)? What is clearer is that an increasing level of abstraction and the detailed focus on bodily fragments allow Lorca's late drawings to elevate the wound — and its focus on the life/death interrelation and the transgression of normativity — to a prominent examining position for the viewer's pleasure, shock and interrogation.

Notes to Chapter 3

1. For a general overview of Lorca's pictorial *oeuvre* in relation to important stages in his life and career and in connection with a selection of his works, see Oppenheimer (1986).
2. The Dalmau exhibition ran from 25 June to 2 July 1927, and the *Semana del Arte Nuevo* in Huelva took place on 26 June, lasting until 3 July 1932 (Buxán Bran 2003: 323). For a more thorough description of the first Lorca exhibition, see Oppenheimer (1986: 61–64), Gallego Morell (1988: 195), and Lahuerta (2010: 251).
3. The project that Lorca and Dalí worked on, 'Los Putrefactos', the lectures they attended and the letters they wrote to each other during these years attest to their learning process and mutual enrichment in their artistic styles. For more details of their collaborations and artistic ventures at the Residencia, see Sociedad Estatal de Conmemoraciones Culturales SECC (2010).
4. 'El hecho de que durante cierto tiempo pensase insistentemente en reunir sus dibujos en un volumen resulta especialmente significativo de como para Federico su obra plástica era un proyecto artístico coherente y absolutamente reflexivo e intelectualizado, nada que ver con un mero divertimento, un hobby, o meras obras de un dominguero' (Buxán Bran 2003: 323).
5. An important study by Paul Ilie (2009) focuses on the grotesque aesthetic in Spanish literature, ranging from the Golden Age to Modernism. For a in-depth study of the grotesque in modern art, see Astruc (2010).
6. See Ilie (2009: 217–64) for an examination of the grotesque in Valle-Inclán.
7. Lorca's preference for male portraits during his North American period must be added to the drawings depicting urban scenes, fantastical animals, calligrams and more abstract and grotesque visions, some of which will be discussed further in Chapter 5.
8. Olivares gives a detailed account of the many social events Lorca attended while in Argentina: his fame had reached the main circles of artists and intellectuals there, all eager to meet and interact with the Spaniard (2001: 41–45; 51–60; 84–87).
9. The other two were Mexican poet Salvador Novo's work, entitled *Seamen Rhymes*, and Argentinean Ricardo Molinari's *Una rosa para Stefan George* (Plaza Chillón 2016: 532). Most of the drawings that illustrated the works by these two poets featured sailors like that of 'Material Nupcial' from Neruda's collection.
10. Barradas was interested in the visual effects achieved by Futurist painting through the recycling of Cubist language, which in his genuine style he translated into the attempt to capture the continuous transit between subject and object, between individual consciousness and the surrounding world (Plaza Chillón 2014: 219).
11. Borkent further posits that these types of 'multimodal artefacts' serve to demonstrate the

syncretism between body and mind, which 'motivates meaning through connections between perception and conception' (2010: 148).

12. After Lorca's 1927 exhibition in Barcelona, art critic Sebastián Gasch noticed the parallels between Lorca's drawings and artists like Cocteau, Max Jacob or Miró (1928: 4).

13. Lahuerta (2010: 149) identifies recurrent pictorial motifs, such as the sailor and Venus, which were amply developed by Dalí and other contemporary artists Lorca came in contact with or whose work he studied during his years at La Residencia in Madrid.

14. A previous 'Venus' drawing from 1927 depicts the female protagonist as a collage of body parts, making use of a number of motifs evidencing Dalí's influence (Plaza Chillón 2006: 836–39).

15. Writing for *La gaceta literaria*, Gasch praised the many accomplishments of Lorca the 'dibujante': 'Dibujos presentados, dibujos adivinados, dibujos vistos en un momento de inspiración, y que pasan directamente de lo más profundo del ser del poeta a su mano. Una mano que se abandona. Una mano que se deja hacer, que no opone resistencia, que ni sabe ni quiere saber a dónde es conducida (1928: 4).

16. There are a number of variations of this drawing accompanying various artefacts, such as Lorca's autographs, book edition covers, dedications to friends, etc. Two of them have a significant amount in common with the piece analysed here: 'Manos cortadas' variation (ca.1935–36, ink on the title page of *Llanto por Ignacio Sánchez Mejías*, a first edition copy dedicated to Manuel Muntañola Tey in Barcelona) contains the severed hands but this time there is a bleeding rose next to them instead of growing roots. A third variation, 'La mano', is also very similar to 'Manos cortadas' in that one severed hand this time dominates the drawing. The latter hand is not dripping blood; but a group of straight lines simulating roots come out of it, reaching the bottom of the drawing. Also, it is not open, but has a firm grasp on a thin branch from which little red fruits, cherries or red grapes, spring out of horizontal branches in turn. The tips of these branches end in long green leaves which become purple peacock feathers. This last version is uncatalogued.

17. Cavanaugh sees the representation of hands as an allusion to the act of reaching out, touching, searching for something (2003: 195); similarly, Oppenheimer identifies the hands as Lorca's expressive agents, since 'without hands an artist cannot express himself, either sexually or creatively' (1986: 31).

18. There are various Lorquian drawings developing the idea of Saint Sebastian, the martyr pierced by arrows. The least figurative of them, which resembles his later face-arrow drawings, was produced in 1927, and its depiction relates to a dialogue Lorca had with Salvador Dalí for some time about the figure of the well-known saint and its aesthetic implications (Lahuerta 2010: 239–50). It concentrates on the act of wounding, on a group of lines with arrows which generate the composition and movement in the drawing. These straight lines all end in a dark circle of ink, pointing in different directions. In the centre of the drawing, there is a human eye and a circle with another dot in the middle, like a bullseye. The whole scene of the martyrdom is reduced to a suggestive image in which the central point is the violent moment of wounding, the stabbing of the saint's body and the suffering implied. However, there is no dripping blood in the drawing, the moment of violence is frozen or crystallised in time. See Plaza Chillón (2019) for a thorough study of the iconography of Saint Sebastian in Lorca's and Dalí's work.

19. Plaza Chillón relates these drawings to 'El beso' and 'San Sebastián', and reads the faces as 'la perenne máscara del drama lorquiano que oculta la auténtica cara como espejo del alma' (2014: 232).

CHAPTER 4

❖

Viaje a la luna:
(Anti-)Narrative Tableaux
and the Spectacle of Death

El escenarista, el constructor literario
de films debe ser ante todo un poeta
que piensa en imágenes visuales.
(De Torre 1925: 387)

Jumping backwards in time, as is usual in Lorca's later works, to the crucial journey
the poet made to New York in 1929, this chapter will analyse the film script *Viaje
a la luna*, an intermedial artefact halfway between poetry and cinema. As a work
whose cohesiveness 'depends much more on the symbolic rather than the narrative'
(Anderson 2017: 1), the film script can be considered a non-linear spectacle of death,
exploring ideas of the human body and identity as fluid and metamorphic. In my
approach to the film script, I will first consider Lorca's initial steps in his journey
into the film medium, examining the influence of early cinema on his work
before his trip to the United States, especially on the short play *El paseo de Buster
Keaton*. I will then focus on *Viaje a la luna*'s tableau structure and spatiotemporal
transgressions, both of which mirror the fragmentations and transformations of
bodies in the film script, and on how the poetic (anti-)narrative of *Viaje* hinges on
ideas of artificiality and spectacularity, which are subverted and questioned in this
particular approach to cinema. Finally, I will focus on the Lorquian interrelation
of desire and death, which is aptly represented as a cyclical intertwining mirroring
the circularity of the moon and that of the trip(s) depicted.

Like many of his fellow students at the Residencia de Estudiantes in Madrid,
Lorca's introduction to cinema took place through the pioneering 'Cineclub
Español' organised by the magazine *La gaceta literaria* (Sánchez Vidal 1988: 142).
Founded by Ernesto Giménez Caballero in 1928, the Spanish cinema club hosted
the projection of several European and North American films (such as Sergei
Eisenstein's *The Battleship Potemkin* (1925), Fritz Lang's *Metropolis* (1927) and the
silent comedies of Buster Keaton and Charlie Chaplin), and held many lectures and
discussion sessions with students, scholars and artists attending.[1] This experience
helped Lorca and his contemporaries acquire an affinity for the new medium and
for some of the genres gaining recognition around the world at the time. Silent

comedy and especially Buster Keaton's films, seem to have fascinated Lorca's generation, due to their mixture of subversion, melancholy and slapstick comedy, which in one way or another started permeating the group's work (see Felten 2005).[2]

In the case of *Viaje a la luna,* one of the elements that evidences this influence is the use of montage — as opposed to continuity editing — to create the effects of rapid movement and incongruous juxtapositions, while emphasising the interrelations among the images that form it.[3] Films such as René Clair's *Entr'acte* (1924) and *Un chien andalou* (1928–29) by Luis Buñuel and Salvador Dalí are very close to Lorca's film script in their unexpected associations of unrelated images and the shocking effects and plurality of meanings they achieved when assembled together through montage. The commonalities between *Viaje a la luna* and *Un chien andalou* go beyond the (then already deteriorated) friendship between Lorca, Buñuel and Dalí. Lorca had not seen *Un chien andalou* but had probably read the script and had a clear idea of the nature of the film (Carnero 2005: 30).[4] While both works make use of montage, dissolves and superimpositions and many symbols and image associations recur across them, it can be argued that *Un chien* adheres more closely to classical modes of editing and narration (Smith 2014). Although spatial and temporal transgressions are notable in *Un chien,* *Viaje* presents a more sustained preference for narrative discontinuity and spatiotemporal disruptions throughout. Both works do, however, propose an elimination or disruption of linear narration, presenting instead a series of episodic vignettes which favour metaphoric, metonymic or other associative interrelations of images like analogy, simile, metaphoric montage or contiguity.

Viaje a la luna's preference for incongruity and shock rather than narrative continuity resonates with the early cinema of the 1900s and especially the prominent filmmaker and magician Georges Méliès and the lesser-known but also pioneering Spanish cineaste Segundo de Chomón.[5] Reminiscent of the eponymous *Voyage dans la lune* by Méliès (1902), Lorca's film script bears many resemblances to Méliès's and de Chomón's trick techniques and illusions in its recourse to multiple dissolves between scenes and superimpositions. De Chomón filmed a remake of *Voyage dans la lune* entitled *Excursion dans la lune* (1908), which imitates Méliès's film quite faithfully but introduces some new techniques such as a more advanced use of colour. The two filmmakers are well-known for being pioneers of cinema and both their films are examples of the wish to explore exotic, legendary and fantastical worlds through cinema and to present them to audiences as a form of cathartic evasion (Powell 2012: 41). The French cineaste usually experimented with comic grotesque images and fantastical or demonic characters, of which Mephistopheles, Beelzebub or Satan and magicians or sorcerers are some examples (Robinson 1993: 33); conversely, the Spaniard was very interested in exploring animal transformations, double expositions and dissolves and presenting inanimate objects springing to life and moving independently through the development of stop motion techniques. Both Méliès and de Chomón used cinematic tricks often involving dismembered bodies and metamorphoses, transpositions and mysteries: 'in an instant, objects turn into people, butterflies metamorphose into chorus beauties, men become women, anyone may vanish in a puff of smoke' (Robinson 1993: 55), elements which are integral to Lorca's *Viaje a la luna*.[6]

The aim of early cineastes to shock and amaze, what has been termed the 'cinema of attractions' model, is closer to an avant-garde film script like *Viaje a la luna* than Hollywood's storytelling could be.[7] Continuity editing is rarely used in *Viaje*, and Lorca's use of montage and superimposition points to a preference for a tableau narrative highly reliant on image associations rather than linear narration. The shock and disorientation produced by spatiotemporal transgressions and random image juxtapositions contribute to create an effect of amazement, attraction and even repulsion at times. In his work *Body Shots: Early Cinema's Incarnations*, Jonathan Auerbach presents Tom Gunning and André Gaudreault's 'attractions' theory as emphasising 'visual shock and display rather than spectatorial identification and narrative integration' (2007: 86), a way to attract the viewer to the images displayed in front of them. The obscure or random connections between images in *Viaje a la luna* respond to a poetic rather than causal logic, which serves to highlight the display of the images themselves and their aesthetic effects without any strict narrative constraints. Lorca's film script is indebted to this initial era of cinema and its great innovations within the medium, while also establishing a dialogue with the avant-garde in its typically Surrealist oneiric atmosphere and its use of montage and superimposition.

Lorca's proper incursion into the cinematic medium took place in New York in 1929–30.[8] His new friendship with Mexican graphic artist Emilio Amero resulted in Lorca's scriptwriting venture, but this was an idea which he might have been already considering when he wrote his short theatrical piece *El paseo de Buster Keaton* (1928), published in *Gallo* magazine.[9] In this short play, a dramatic dialogue is interspersed with cinematic elements, such as references to well-known film director and actor Buster Keaton and to the silent comedy tradition of the time, as well as to motifs and techniques Lorca had come to know in these films. Absurd and disconcerting scenes combine at times with a humorous tone and at others with lyrical images announcing the oneiric and apocalyptic urban poems of *Poeta en Nueva York*, as well as the images of *Viaje a la luna*. A strange relationship is established between Keaton's desire and images of suffering and death, which ultimately unveils his inherent anguish and sorrow. His stroll, the overarching premise of the short play, is presented as a series of encounters with different characters, whose interactions with Keaton are ambiguous and uncertain at best but which become ominous and disturbing when analysed closely.

The play, set in Philadelphia, also contains many references to modernity and American society, such as technological innovations like the *Singer* sewing machine and the gramophone, the marginality and discrimination of black people (one of the characters is a black man who is eating his own hat) and popular fashion of the time (shoes made of crocodile skin, Keaton's pork pie hat, shirt and tie), all of which help to evoke the settings and tropes seen in Keaton's cinema and the place where it originated. *El paseo de Buster Keaton* can be considered a proto-montage, juxtaposing unrelated or random scenes in a rapid succession without narrative causality or resolution, also mirroring some other filmic representational devices such as magic tricks, close-ups and cutaways. Cinema was the source which enabled Lorca to incorporate these tricks and devices into his play, expanding the range of his imagination and allowing him to 'visualize movements that, however rapid or strange, were inspired or authenticated by what he had observed on the screen' (Morris 1980: 125). In the play, Keaton falls off his bike and it magically flies chasing after two butterflies, a trick which supposes a transgression of the laws of physics and which might have proved challenging in a theatre play but would fit perfectly into a film by Georges Méliès or Keaton himself. Stage directions describe the protagonist smiling while looking *'en gros plan'* (García Lorca 1996 II: 25) (in close-up) at a young American girl 'con los ojos de celuloide' (García Lorca 1996 II: 24), who wears crocodile-skin shoes. All these elements resolutely refer to the filmic medium, as do the stage directions relating to the *mise en scène* of the play which surpass the actual dialogues in it in length and quantity. The influence of the film medium thus becomes palpable in Lorca's work, announcing some of the elements he then developed when he arrived in New York a year later.

Viaje a la luna, Lorca's *guion cinematográfico*, is the equivalent of what we consider a film script, scenario or screenplay.[10] The text presents a fragmented and discontinuous structure which deliberately transgresses narrative linearity and resembles a collage of vignettes or tableaux. It is formed of a series of seventy-two numbered units separated graphically in the text by blank spaces.[11] These units can be identified as segments or sections equivalent to film shots or shot sequences, some combined to create scenes varying in length and complexity. They are referred to as 'cuadros' (frames or tableaux) in the text and they contain descriptions of settings and the (potential) cinematic *mise en scène* ('Pasillo largo', section 6; 'Vista de Broadway de noche', 7; 'Un plano blanco sobre el cual se arrojan gotas de tinta', 21), of the characters or objects in the shot ('Sale un hombre con una bata blanca', 23), visual details of the shot ('Gran plano de manos y traje de arlequín', 26) or transitional devices sequencing the segments ('Se disuelve sobre una doble exposición de serpientes de mar', 27). The stage directions or technical indications referring to transitions between shots appear in more than two thirds of the scenario, and they are mostly integrated seamlessly into the narrative. Through these complex segments, Lorca achieves great depth in the visual and poetic content of each shot, articulating the intended filmic result but also establishing poetic connections between the images represented through language and the film medium itself. Film scholar Román Gubern argues that *Viaje a la luna* must be considered:

> un guión literario, aunque con algunas someras indicaciones técnicas, lo que nos obliga a recordar que un guión no es un film, sino un texto instrumental o transitorio, una matriz literaria preliminar para un proyecto de film, es decir, una larva o embrión textual para su ulterior desarrollo audiovisual, en un sistema semiótico muy distinto. (Gubern 1999: 451)

This emphasises the intermedial relationship established between language and image in the film scenario, although Gubern somewhat downplays the importance of Lorca's use of editing elements. Despite considering the script an instrumental tool or a transitory stage between literature and film, a cinematic embryo, it is obvious that 'Lorca was well aware of the particular suitability of film, as poetry in motion pictures, to convey psychic processes through symbolic images, as in a dream' (McDermott 1996: 123). What Gubern calls perfunctory technical indications constitute a significant part of *Viaje a la luna* and therefore should be seen as the author's preferred expressive medium in their own right. The film script is a particularly intermedial artefact. Lorca is making use of elements that would usually be associated to two distinct media: poetry and film. Its linguistic component (the film script is pre-eminently a written text) and its vignette or tableau structure hinge on poetry's stylistic economy and sense of visuality.[12] This immediacy of the poetic image brings poetry close to cinema's visuality, which Lorca exploits in the film script by combining it with cinematic devices such as dissolves, superimpositions and image juxtapositions and associations. In Larson's view, *Viaje* is a unique example of the translation of cinematic effects into writing, of 'cinegrafía', because it theorises 'the relationship between the written word and the film image' (2011: 303). The text of the film script achieves a sense of 'watchability', since the cohesive relationship between the poetic images and the potential cinematic images makes their separation almost non-existent, forcing the reader/viewer to draw from word and image simultaneously in order to make sense of them.

Viaje a la luna may thus be examined taking into account its linguistic component, which presents the characters, images and tableaux and their poetic interrelations and which also establishes the visual and cinematic effects intended for its filmic production. In parallel, its cinematic qualities can also be analysed in themselves, insofar as Lorca's technical directions suggest (to an extent) the potential spectatorial position proposed were the film to be realised. A further perspective can also be adopted if Frederic Amat's film adaptation (1998) is taken into account, bearing in mind that the latter is just one possible interpretation of Lorca's script and that, albeit quite faithful to the text's structure and content, it inevitably makes use of modern technological resources that would have not been available to Lorca at the time of writing.[13] Nonetheless, Amat's film contributes to creating a clearer sense of what Lorca's intended artistic project would have been if he had lived to see it fully realised on the screen, so throughout this chapter I shall have recourse to the film adaptation to illustrate certain points in the film script.

Since the film script lacks a clearly linear narrative development, it is instead possible, albeit problematic, to establish a division of the text into sub-sections and to engage with some of its narrative elements. It could be divided into three parts or blocks of segments, following the more or less recurrent characters and events at different points in the script. The first part would run from segment 1 to segment 30, in which a sign with the title *Viaje a la luna* appears; the second part would follow until section 43, in which the recurrent character of the Man of Veins appears for the first time; finally, the third part focuses on this character in different scenarios until it ends with a shot of the moon above a group of trees being waved by the wind in section 72.[14] Although by no means chronological or linear, a broad storyline emerging from certain diegetic episodes can be identified in the scenario.[15] In the first part, the urban setting of New York is introduced and a multitude of body parts are juxtaposed, suggesting that fear, horror and violence are threatening consequences of sexual desire. There is a stark tension between images of nature, animals and childhood and contrasting images of modernity, technology, science and the human body. In the second part, which starts with a 'letrero' serving as the title card of the film, female figures abound, associated with images of motherhood, suffering, sexuality, violence and death. The third part, arguably the most narratively coherent, follows a young man who seems to rebel against social impositions and chooses to show a form of heterodox identity which is closely connected with non-normative sexual desire and with the imminence of death. After he dies, a short epilogue alludes self-reflexively to the artificiality of cinema as desire and death themselves are ambiguously fused. The film script's fragmented narrative is characterised by disorienting jumps across space and time, and there is a profusion of transitioning techniques which fuse or dissolve images into one another, as well as showing double or multiple images simultaneously by superimposition. In parallel, the segmentation of the text mirrors the representation of bodies in a constant state of metamorphosis, also destructured but able to morph into other bodies. The first part of the film script, which may be considered a prologue preceding the title in section 30, is characterised by short segments in which isolated scenes focus on elements in close-up, most of them human bodily fragments.[16] An exception to this is section 7, in which there is a long shot of Broadway at night. This scene follows a view of a long corridor which ends in a window, and after the wide shot of the city has been shown, it dissolves back into the view of the corridor. This corridor appears again in segment 12, serving as a spatial signpost amongst the rest of the close-ups. The spatial setting of the first part of the script thus superimposes a domestic enclosed space on an urban space, that of the metropolis *par excellence*, New York City. In addition, this spatial tension is accompanied by the enormous speed in which the shots succeed each other, which is in keeping with the allusions to modernity and technology implied by the urban scenarios. As Doane posits, 'the acceleration of events specific to city life was inseparable from the effects of new technologies and a machine culture made possible by developments in modern science' (2002: 4). Cinema is very much the machine that drives these spatiotemporal transgressions, as evidenced in Lorca's references to the moving camera as 'la máquina' (6, 12). Whilst the urban space accentuates the idea of movement and speed suggested by the successive corporeal transformations and the shocking appearance of the machine, the domestic spaces in the script serve to disorient and confuse, since the images keep changing scenarios so that the oneiric and grotesque atmosphere being created by the dismembered bodies is strengthened. The camera is the force enabling the images to move frenetically and to mutate and fuse into other images, at once threatening to disintegrate and annihilate them but also with the ability to recreate them.

The first section of *Viaje* represents a white bed against a grey wall (1), where sets of numbers 13 and 22 start dancing around the bed magically, multiplying and invading it until they resemble small ants. While the bed may carry connotations related to sexual activity or sleep (Anderson 2017: 6), its whiteness inevitably evokes purity, cleanliness and peacefulness.[17] The 'avalanche of numbers' may be suggestive of 'scientific knowledge, money and the importance given to statistics, norms and rules in modernity' (Hacking 1987: 52–53), which here disturbs the clean white canvas created by the bedsheets and simulates ink writing on a blank page or projections on a screen.[18] The numbers on the bed can be associated with modernity's obsession with statistics and the representability and measurability of abstract concepts like time. However, 'modernity is also strongly associated with epistemologies that valorize the contingent, the ephemeral, chance — that which is beyond or resistant to meaning' (Doane 2002: 10).[19] The two numbers on the bed are open to a wide variety of interpretations as a contrasting pair: Anderson suggests 'odd/even, unbalanced/balanced, alone/together, divided/unified, and perhaps also female/male, heterosexual/homosexual' (2017: 6), and to those must be added the *chiaroscuro* created by the white bedsheets under the black numbers as well as the rationality evoked by mathematics against the irrationality of its animation. As Lorca aptly suggested, the poetic creation he favoured 'rechaza toda la dulce geometría aprendida' (*OC* III: 310), Geometry taken here as a metonymical term for mathematical or logical thought. The poetic logic at work, aided by the cinematic power to represent the illogical as possible, challenges the urge to measure and count or the tendency towards symmetry and linearity.[20] Instead, *Viaje*'s poetic narrative 'allows for multiple and personalised readings in contrast to the privileging of a single reading as practised by the traditional Hollywood narrative' (Powell 2012: 64). In the film adaptation, Amat emphasises this tension and the anxiety generated by superimposing the ants on the numbers, both in the foreground and in close-up and in the background covering the white bed, accentuating this superimposition through scratches on the film which give a sense of degradation and fragmentation. The camera tilts and zooms in to reposition the bed from a long shot to a medium shot and from an eye-level angle to a high angle, which increases the sense of anxiety produced by the ants invading the bed and the entire frame.

In this first block of sections, spatiotemporal disruption is often evident, along with an increasing sense of threat, horror, fear and violence, perhaps stemming from the threat to linearity and rationality announced in section 1. The totality of the body is disrupted by the random succession of body parts and their destructuration and transformation, suggesting again the urge to capture reality through cinema and the impossibility of doing so.[21] This inevitably results in fragmentation, dismemberment and fear. Auerbach suggests that 'editing threatens the body, threatens to dismember it' (2007: 98), so the montage-like succession of shots containing close-ups of bodily fragments represents a composite body taken apart and recreated. A fragmented hand (2), big feet running fast (3), a frightened head that dissolves into a head made of wire (4), an image of female genitalia (5), a group of six dangling legs (8) and these dissolving into a group of trembling hands (9). The invisible hand (2) tears the sheets off the bed violently, acting as a sequencing force that moves the action forward but blurs the previous space and time coordinates. The hand alludes to artistic agency and performance, as seen in Lorca's drawings, and here perhaps also to the 'sleight of hand' taking place, the magic tricks and illusions of film. The feet — supposedly a pair but possibly more — wearing argyle black and white socks foreshadow the harlequin costumes and motifs appearing later, so their exaggerated theatricality ('exagerados calcetines') is conflated with the mounting sense of threat. In addition, the vision of fear in the frightened expression in section 4 is echoed by the words 'Socorro Socorro Socorro', superimposed on a vagina tilting up and down (5), and by the metallic head, a fusion of man and machine, dehumanised or monstrous (4).[22] Interestingly, the spatiotemporal transgressions made possible by film's technology, which threaten to dissolve totality and continuity, are used to represent fusions between technology itself and the body, creating an unexpected hybrid, a bionic human of sorts. This fusion will be repeated at the beginning of the second part of the script, in which two women have hands whose fingers are morphing into metal wires (30–31). In sum, the increasing fear and panic in this initial sequence may be related to the awareness of sexuality, to female sexuality in particular, or to the impending physical threat that mortality poses. In parallel, the allusions to theatricality, non-realistic bodies and modernity suggest that the fear might be caused by cinema itself, by the inauthenticity of representation.

These sequences focus on boundaries separating the fragments from a corporeal whole, announcing the fragmentary and threatening nature of film editing and its cutting and dismembering of reality. Whatever is left out of the screen seems to be destroyed or eliminated by the camera, but *Viaje*'s swift movement between tableaux also emphasises the alternative cinematic body simultaneously being created. The bodily fragments represent mutilated or unfinished bodies, which together with the rapid dissolution of segments into one another and the allusions to water and a roller coaster give a sense of fluidity and motion. Put together, these fragments form a distorted body, changing and becoming something else, dismembered but recreated. Perhaps the Man of Veins is a result of this creation, like *Frankenstein*'s creature, as will be seen later. The film script often focuses on these corporeal limits in the depiction of bodily orifices or issue: figures vomiting (18, 55, 56), bleeding (38, 41, 42, 43), or even cannibalistic violence (59). This imagery resonates with the tradition of the grotesque in modern art, recalling those Lorquian drawings which signalled Bakhtin's life-death and body-world confluences.

Following the dismembered bodies, a longer sequence in segments 10–12 transforms the fragments into human characters that will momentarily acquire fully visible bodies, although double exposure and superimposition mix the characters in the tableau with each other. A crying child and a woman beating him violently are superimposed by the camera or 'máquina', which captures them in a fluid movement of fast sequences:

> 10
> Las manos que tiemblan [se disuelven] sobre una doble exposición de un niño que llora.
> 11
> Y el niño que llora sobre una doble exposición de una mujer que le da una paliza.

12
Esta paliza se disuelve sobre el pasillo largo otra vez, que la máquina recorre con rapidez. (García Lorca 1994: 61)

This image subverts the traditional Madonna and Child icon (McDermott 1996: 124), and may remind us of the pain associated with futurity and reproduction seen in Lorca's late poems.[23] The brutal act of violence is nonetheless so quick — and unstable or blurry due to double exposure — that it barely allows for its implications to be fully grasped before it has vanished into the preceding image, the corridor (12), and the following segments, thus incorporating the image into the general chaotic atmosphere. The two interrelated bodies (the child and the woman) appear momentarily into the collage of bodily fragments to add a further transgression of time and corporeal totality. Just as the dismembered and vomiting bodies in *Viaje* suggest the dissolution of boundaries between bodies and the outer world, so does this image refer to an elimination of the boundaries between the child's innocence and the woman's violence; between both their bodies which are in brutal contact; and between cause and effect and temporal linearity (the child is crying first and then the woman hits him, the two images becoming blurred and simultaneous by superimposition). The event is finally left unresolved, as if it were the fragment of a dream, and the camera resumes its race along the corridor. Because the outcome of the sequence is not made explicit in the script (nor in the film adaptation), its connection with previous or later images is also uncertain, it is only suggested by their contiguity and their presence in the spectacle. It may be connected with the brutality of the Man in the white coat towards the Young Man (23–25), or with the violence of the Man of Veins towards the Young Woman (59; 61–62).

In section 23, a man in a white lab coat and a young man in swimming trunks — in black and white like the earlier socks, but checkered this time — inhabit a violent scene in which the man attacks the boy after he refuses to wear a harlequin costume, grabbing him by the neck and gagging him with the costume as he tries to scream. To the common reading of the harlequin suit as a symbol of imposed (hetero-)/(bi-)sexuality by institutional authority must be added the recurrent Lorquian idea of desire as the inevitable advent of temporal transience and suffering/death.[24] The Muchacho may represent a freer vision of sexuality, which is disrupted — here orally, rammed down the Young Man's throat — by the awareness of temporality — the doctor/scientist and his rational logic — as well as by the falsity or artificiality that comes with this awareness, signalled by the harlequin costume. This reading would confirm the possible reappearance of the Young Man as the Man of Veins in the third part (43–72). Aquatic animals are interspersed in the sequence, first fish and then snakes and crabs. Fish, usually phallic symbols, and water have a special symbolism in Lorca's works relating to sexuality, fertility and life-giving powers (Feal Deibe 1973: 110). These watery symbols are nonetheless juxtaposed with images relating to death and the metamorphic grotesque: the violence of the man, the fragmented elements in the scene mutating rapidly and the image of a fish dying and then multiplying into more and more fish in agony in an exaggerated kaleidoscopic close-up:

28
Pez vivo sostenido en la mano en un gran plano hasta que muera y avance la boquita abierta hasta cubrir el objetivo.
29
Dentro de la boquita aparece un gran plano en el cual saltan, en agonía, dos peces. Estos se convierten en un caleidoscopio en el que cien peces saltan o laten en agonía. (1994: 65–66)

It seems that the circularity and fusion favoured in these sections are striving to convey the inevitable interrelation of desire and pain/death.[25] The fluidity of water, a symbol of sexuality and of temporal transience, connects desire and mortality throughout the entire script. In the adaptation, Amat accentuates the kaleidoscope effect by zooming out the camera from the close-up of the two first fish gradually until the large group of fish is visible, using an alternating colour scheme which simulates the agonic beats or jumps suggested in the script. The use of colour in the film adaptation creates a contrast between the recurrent monochrome images and those in colour (notably the red/green harlequin costume in this sequence, which suitably matches the deathly undertones of red and green in Lorca's works), an effect absent in the film script for obvious reasons.

The killing of animals is a recurrent image in the film script. Fish, frogs and a bird are meant to be 'killed in front of the camera lens' (28, 45, 52), underlining the frailty of the animal victim and creating a parallel with the children or young people being physically harmed by adults. In addition, the phallic symbology of fish and birds may evoke masturbation or emasculation (Anderson 2017: 16–17), as well as the recurrent confluence of desire and death. These acts of violence may thus respond to the Lorquian vision of death as a source of creative substance.[26] The aesthetics of death in Lorca relates to the inevitable immanence of death in human imagination and to the poetic force that death's interrelation with human life brings about. Any symbol of life processes and energies acquires a more powerful dramatism when confronted with death, life's counterpart, and in Lorca's poetics that coalescence of radical opposites is sought as a factor of transgression. In *Viaje*, the representation of the repulsive, the disgusting or the violent serves to transgress the norms and canons of idealised beauty and to cause an extreme reaction in the spectator, something often characteristic of the historical avant-garde as well as of the 'cinema of attractions' at the turn of the twentieth century. None of the scenes of violence in the film script seems to be condemned or resolved or to have a narrative *dénouement*; instead, they are presented as tableaux in a spectacle within the kaleidoscope of images that is *Viaje*, a web of spiralling recurrences and interpolations.

Whilst most sections in the first part are juxtaposed by jump cuts, transitions between images often contain superimpositions or dissolves, creating composite and metamorphic images and accentuating the rhythmic movement. Furthermore, corporeal fragments are combined with references to movement and motion (13–21), following on from the previous corridor sequences (6–12). The diegetic motion is reinforced by Lorca's self-reflexive allusions to section transitions (21, 36), which explain the spatiotemporal movement called for in the shots. A roller coaster

(14), perhaps that from Coney Island's Luna Park, initiates a frantic movement downwards, while footprints (15) recall the feet running earlier (3) and announce a forward motion.[27] Silkworms on tree leaves (16) allude to the cyclical movement in nature (Anderson 2017: 15), but announce death as the consequence of that transient cycle, symbolised by the ominous circularity of a dead head and that of the moon (17). A further forward motion, 'dos niños que avanzan' (19), and the throwing of ink drops (20, 21) connect this ongoing journey with writing, perhaps with the poetic narrative taking place. The instructions about tableau transitions and the 'letrero' in section 21 refer back to the previous shots, explicitly to their rhythmic succession. This may apply either to all shots before this one (which would be plausible since jump-cuts abound in this first section), or more specifically to the immediately previous sequence of shots:

> 21
> Un plano blanco sobre el cual se arrojan gotas de tinta.
> (Todos estos cuadros rápidos y bien ritmados.) Aquí un letrero que diga *No es por aquí*. (1994: 64)

The apparent incongruity of the elements in the sequence reveals some correlations among them nonetheless: circularity, nature, temporal transience, childhood and death, while the rhythmic juxtaposition and the allusions to forward movements reinforce their analogy. The head in section 17 evokes the circular shape of the moon it transforms into, which in turn transforms into another head (18). This second vomiting head (are its contents being split from it as it vomits, mirroring the split moon?) is opening and closing its eyes, which relates to the next shot in which the children have their eyes closed.[28] In turn, the ink drops (whose liquid nature in turn connects with the vomit), fall both on the heads of the children and then on a white background, a further allusion to writing (linking with the numbers in section 1 and the repeated signs of 'Socorro'). Finally, this writing materialises in the next shot with a verbal sign (21). The images of motion and the mixture of language and image present throughout the sequence of shots paradoxically lead to a sign which warns the reader not to make that connection of meanings (is the sign literally saying that this is not the right way to read this film script?) and which warns against the spatial movement followed up to this point. This may be the wrong direction, since the next shot contains a door into a different space, and therefore, a change of direction and setting.

As seen earlier, the sequence of sections 23–29 introduces a Young Man who takes on a prominent, though obviously intermittent, role in the narrative. As the second and third parts of the script develop, metamorphic bodies, harlequin costumes, deceitful identities and the same Young Man without his skin all point to the destabilisation of boundaries between bodies, objects and subjects, suggesting not only uncertainty and instability but also purposeful transformations and reversals. Bodies are presented not as immutable entities, but, as seen in Lorca's poetry and drawings, as 'processes which extend into and are immersed in worlds' (Blackman 2012: 1).[29] The instabilities to which *Viaje*'s bodies are subjected signal an attempt to do away with any body-world boundaries through cinematic representation, fusing the elements of both realms together in a collage of sorts. The seamless illusion of cinema makes this possible, but it inevitably renders the result artificial and unreliable, in that its theatricality is exposed and its ostensibly faithful representation of reality is denied.[30] Corporeal limits, spatiotemporal coordinates and emotional states are unstable and change at random.

As seen earlier, the first part of the script depicts images of fear and panic, but their rapid succession and fluid transitions merge rather than distinguish them, adding the disconcerting element of the absurd and the humour of the carnivalesque. Similarly, the second part (30–43) contains recurrent meta-textual comments on the writing process and has the most elements showing the artifice of the text and the cinematic quality and 'watchability' of the sections. In tune with the spatial multiplicity of previous shots, segment 30 is explicitly set in a previously unseen nondescript room. The segments in this part are very descriptive nonetheless, emphasising the movements of characters, objects in the tableaux and the camera:

> 30
> Letrero: *Viaje a la luna*
> Habitación. Dos mujeres vestidas de negro lloran sentadas con las cabezas echadas en una mesa donde hay una lámpara. Dirigen las manos al cielo. Planos de los bustos y las manos. Tienen las cabelleras echadas sobre las caras y las manos contrahechas con espirales de   alambre.
> 31
> Siguen las mujeres bajando los brazos y subiéndolos al cielo.
> 32
> Una rana cae sobre la mesa. (García Lorca 1994: 66–67)

The agony of the crying women dressed all in black, whose bodies combine the vulnerability of their suffering with the sharp and resistant quality of their metal fingers (an oneiric vision of bionic humans), is suddenly contrasted by the absurd and incongruous, even comical, appearance of a frog. As seen earlier, the frog may be a further symbol of the fusion of desire and death, although it also has biblical connotations relating to the plagues sent to punish humanity in Exodus (Anderson 2017: 17).[31] The frog's usual green colour suggests typically Lorquian deathly undertones, but it may also symbolise the sexual fluidity ascribed to water. It ties in with ideas of repulsion and disgust derived from the grotesque, so the monstrous and the metamorphic are juxtaposed with the enigmatic ritual, perhaps a prayer, that the women are entranced by, also suggesting melancholy and suffering. There may be a link between the women and the violent mother glimpsed earlier (11), or with the crying Marys at the scene of the crucifixion (McDermott 1996: 126). This enigmatic scene is interrupted before reaching any *dénouement*, initiating a further series of transformations and fast movements through multiple opening and shutting doors and up and down a staircase. The repulsive extreme close-up of the frog is dissolved into a bunch of orchids and then into a female head vomiting compulsively, whilst the light and contrast of the image changes the exposure from positive to negative and vice versa (33). While the frog and the orchids can be connected through their allusion to genitalia (Anderson 2017: 18), they seem also to return to the image of nature's cyclical transience and its dual association with life and death, emphasised in the positive/negative contrast which seems to echo the earlier black-and-white elements. The prominence of female characters in this second part is reinforced with the allusions to the name 'Elena' and to Lorca's drawing of 'Santa Radegunda'. I will return to these two elements in the next chapter as I discuss the intermedial connections taking place in this part of the film script. For now, it is worth noting that both references tie in with the fusion of desire/sexuality and suffering/disgust/death. As multiple variations of the name 'Elena' appear, on intertitles shown after four successive doors slam shut, the forward/up/down motion is accelerated ('se cierra violentamente', 'se dirige rápidamente', 'con gran ritmo acelerado') and the fusions and distortions are intensified with double and triple exposures. The drawing 'Muerte de Santa Rodegunda' (38) — shown behind prison bars — and its graphic depiction of pain, bodily issue and female sexuality mirrors the mourning women's physical and emotional suffering, also anchoring both elements in a Hispanic context through the allusions to religious traditions like the worship of saints and Spanish clothing traditions for mourning ('enlutada', 39; 'pañuelo en la cabeza a la manera española', 41). As he would later explore theatrically in the rural plays, Lorca links the experience of suffering and mortality with iconography binding women to repressive gender roles and norms.[32] In section 42, one of the women falls down the staircase and there is a close-up of her face and then her nose bleeding profusely. Even though a narrative development is resisted through jump-cuts and spatiotemporal disorientation, the speedy motion evoked through the doors, the staircases and the section transitions leads to a culminating moment with the climactic introduction of the Man of Veins (43).

The most prominent character in *Viaje a la luna*, the Hombre de las venas, is revealed by a swift tilt of the camera upstairs (43), briefly foreshadowed by the previous sequence in which the 'enlutada' falls down a staircase — supposedly to her death — and her head is superimposed on a drawing of veins and grains of salt in relief.[33] The Man of Veins is a metamorphic body, a naked man/anatomical dummy whose internal muscular and circulatory structures are exposed as an outside layer denoting an ambivalent process of destructuring and recreation:

> 43
> [...] En lo alto aparece un desnudo de muchacho. Tiene la cabeza como los muñecos anatómicos con los músculos y las venas y los tendones. Luego sobre el desnudo lleva dibujado el sistema de la circulación de la sangre y arrastra un traje de arlequín. (1994: 69)

The Man of Veins syncretises both human corporeality and its inevitable decay and mortality. He is alive, as evidenced in the functioning blood system he wears for a suit; but he is also an image of decomposition and putrefaction, devoid of skin and half-dead. The Man of Veins is also a sign of the tension between excess and omission of meaning in *Viaje a la luna*. His body is, on the one hand, a composite of the previous images that have been metamorphosing throughout the film script, an excessive amalgam of a multiplicity of bodies, like the monster Dr Frankenstein creates (Shelley 1941). On the other hand, he has taken off the harlequin costume (which he is now dragging along) and has done away with the external layers of his body. The harlequin costume alludes to the theatricality and artifice of the carnivalesque, which suggests that by ridding himself of his costume and his skin he is somehow showing a 'truer' self, not the falsity of masks, make-up and theatrical personae. This idea is reminiscent of the metamorphic dance in Act II of *El público* and of Act V, in which a similar character and a male nurse discuss truth and appearance in theatre or in art. The Desnudo Rojo, another nude young man figure being crucified, tortured and physically maimed, bears many resemblances with the Man of Veins in that their bodies are in a process of decomposition and their wounds and internal parts are being exposed. They are both naked (exposed) and red (bloody, skinless), and their insides are visible, announcing their imminent destructuration/death. The Desnudo Rojo alludes to the figure of Christ being crucified and tortured, with wounds all over his body and a crown of thorns on his head. In turn, the Man of Veins adopts the position of the cross (47) evoking the crucifixion and martyrdom of Christ as he stands in a solitary street. In the play, the Desnudo Rojo embodies the 'theatre beneath the sand', a kind of theatre without masks, devoid of artifice and falsity (Amat 1998) which his alter ego Hombre 1/ Gonzalo links with heterodox desires and fluid gender identities. He is doomed, nonetheless, since this kind of earnestness is bound to bring suffering and death (Anderson 1992). However, the incongruity and mixture of tragic and humorous elements in the scene in which he appears suggest that these clear-cut principles are being challenged and shown as ambiguous:

> DESNUDO. Yo deseo morir. ¿Cuántos vasos de sangre me habéis sacado?
> ENFERMERO. Cincuenta. Ahora te daré la hiel, y luego, a las ocho, vendré con
>   el bisturí para ahondarte la herida del costado.
> DESNUDO. Es la que tiene más vitaminas.
> ENFERMERO. Sí. [...]
> DESNUDO. ¿Cuánto falta para Jerusalén?
> ENFERMERO. Tres estaciones, si queda bastante carbón.
> DESNUDO. Padre mío, aparta de mí este cáliz de amargura.
> ENFERMERO. Cállate. Ya es éste el tercer termómetro que rompes. (OC II:
>   648)

The tragic martyrdom that the character performs is opposed to his and the nurse's comments, at times humorous, sarcastic or absurd and at times devoid of feeling or compassion. The scene blurs the lines between tragedy and comedy and brings all the elements down to the spectacle, suggesting that not even the seemingly 'truer' theatre can be devoid of artifice. Underneath 'the sand', the mask, the costume or even the skin, there is nothing but further masks and artifices, not least those showing the interconnectedness of desire and mortality. In *El público*, the moribund man's blood and wounds are coldly measured in glasses, in appointment times and in the number of thermometers used (an echo of *Viaje*'s numbers and science?). The Red Nude himself 'desires to die' and concurs with the nurse that the wound on his side (that which in the Passion of Christ was caused by a lance and became the fatal wound) is the one with the most vitamins, a colloquial expression meaning it is the healthiest or most wholesome one. The parodic tone continues with a pun on the Stations of the Cross — here, three stations away from Jerusalem — which correlates to *Viaje*'s man dissolved into a triple exposure of fast-moving trains crossing one another (48) (Anderson 2017: 9). Further signs of artistry or artificiality follow, with a double exposure of piano keys being played by disembodied hands (49), which may evoke masturbation (McDermott 1996: 127–28).

Before the Man of Veins's 'crucifixion' in the street, a sequence is interpolated which highlights the significance of sight and the gaze, returning to the circularity of *eros* and *thanatos* and its spectacularity on the (potential) cinema screen. Three mysterious men wearing overcoats stand in the same 'calle nocturna' (44, 45). The sequence makes use of cross-cutting to present different superimpositions of images on the moon itself (Monegal 1994a: 25). The first man's gaze is juxtaposed with a close-up of the moon; the second one looks up and the camera cuts to a close-up of a bird's head whose neck is then squeezed until it dies; finally, the third man is shown followed by another shot of the moon which dissolves into a close-up of 'un sexo' (male or female?) which in turn dissolves into a screaming mouth. Each gaze is associated with a different image, all of which could be connected to one another metaphorically. By analogy, the circular shapes of all the images coincide (the moon, a bird's head, the head of a penis, a mouth), but they can also be taken as symbols of death, sexual desire and horror respectively by metaphorical substitution. In addition, the contiguity of the men's gazes to the images superimposed on the moon relies on the 'Kuleshov effect'.[34] The three men look at the moon, and the moon in return offers them varying meanings. Is each man projecting a different meaning onto his gaze at the moon or is the moon itself mutating? Whether it is the moon or the men's attitudes that are changing, the metamorphosis and polysemy evoked suggest that desire adopts many guises and is too fluid and unstable to pin down through logic or rationality.[35] This is a vision of desire as a malleable and multifaceted process: at times evoking fear, danger or repulsion and at times pleasure, humour and parody. The 'circular gaze' of the Moon is indeed the vision that *Viaje a la luna* proposes throughout: rather than offering a linear narrative in which events and characters develop in front of the spectator, Lorca presents the spectator with a plethora of meanings that can be transformed at will, challenging and questioning the very act of cinematic representation as a stable and truthful source of meaning.

In the third block, the Man of Veins's seemingly 'truer' self becomes a sign of death and a sight too unbearable to contemplate, which implies that, like the 'theatre beneath the sand' in *El público*, an absolute truth without artifice is impossible. Certain truths will dismantle social norms and assumptions, causing rejection (disgust, repulsion) and revealing the coalescence of death and life. In section 50, the action jumps to a bar. The tuxedo-clad customers are being served wine in their glasses by a barman, but they keep failing to lift the glasses to drink. The barman keeps topping up the full glasses with more wine which they cannot drink, rendering the situation absurd. Later, they are all shown vomiting (55). This vision of unfulfilled desire resembles previous tableaux in that desire leads to suffering (the men cannot quench their thirst), absurdity and death, but the conflict is never resolved and becomes cyclical. In the men's vomiting, as Bakhtin suggests, the confines of their bodies and the outer world are 'linked and interwoven' (1984: 317): the expulsion of part of the body (which had previously been ingested in the form of food or drink) transforms it into another body which is expelled violently, causing further repulsion and physical pain. However, the reasons and consequences of this bodily pain are not explained or resolved, since the wine that the characters wanted to drink had not been ingested.[36] This repulsion might signal the repression and censoring of heterodox desires and identities, which are now visible in the public social scene of the bar. In tune with *El público*, visibility here serves the function of transgressing socially accepted constructs and to signal multiplicity and polysemy as governing agents of existence and identity, ideas which require audiences to reflect critically and re-evaluate their belief systems, which may cause fear, uncertainty and rejection.

The heterodoxy of the Man of Veins is present all throughout the second half of the film script (43–72). He is a monstrous and ominous character, whose interactions with other characters produce fear, repulsion and death. He kills a frog by gripping and squeezing its neck until it dies in front of the camera, he violently attacks the Young Woman in the lift and then kisses her passionately after she turns into a statue, and people around him vomit convulsively. However, he is an image of suffering and is crying for help amongst the sleepy and emotionless faces of the people in the bar scene (50–52), and he finally suffers a mysterious death that leaves him lying in the street on a bed of newspapers and fish, perhaps symbols of the ephemeral and fluid nature of 'truth' (news) in modernity. His humanity and non-humanity are fused, revealing a polymorphous and heterogeneous identity. He epitomises metamorphosis in that his role in the film, like his body, is in a constant state of becoming: from harlequin to decomposing man, from villain to victim, from life to death, from human to non-human and vice versa. The most frightening of his traits, though, may be his exposure of the very idea of human mortality and the horror it causes, the 'constant awareness of death's proximity' (Nandorfy 2001: 267). Nonetheless, death is not presented as the ultimate end of life and meaning, but as a crucial part of both. It is re-inscribed and positivised as a site of spectacularity and transgressive creativity, exposing the artificiality and illusion cinema attempts to create. By opening up the boundaries between truth and artificiality, humour and horror and desire and death, Lorca is suggesting that death has an ambivalent role as destructor and creator of aesthetic value. The fusion of life and death is a 'dramatic enactment of irreconcilability and the celebration of *thanatos* and *eros*' (Nandorfy 2001: 267), a complicated interrelationship which has acquired a prominent place in Lorca scholarship, and which becomes dramatised in *Viaje a la luna* through a new artistic medium.

This is made clear in the final sections of the film script, where it becomes evident that the 'trip to the moon' is actually a disorienting circular trip shattering assumptions of linearity and stability. When the Man of Veins is lying dead in the street, the camera cuts to a bed where a pair of hands is covering a different juxtaposed corpse. A young man in a lab coat and rubber gloves (a younger version of the man in 23–26) and a young woman in black (mirroring the *enlutadas* in

30–42) approach the bed, draw a moustache on the 'terrible corpse's head' and kiss each other while laughing out loud. Their kiss is relocated to a cemetery by a dissolve and this scene then cuts to a 'cinematic' kiss with another couple. The Man of Veins's death is re-appropriated in the next tableaux to depict an ironic view of mortality, re-inscribing the meaning of death into a comical and absurd parody. The first couple's laughs and mockery of mortality (referencing Dalí's infamous moustache or Duchamp's *L.H.O.O.Q.*?) divest death of its tragic meaning and infuse it with theatricality and irony. However, their own act is itself further ironised by another kissing couple, this time explicitly artificial and parodic. Thus, both the couple's desire and the Man of Veins's death lose their original significations by being spectacularised and made artificial through cinema, in order to be shown as unstable and heterogeneous. For instance, the 'beso cursi de cine' (71) ironises the tendency of Hollywood films to use sex (or rather the less taboo romantic kiss suggesting sex) as such a cliché to represent sexual desire and as an evocation of the (hetero)normative socially accepted modes of conduct. The adjective 'cursi' suggests both the distasteful and the kitsch, hinging on the appropriateness and morality that this kind of representation purports to maintain in the context of film.[37] The passionate kiss between the Man of Veins, disguised as a Harlequin, and the Young Woman (56–64) is transgressed as a violent scene of brutality and rape, and later it is also ironised by the Man's passionate impulses towards the Woman's statue alter-ego, a scene reminiscent of the Greek myth of Pygmalion and which Cocteau used similarly in *Le sang d'un poète*.[38] Lorca's self-conscious questioning of art's 'truthfulness' nonetheless embraces theatricality and the spectacle as liberating qualities that ultimately manifest and positivise identity's instability and multifaceted-ness.

Lorca's *Viaje a la luna* is ultimately presented as a circular process, constantly re-inscribing and recreating that which it destroys. After death is approached but not resolved, its circular re-enactment produces constant metamorphoses into further images, never breaking the circle of the spectacle. Faced with this threat to meaning and representation, the spectacle's unstable quality simultaneously refers to that which it reinterprets, always 'leaving the wound open' for a new transformation to take place. *Eros* and *thanatos* are nothing but a cyclical process, a circular gaze where there is no beginning or end, but an ongoing spiral that keeps mutating and recreating itself. Death is not presented as the ultimate end of representation, but instead transposed into further images of desire and death, culminating with the aptly circular shape of the moon and its mystical undertones which, like the images in the script, represent a mystery unsolved.

Notes to Chapter 4

1. Puyal compiles a list of Lorca's wide-ranging experiences as a cinema spectator: 'de las vanguardias del cine francés (impresionismo, cine puro) a los filmes americanos de Hollywood en su género burlesco, pasando por el documental o el cine soviético. En suma, todo el gran periodo de cine mudo' (2011: 768). Also, Lorca might have had access to Gilberto Owen's 1928 film script *El río sin tacto*, which Emilio Amero had in his possession (Anderson 2017: 2).

2. For a more comprehensive approach to the influence of cinema on the 'Generación del 27' and other Spanish writers of this period, see Morris (1980).
3. Montage was introduced by Soviet filmmakers, such as Sergei Eisenstein and Lev Kuleshov, and was characteristic of avant-garde filmmaking of the 1920s and 1930s, which to a large extent wished to experiment with new modes of representation and to create films that focused on purely cinematic elements (motion, visual composition, camera moves and editing) rejecting conventions like story, characters and narrative continuity (O'Pray 2003).
4. According to Gubern, the film script was available in a number of publications: the Belgian Surrealist magazine *Varietés* in July, the French *Revue du Cinema* in November, and *La Révolution Surréaliste* in December 1929 (1999: 448–50).
5. Segundo de Chomón (1871–1929) worked in Spain, France and Italy and was best-known for his associations with Pathé Frères and Itala Films. He is believed to be the first filmmaker to use the travelling dolly shot as well as developing the Pathé stencil process of film colouring and techniques of stop motion. For a thorough study of his work, see Sánchez Vidal (1992; 1999).
6. Interestingly, Segundo de Chomón's short films *La Grenouille* (1908) and *Métamorphoses* (1912), amongst others, contain elements that appear extensively in Lorca's film script, such as the comical/repulsive frog or rapid transformations of animals and objects. Despite the many correlations between *Viaje a la luna* and de Chomón's films, there is no proof that Lorca knew the early cineaste's work.
7. Tom Gunning's work on the 'cinema of attractions' is seminal to the study of early film (see Gunning 1993, 2006).
8. Written between December 1929 and January 1930, the original Spanish manuscript was not known until it was found at the home of Emilio Amero's widow in 1989 and from which the current edition by Antonio Monegal was finally published in 1994. The manuscript was translated into English by Berenice G. Duncan and first published in the New York journal *New Directions in Prose and Poetry* (no. 18, 1964) by Richard Diers (Monegal 1994a: 9). Although the current edition of *Viaje a la luna* by Monegal cites *New Directions* as the first journal where Duncan's English translation of the manuscript appeared, Diers himself published an earlier article on the film script in the magazine *Windmill* (issue 5, 1963) (Diers 1998: 183).
9. Willard Bohn notices the thoughts about intermediality and multimodal expression Lorca had at the time he wrote the short play, which he defined as 'a poem — a critical poem in which poetry, criticism, and film intersect' and which he conceived as a 'diálogo fotografiado' (2000: 414). In parallel, Xon de Ros relates the appearance of visual strategies on stage with the entrance of the cinematic medium into *El público* (1996: 115).
10. McDermott (1996) and Anderson (2017), among others, refer to it indistinctly as film script or film scenario, both terms defined as 'outline or synopsis of the plot or scenes of a film; [...] a screenplay or synopsis annotated with the details of the scenes, stage directions, etc., necessary for shooting the film' (*OED Online* <https://www.oed.com/view/Entry/172215?rskey=u5aIh3&result=1#eid> [accessed July 2021]).
11. The edition by Antonio Monegal (1994) is today considered the definitive version and is the one I cite throughout, although a previous one exists by Marie Laffranque (1980) in which the section numbering varied.
12. Poems often rely on rhetorical devices to produce a visual effect through the use of language, often through means such as synthesis, metonymy, spacing and typographical effects, etc. For an insightful analysis of poetic techniques in relation to cinema and visual media, see Whittock (1990).
13. Also in 1998, Javier Martín Domínguez, photographer Javier Aguirresarobe, and musician Juan Bardem filmed another version of *Viaje* (Samaniego 1997; Carnero 2005: 30).
14. Laffranque (1982: 81–83), McDermott (1996: 123) and Anderson (2017: 6) all establish a similar division into these three blocks of sections.
15. Monegal finds that the 'hilo conductor, mínimamente narrativo' in the script is the recurrent character of the Hombre de las venas (1994a: 31). McDermott considers the scenario a parody of an *auto sacramental*, with the prologue serving as the *loa* and the 'viaje' proper as a parody of an *auto de la pasión*' (1996: 125). Anderson goes further and establishes a triangular connection

between the Young Man, the Young Woman and the Man in the Lab Coat, which, in his view, can be traced back to the first two blocks and sheds light on some of the interpolated images and sequences (2017: 7–8).

16. McDermott reads the first part of the scenario (1–29) as a 'parody of an *auto de nacimiento*', which demythifies 'the birth and childhood of the divine hero which at the same time mythifies common humanity: the birth of everyman is a heroic journey into an unknown world of peril' (1996: 123). The bed in the opening sections would thus allude to conception in her view, and the succession of body parts would convey 'the panic of delivery and the expulsion of the baby into the world' (1996: 123).

17. Monegal notices this 'plano contrastado de negro sobre blanco', the only available colour palette in the cinema of the time and a very recurrent opposition throughout *Viaje* (1994a: 30), especially in the harlequin motifs. There is a wide variety of associations with the black/white contrast that can be drawn from Lorca's *oeuvre*: some obvious ones are life/death, light/darkness or male/female, all of which are present in the film script (see Chapter 1 on Lorca's poetry and Chapter 3 on the drawings). See also Peral Vega (2015: 117).

18. Anderson notes that the bed must be positioned vertically rather than horizontally ('Cama blanca *sobre* una pared gris' (1)), mirroring the scene from *El público* in which the Desnudo Rojo is crucified in front of the audience (2017: 6). He suggests that Lorca might have been inspired by the Murphy bed, 'an invention that he would have encountered in Manhattan apartments and in slapstick comedy films of the 1920s' (2017: 6), linking the vertical bed with the image of the white cinema screen.

19. With the emergence of cinema at the turn of the twentieth century, the representation, rationalisation and standardisation of time became prominent issues in the Western world. In her important work *The Emergence of Cinematic Time*, Mary Ann Doane explores the obsession with capturing time, especially in relation to 'immortality' and 'the denial of the radical finitude of the human body' (2002: 2) as a general preoccupation at the turn of the twentieth century, prompted by the changes in society stemming from industrialisation and the new organisation of the world of labour. A distinction between spatiotemporal presence and absence was challenged by the new medium, since distant places and past events (even non-existent ones) could be made present in the 'here and now' of the cinema screen. As Elizabeth Freeman posits, 'the photographic media negotiate the relationship between past and present: a photographic image consists of the trace of an object and presents that object in a moment other than the moment of recording' (2010: xviii).

20. See the discussion in Chapter 2 of unity against multiplicity in *El público*, an idea that resonates with the contrast between the Apollonian — rational, symmetrical beauty — and the Dionysian — irrational, uncontrollable desire. Monegal also notices this link (1994a: 29). Anderson suggests that there might be an underlying mathematical logic to the choice of 13 and 22: 'both numbers are composed of two digits; in one case both digits are odd and in the other even; the sum of the two digits is in both cases 4' (2017: 6). The prose poem 'Suicidio en Alejandría' clearly suggests this in the subheadings of its sections (*PC*: 448–50).

21. Film blurred the limits between reality and illusion, transgressing what were believed to be fixed and immutable realities such as human bodies or life and death. Inanimate objects could spring to life, heads could be detached from their bodies and sorcerers could conjure the dead back from the underworld. Also, time could be stopped, accelerated or decelerated by the magic of cinema. As opposed to the spectators watching a film, whose bodies will inevitably age and die, the filmic artefact is itself immortal: it can be played a myriad of times over and will always remain the same even after time has gone by and those bodies who appear in it are departed.

22. McDermott reads this section as a womb's-eye vision, in which water symbolises the amniotic fluid in which a foetus (the human head) is floating (1996: 122). This would connect the initial images in sections 1–3 and in section 5 with sexual activity and procreation, as well as the corridor in 6 with sexual intercourse and the birth canal.

23. McDermott also suggests that, in Freudian oneiric interpretations, 'a woman beating a child signifies masturbation' (1996: 124); Carnero's Freudian reading relates childhood and psychopathology with Max Ernst's 1926 Surrealist work *The Virgin Spanking the Christ Child before Three Witnesses: André Breton, Paul Éluard, and the Painter* (2005: 31).

24. Anderson suggests that '*el hombre de la bata* wishes to impose a conforming, harlequinesque model of heterosexuality on him, or else that he wants him at least to "try it on" like a garment, to experiment with it, but that the *muchacho* refuses and resists' (2017: 8). Both Martínez Cuitiño (2002: 120–23) and Peral Vega (2015: 31–42) read the contrast between Harlequin (dressed in black-and-white rhomboids) and Pierrot (dressed all in white) as that between heterosexuality and homosexuality in Lorca's work.

25. José Ángel Valente (1976) first examined the image of the 'pez-luna', which appears in *El público* and is evoked throughout the film script, as a symbol for the duality/circularity established between *eros* and *thanatos*, as well as an image of androgyny or male/female intertwining. See also Martínez Cuitiño (2002).

26. In *Juego y teoría del duende*, Lorca claims that 'España es el único país donde la muerte es el espectáculo nacional, [...] y su arte está siempre regido por un duende agudo que le ha dado su diferencia y su calidad de invención' (*OC* III: 317).

27. The roller coaster ride *Trip to the Moon*, which Lorca visited during his stay in New York, is commonly thought to be one of the possible sources of inspiration for the film script's title (McDermott 1996:123; Anderson 2017: 20), as well as for the poems alluding to Coney Island in *Poeta en Nueva York* (Llera 2011).

28. The eye is reminiscent of the Surrealist movement, and especially of the iconic scene from *Un chien andalou* in which a razor slits a woman's eye, which is mirrored through cross-cutting by the moon being split in half by a cloud. Remy refers to the representation of eyes, very often blinded, damaged or closed, as a 'fundamental principle of Surrealism, i.e. the freeing of the eye from any kind of authority. [...] The fragmentation of the bodies, the multiplication of the eyes, the splintering of our gaze, all this bars the spectator from reaching any totality' (1996: 159–60). Similarly, during the fight between the Harlequin/Man of Veins and the Young Woman in the lift (56–64) — an erotic/violent fight also reminiscent of *Un chien andalou* — he tries to blind her by pushing her eyeballs in with his thumbs.

29. Lisa Blackman's (2012) vision of embodiment focuses on the constant 'entanglements' taking place between human bodies and the world surrounding them, which make it difficult to draw boundaries between the human and non-human, self and other, material and immaterial.

30. The rapid transitions and mutations in *Viaje*, Gómez Torres argues, 'revelan un mundo de incertidumbre donde todo es inestable, un universo sometido a las metamorfosis y a los disfraces, donde las cosas y las personas no son lo que parecen' (1999: 52). The self-moving bodies on the screen 'blur categorical distinctions between the animate and the inanimate, and [...] question our very being' (Väliaho 2010: 26), confronting the reader/spectator with polymorphous bodies, half-dead characters, unexpected acts of violence and identity transformations.

31. In Anderson's view, the frog is 'conventionally associated with fertility (the number of eggs laid) and metamorphosis (the transitions from egg to tadpole to adult amphibian)' (2017: 17), whereas for McDermott it links with 'procreation in the flesh as infernal incarnation' (1996: 126).

32. In Anderson's view, 'women, too, are defined and trapped by traditional roles, both biologically and socially, and destined to suffer (2017: 19).

33. Anderson suggests a stronger link between the woman and the young man, in that '[the] repetition of motifs and the spatial contiguity imply a strong connection: he may well be her son, and his manifestation of this "authenctic" incarnation may only be possible with the "liberation" brought about by her death' (2017: 19).

34. Soviet filmmaker Lev Kuleshov (1899–1970), as well as other masters like Eisenstein and Hitchcock later, theorised about the power that editing can have on film narrative and the meaning of images. Kuleshov 'had shown the same picture of a baby followed by a series of different images, discovering that the baby was perceived differently in each case. The meaning lay in the relation between the pictures rather than in the images themselves (Butler 2005: 17). Juxtaposing the same close-up shot of a person's face with different images can change the perception that spectators have of their interrelation, suggesting radically different meanings of the character's gaze (although their expression remains the same).

35. Because in *Viaje* narrative continuity is rare, if not purposely transgressed, the Kuleshov effect is magnified by the incongruity and randomness of the images juxtaposed, proposing a revision of the reliability of logic and meaning. Lorca declared after seeing Jean Cocteau's *Le sang d'un*

poète in 1932 that films in which storytelling and narrative continuity are transgressed 'defy explanation; their greatness lies [...] in the freedom we all enjoy to interpret them as we will' (Morris 1980: 123). Anderson attempts to thread the three moon gazes together allegorically: 'one is literal, one sees a phallic symbol that is crushed, and one sees, more indirectly, female genitalia that inspire fear or panic' (2017: 12). Assuming that 'un sexo' is female here, the three gazes would plausibly be read as a triangle (male, female, the moon as both?) and would tie in with previous images connecting female genitalia and fear/screaming.

36. Nicolás Martínez associates vomit in the script with 'la repugnancia que la gente siente hacia la heterodoxia en los hábitos o, en este caso, al rechazo irrespetuoso ante cualquier tipo de novedad artística, bien sea la que él propone o la que plasmaron sus, hasta hace poco, amigos en *El perro andaluz*' [*sic*] (2006: 268).

37. For an insightful look at the concept of 'cursilería' in Spain's twentieth century, see Noël Valis's study on Kitsch and bad taste in modern Spain (2002).

38. It has been documented that kissing on screen produced an immense fascination in early cinema spectators, to the point that it was even elevated to a science by the Hollywood film industry. The Spanish 'Cineclub' paid tribute to it in an 'Antología del beso' during its twenty-first session in May of 1931. Morris argues that 'the interest shown by magazines in the way stars kissed on the screen was part of the mental and moral freedom induced and inspired by films' (1980: 10). However, this was seen, both by Spanish artists and critics in this milieu and by Lorca in *Viaje a la luna* as an object of mockery and satire. Morris cites Enrique Jardiel Poncela, a Spanish humorist, and several Spanish magazines of the 1920s and 30s as producing multiple satires of the kiss motif and other tropes introduced by cinema, especially Western films and other Hollywood productions.

CHAPTER 5

❖

Intermediality and Multimodal Representations in the Post-New York Works

El duende no se repite,
como no se repiten las
formas del mar en la borrasca.
(OC III: 316)

While Lorca's later years were characterised by his simultaneous production of literature, theatre, art, photography and cinema, he had always been a multi-faceted artist and some of his earlier works already played with the limits of media and often tried to bring words, images and music together. In parallel with the experimental *Poemas en prosa* and with the multimodality of *Poeta en Nueva York*, in whose edition Lorca planned to include drawings and photographs, earlier works like *Poema del cante jondo* contained poems imitating the rhythms, sounds and performance of flamenco, while in *Canciones* or *Romancero gitano* he played with the visuality of poetic images or sought to mix the five senses to explore different levels of perception.[1] Approaching the later works from a comparative perspective, this chapter will analyse the transgressive effects of Lorca's aesthetics on the limits of artistic media.[2] Firstly, visual-verbal links, sensory imagery and poetic devices will be examined as they emerge in the late poetry, with counterparts in the calligrams and the more experimental quasi-concrete late poems, as well as in the performative and visual media. Subsequently, I will focus on motifs that can be examined transmedially and comparatively in all the post-New York works: processes of fluidity and transformation, roses, hands, roots, doublings and fusions.

As the previous chapters have shown, Lorca's poetic works, plays, drawings and film script all share a particular relationship with the performative. While they hinge on the visuality of performance as poetic or theatrical artefacts, they may be seen as embryos each in their own particular way: in an intermediate state between the page or canvas and their actualisation through, say, a performed play, a recited or graphic poem, or an edited film. The thrill of performance, the excitement of the moment in which the artwork is actualised was to Lorca a substantial and transformative experience. These four different creative practices all have the 'potentiality' of performance that Lorca instilled in their creation. By putting them in dialogue in light of the aesthetic principles explored in his lectures, we can examine Lorca's overarching preoccupations and how his poetics was channeled through interconnected media. In his view, all arts are capable of *duende*, so even the least performative media can perform the play of this impish spirit by transgressing the limits and norms governing creative practices and their differences. This is one of the issues which critics of the *duende* lecture have found problematic: in Mayhew's view, 'Lorca repeatedly emphasizes the performative dimension of the *duende*, but at the same time adduces multiple examples from literature or the visual arts, in which performance does not seem particularly relevant' (2018: 71). The intermedial/transmedial nature of *duende* is a unique aspect often overlooked and worth exploring through further research. As will be shown here, these arts in intermedial dialogue coincide in showing the cyclical and interrelated nature of desire and death, anchored in the poetic transgression of spatiotemporal limits, which must be considered staples of Lorca's poetics.[3]

In the later corpus, Lorca's works become more evidently aware of the media transferences and combinations at play. Elements conventionally ascribed to distinct and multiple media can interact with one another in order to produce a broader and multi-layered meaning within a single medium. His return to canonical forms in the late poetry helps to make the form/content connection much more intricate and self-conscious. Traditional poetic forms and their technical restrictions allow the poet to mix the unconventionality and novelty of poetic images with well-known formats, and to explore new perceptive possibilities emerging from recognisable formal aspects. The poems are also characterised by their emphasis on visuality: the imagery relies heavily on metaphors and metonymies featuring elements like synaesthesia, *chiaroscuro* and multiple colour contrasts, but the organisation of the imagery and its semantic interrelations follow a less logical structure and are therefore more ambiguous and obscure. Conversely, Lorca's drawings are an attempt to let his poetic voice speak through an entirely different medium, combining image and language intra-compositionally but also reproducing images from the poems via graphic elements. His expanding late corpus of drawings contained graphic works that have been defined as linear poems or pure lyrical abstractions (Plaza Chillón 2014: 217). Exploring through a new medium some of the images created in his poetry as well as original ones, his later drawings become artefacts with a myriad word-image combinations full of depth and complex connotations — they are 'plastic poems' or 'poetic drawings'. In the so-called 'impossible theatre', the stage directions and even some characters themselves hinge on intrinsically visual aspects already articulated by Lorca before any actual performances had taken place. Last but not least, *Viaje a la luna*'s film script is an example of an ontological intermedium (Schröter 2011: 3): a medium which is not quite poetry and not quite moving images, but which combines elements of both and becomes an intermediate state between literature and film.

Whether looking at media as always dependent on other media, as semiotic systems of communication containing transmedial elements, or in terms of each medium's particularities of representation, there are often multiple levels of perception and sensory meanings being activated within and across creative practices. Issues of perception and embodiment deal more directly with the medium's process of representation and transmission of (multi)sensorial meanings: visual, verbal, auditory or a combination of some or all at once. Looking closely and comparatively at the later works in search of these principles, we may begin by examining the visual-verbal connections in the poems, which find a suitable ally in Lorca's frequent use of synaesthesia and the blurring of the five senses. His sensory poetics emphasises the multimediality of the perceptive process. Thus, he describes clouds and their shapes in terms of animals (Anderson 1990: 105), he creates apple trees with sighing/sobbing apples or shadows of dusk which sound like elephants stomping:

> El Tamarit tiene un manzano
> con una manzana de sollozos.
> [...]
> La penumbra con paso de elefante
> empujaba las ramas y los troncos.
> ('Casida de los ramos' *DT*: 161, ll. 5–6; 15–16)

In this casida, the personification of animals and plants creates an additional layer of sensory perception: while accentuating the usual emphasis on the cyclical temporality of nature, the human experience of transience and mortality is 'felt' figuratively (manzana de sollozos) by the natural world or articulated in animal terms (the elephant-like shadow may stand for impending, unstoppable transience and death).[4] This was also seen, for instance, in the 'Gacela del amor que no se deja ver' and its choruses personifying and animalising Granada, and in '[Ay voz secreta del amor oscuro]' in the *Sonetos* (¡ay balido sin lanas!', '¡ay perro en corazón!'). Metaphors, metonymy, alliterations and sensory associations reinforce the attempt to combine visual and verbal elements within the poetic medium to fuse and blur the five senses. Seeking to create images that shock and produce a sense of novelty, the poetic voice finds ways to apply new qualities to sensory images:

> Vino la noche clara,
> turbia de plata mala,
> con peladas montañas
> bajo la brisa parda.
> ('Casida de la muchacha dorada' *DT*: 167, ll. 8–11)

Reversing the image of the night to make it first clear — presumably illuminated by the moon (Anderson 1990: 131) — and then muddy or shady as bad silver, with all the connotations of inauthenticity, threat, and lunar ill omens the image carries, the sense of sight is challenged to adapt to each new poetic image, while the subsequent metaphors play with sight through personification (the bare mountains are 'peeled') and synaesthesia (a breeze can be heard or felt, but can rarely be coloured a greyish brown). These unexpected semantic associations, describing visually the unsettling and ominous feelings the night evokes in the poet, prompt the reader to think in visual terms in order to grasp the meanings that, despite syntactic coherence, elude mere linguistic referentiality.

In some of Lorca's late poems, there is a semantic opaqueness in the free associations, sudden metamorphoses and unexpected image juxtapositions he creates, which 'brings them very close to Surrealist practice' (Harris 1998: 98) and contrasts with the rhythmic and metric adherence to traditional poetic forms. Images often flow unconstrained by logical relations or narrative progressions:

> Flor de jazmín y toro degollado.
> Pavimento infinito. Mapa. Sala. Arpa. Alba
> La niña sueña un toro de jazmines
> y el toro es un sangriento crepúsculo que brama.
> ('Casida del sueño al aire libre' DT: 164, ll. 1–4)

Alluding to the oneiric in the very title of the poem, despite Lorca's emphatic rejection of Surrealist practices like automatic writing or painting and the primacy of dreams, 'Casida del sueño al aire libre' should either be taken as a dream described in poetic terms or as simply a series of juxtaposed images with no apparent relation to one another.[5]

The asyndetic succession of short phrases and nouns in the first stanza does, however, hinge on the visuality of the images created and on the graphic and phonic relationships among them. First, the jasmine flower, the decapitated bull and the infinite pavement, while unrelated, share aspects suggesting a sensory proximity: they can all be contemplated in nature and they offer a sharp colour contrast. The whiteness of the jasmine against the black bull leads the way to the possible greyness of the pavement, while anticipating the bright red blood that soon reappears as the bull bleeds in the colour of twilight. The ground or paving image can be read as a 'blank dreamscape, an intermediate and indefinite background between ground and sky' (Anderson 1990: 116), which is precisely the plane the poetic voice seems to be inhabiting, outside time, space and logic. The pavement, the bull's assassination, the girl and the homophonic words all suggest man's presence against nature, conjuring a natural/artificial opposition. This is reinforced by the four isolated nouns in the second line: 'mapa', 'sala', 'arpa', 'alba' (map, room, harp, sunrise). This play on the assonance of the words and their phonic and graphic amalgamation clearly reinforces the form/content and verbal/visual connection in the poem. The poet goes from one word to the next by simply changing the consonants while the vowel 'a' is repeated. In a declension of sorts, he explores the multiple possibilities allowed by poetic language while also adding further contrasting images to the stanza. In addition, the graphic brevity of the successive images in the first two lines gradually accelerates the rhythm of the juxtapositions, and hence the sharp contrast and sudden transformations they suffer. Ever since Ancient Greece, poetry was meant to be recited, providing it with an aural sensory meaning through performance which Lorca consciously includes here.[6]

The elements in the casida also find a way into Lorca's other creative practices: some of the drawings use similar assonant repetitions of words ('Puta y luna' and 'Marinero del amor', both ca.1934); in El público there are recurrent syllabic reversals ('¡Abominable! [...] Blenamiboá' TC: 251) or rhyming chants ('Amor. Amar. Amor. | Amor del caracol, col, col, col,' TC: 269); and high-speed image juxtapositions are frequently created in *Viaje a la luna*. Firstly, in the drawing 'Puta y luna', the suggestive and derogatory term 'puta' is declined, transcribed or transposed to accommodate multiple vowel combinations ('puta', 'peta', 'pota', 'pita', 'pata') while retaining the same consonants and thus creating a clear rhythm within the drawing. Conversely, from the title it may be inferred that either the connection between the words 'puta' and 'luna' is purely linguistic, or that the femininity usually ascribed to the moon is perversely mocked with an insult. Also, the *eros* and *thanatos* communion is intimately related to both words. As seen earlier, the moon almost always carries ominous and tragic consequences and undertones (the images of death juxtaposed with moons in *Viaje a la luna* and *Diván del Tamarit* are immediate ones among a myriad examples), while the rural plays usually pair the figure of the 'fallen woman', judged and condemned by social norms, with fate, suffering and mortality.[7] Nonetheless, both the connotative connection and the linguistic/ graphic/phonic fusion between 'puta' and 'luna' attest to the playful combination created by the poet. The well-known squiggly lines from other drawings are used here to join all these words together simulating a single stroke, a continuous line encircling the whole composition into an irregular shape. Contained within this frame is a fantastical animal coloured in red, resembling a horse in its long tail made up of thin extending lines and its long mouth but also a dog or a lion in its short paws — one of them black and claw-like, reaching up and incidentally pointing at the word 'pata' itself — and its hairy head with a mane of sorts. The bottom-right end of the main circular line ends in the shape of a waxing or waning moon coloured black, directly opposite the word 'luna' at the top of the drawing. Throughout this multifarious composition, Lorca repeats the playful deformation of words into nonsensical elements from his poems, while simultaneously pointing to the rhythmic harmony that their assonance creates. He combines words and images seamlessly but alludes to the sharp contrast between the formal aspects and their signification, the signifiers and the signifieds. While the word 'luna' in the drawing has a graphic counterpart and the 'pata' might be mirroring the drawn animal's paw, the other words are random and only hinge on their nonsensical nature, purely derived from their homographic resemblance to 'puta' and 'luna'. Perhaps even the poet himself could be included in the mix as 'poeta', another plausible combination which could easily be elicited from this varied array. The presence of the words is as unexpected as that of the fantastical animal, all of them objects which become hard to identify or explain. These odd, indeed queer, objects are joined together, literally, by Lorca's line, and they question the logic of the drawing as well as their own meaning within it. What holds them together is the process of creation, the poetics which can give life to these unwonted and incongruous realities and encircle them in a cyclical graphic poem. The intermedial link between visual and verbal elements works seamlessly to close this circular process, since the reader/viewer needs both to make sense of it.

The same link of apparently extraneous elements appears profusely in *Viaje a la luna*. To the many disparate objects juxtaposed as a series of tableaux throughout most of the film script must be added the transformation of words included in

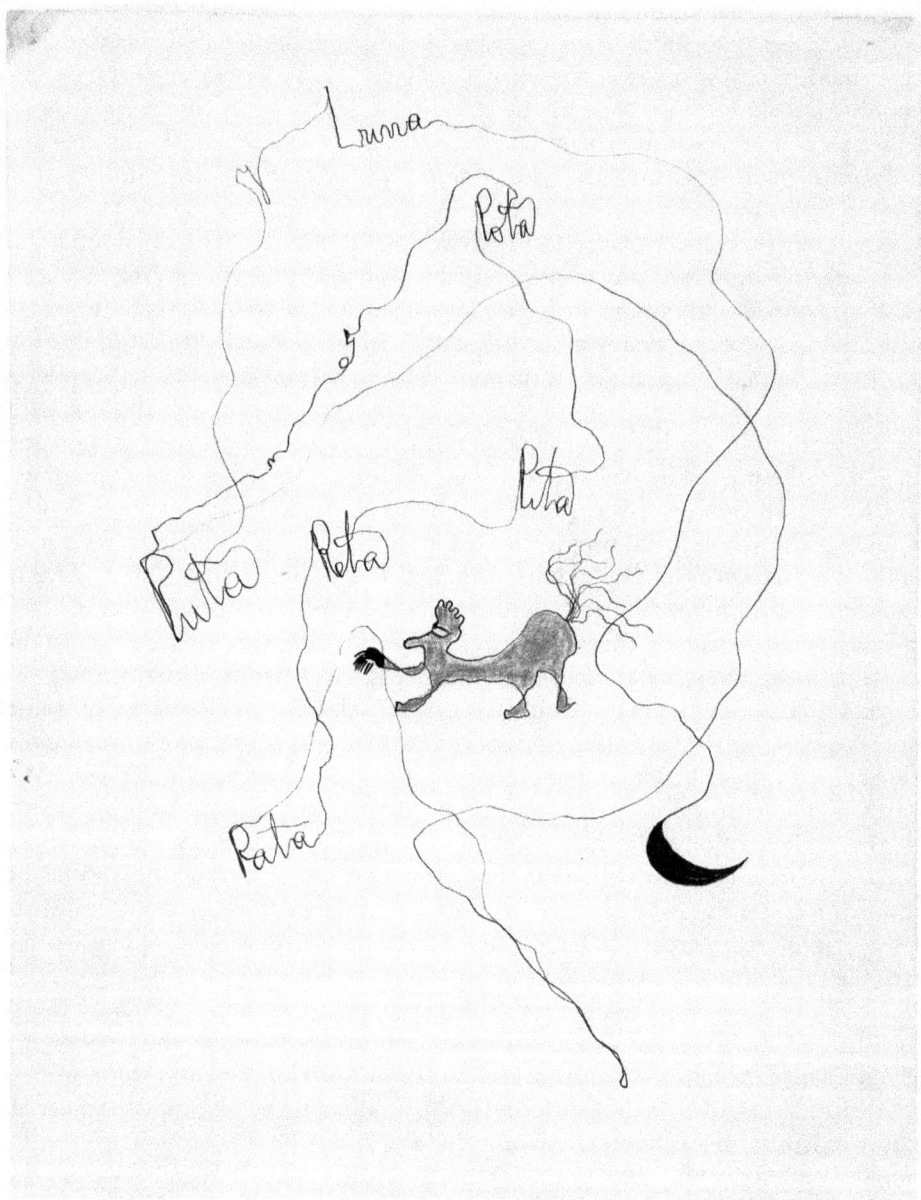

FIG. 5.1. 'Puta y luna' (1934).

some of the segments. In section 34, a successive series of doors being slammed shut presents the female name 'Elena' on each of them, but the word is transposed into a new version with each closing door: 'Helena', 'elhena', 'eLHeNa'. The same repetition, but with smaller alterations (Elena elena elena elena) occurs again in section 65. These 'declensions' do not actually eliminate or alter the letters or sound of the name, but rearrange them and play with their visual aspect, so the distortion keeps the rhythm and meaning of the word almost intact. Lorca, aware that this film script was the embryo of a cinematic work, is able to play with linguistic and visual aspects through yet another medium. For the potential viewer of the finished film, this word distortion would be as disconcerting as those from the poems and the drawings, but this time the visual aspect of the word transformation acquires more prominence. Managing to detach the linguistic meaning from the graphic and visual meanings, unexpected distortions of Elena are created: the word, the name and the character it conjures all become blurry. This mirrors the uncertainty surrounding the female characters in the film script (and in the other media), as it remains unclear whether Elena names any of them.

As seen earlier, the name could refer to a variety of figures or none at all. It could allude to the mourning women in the second part of the film script (sections 30–42) or the young woman who turns into a marble statue in the third (50–65); it could be related to the classical Helen of Troy; to the character of Elena in El público (who in turn relates to classical antiquity, to the character of Juliet in the play-within-the-play and to the Centurión's wife); to the real-life people Eleanor Dove, the woman for whom Emilio Aladrén allegedly left Lorca before he went to New York, or Gala (Elena) Ivanovna Diakonova, the wife of Paul Éluard who later married Salvador Dalí.[8] In the context of Viaje a la luna, the transposition of the name Elena appears after a sequence in which the two 'enlutadas', themselves transformed into monster-creatures with wiry hands, cry desperately and the close-up of a female head vomits. One of the two dark women also falls down a staircase and images of her bloody nose, a close-up of her head upside down and close-ups of veins and grains of salt are juxtaposed (39–42). The drawing 'Muerte de Santa Rodegunda' (1929), in which another agonising distorted female creature vomits violently on a bed, also makes an appearance in this sequence, 'incarcerated' by a set of prison cell bars superimposed (38). I will return to this drawing in more depth later, but for now it is clear that the distortion and destructuration of Saint Radegund add to the non-specificity and veiled identity of most female characters in Viaje and especially to the uncertainty surrounding the elusive Elena, whose name is presented under so many 'guises' that it is hard to establish whether her presence relates to female sexuality (eros, 'puta'); to the ominous awareness of death, sometimes derived from the awareness of sexuality (thanatos, moon); or, as is usual, to the fluidity and circularity among all these ideas simultaneously.

One of the most prominent aspects of Lorca's duende aesthetics is precisely fluidity, understood as the transgression and constant transformation of norms and limits defining or identifying subjects, objects or media themselves. There are examples of this limit-breaking fluidity across Lorca's creative practices which can be analysed in parallel. In 'Gacela del amor desesperado', the poet sets out to disrupt the laws of time, placing his desire for the beloved against the norms of logic and meaning. One of these crucial norms has to do with the limits separating life and death, a norm which in this poem is linked to the logical succession of events or the linearity of time. The language of the poem alters this succession by syncretising the structure of the poems with the meanings of the images represented. Visual and verbal elements work in unison so that their meanings converge, in turn making the spatiotemporal elements of the poem coalesce as well. Conversely, Lorca's calligrams from this time — 'Rosa de la muerte' (1934) and 'Mierda. Caligrama' (ca. 1934–36) — use the interrelation of word and image to explore a similar process of disruption, while the grotesque and transgressive 'Muerte de Santa Rodegunda' appears both in drawing form and as part of the cinematic *Viaje a la luna*.

The cohesion and convergence of multimedia meanings is examined by Mike Borkent (2010) in his study of innovative poetic artefacts such as concrete poems, which he also calls visual poems.[9] He argues that 'many visual poems [...] rely on verbal and visual prompts coalescing into a broader meaning' (Borkent 2010: 147), which points to the idea that media (or elements typically associated with certain media) do not exist in isolation but in relation to other media, since the elements channelled through a certain medium acquire meaning in conjunction with the medium itself. Therefore, some conclude that the medium itself is the message, or more precisely, that the medium certainly contributes to the meaning of the artefact together with the rest of its intra-compositional elements.[10] Lorca's late poems, his calligrams and the multimodality and intermediality of *Viaje a la luna* demonstrate that multiple levels of meaning extracted from different media are at work simultaneously and manage to create a wider meaning through the conjunction of all of them.

Although its typography is conventional, in 'Gacela del amor desesperado', the visual meaning of the images plays an important part in enhancing the verbal meaning expressed and adding spatiotemporal cues. Night and day are the two poles in between which the poet and his addressee are represented. The limits between both times are unclear and undetermined, as are the positions and identities of the lovers. The liminal state of the poet and his lover is described as the only spatiotemporal realm in which their union is possible, although this union takes place inevitably through suffering and death. If desire never achieves the fulfilment it seeks, it will lead to nothingness, but the poet's wish for death perseveres nonetheless. A hypothetical fulfilment would mean a lack of purpose to the poet and his lover, so liminality is the preferable state for them:

> La noche no quiere venir
> para que tú no vengas
> ni yo pueda ir.
>
> Pero yo iré,
> aunque un sol de alacranes me coma la sien.
> Pero tu vendrás
> con la lengua quemada por la lluvia de sal.

> El día no quiere venir
> para que tú no vengas
> ni yo pueda ir.
>
> Pero yo iré
> entregando a los sapos mi mordido clavel.
> Pero tu vendrás
> por las turbias cloacas de la oscuridad. (*DT*: 143, ll. 1–14)

The images in the poem mirror the polarity of night and day through the use of poetic *chiaroscuro*. However, the conventional values of light and darkness are also reversed and disrupted, such that darkness adopts positive connotations at first and then becomes negativised and vice versa. As in many other examples in the late poetry, in this gacela the *chiaroscuro* reinforces the linguistic meaning in the poem making use of visual prompts that situate the reader on a sensory plane of perception. The permeability that light and darkness acquire creates a fictive movement that transports the reader from one to the other side of the visual spectrum. This allows for the final stanza to become an appraisal of death as a creative force rather than a destructive one, a disruption of its conventional meaning, and a reminder that corporeality entails both creation and destruction, desire and death. Not coincidentally, this correlation is one of the key aspects of the grotesque artistic image: 'actions that are both destructive and constructive' (Connelly 2003: 2) are a means to challenge norms and shock or impact readers/viewers. They are also an effective way to transcend binaries: life/death, pleasure/pain, word/image.

As in other gacelas, conflict and unfulfilled desire are needed for the poet to express his longing and desperate passion for his beloved, but the wound of this desire attacks the finitude and stability of the lovers' bodies. The will to overcome this conflict in pursuit of each other results in the representation of the lovers in grotesque forms: 'Pero yo iré, | aunque un sol de alacranes me coma la sien | Pero tú vendrás | con la lengua quemada por la lluvia de sal' (ll. 4–7). The poet's head half-eaten by a sun of scorpions and the beloved's tongue burnt by salt rain construct two corporeal forms in decay, stuck between living and dying.[11] As the poetic voice attempts to articulate the paradoxical emotions felt by the lovers in the poem and how the dichotomy pain/pleasure becomes fluid, these bodily grotesques emphasise the ongoing process of destructuration and recreation. Both the poet and the beloved 'are dying for each other', a purposely ambivalent metaphorical phrase which sums up the desire/death reversibility:

> Ni la noche ni el día quieren venir
> para que por ti muera
> y tú mueras por mí. (*DT*: 143, ll. 15–17)

Leaving the resolution of the conflict open-ended, the final lines of the gacela take place in a non-place and a non-time, since at this point spatiotemporal limits have ceased to exist. Neither day nor night wants to arrive so that the lovers can love/ die for each other.

The fictive movement of night into day and day into night is in turn combined with the propositional movement explicit in the verbs 'ir' and 'venir', which in their future forms 'iré' and 'vendrás' synthesise the alternating movement of going and coming, the alternating musicality of their rhyme (e-a) and the visuality of their also alternating light associations within each stanza (night-sun-day-darkness). The final alternating elements are the poet and his addressee, yo and tú, who are equally included in this pendular motion running throughout the poem. The limits between each other are suppressed, such that their opposition becomes blurred. This idea echoes the Surrealist principles put forward by André Breton in his *Manifesto of Surrealism*, where he describes the search for a state of *surreality*, 'where life and death, the real and the imaginary, past and future, the communicable and the incommunicable, high and low cease to be perceived as contradictory' (1972: 123). In this liminal state, the poem can accommodate a multiplicity of sensorial elements, all of which can work simultaneously. The process of perception is thus multi-layered and the limits between the visual and the verbal are blurred.

This is further exemplified in 'Gacela del amor con cien años', in which visual and linguistic meanings are joined by a musical element from the flamenco tradition (which had also been employed in *Poema del cante jondo* and in the *Poemas en prosa*).[12] Form and content are significantly related in this poem, in that the couplets and choruses are repeated to imitate both the implied pendular movement or transience of the male figures in the poem, walking up and down the street as time goes by, and the musical rhythm alluded to in the structure of the poem, simulating the stanza-chorus pattern of a song. The 'galanes', beaux or suitors, are 'rondando' through the poem, as traditional suitors would walk around a neighbourhood or town wooing their love interests.[13] In the gacela, the objects of desire of these wandering beaux are notably absent from the poem, as is their gender:

> Suben por la calle
> los cuatro galanes,
>
> ay, ay, ay, ay.
>
> Por la calle abajo
> van los tres galanes,
>
> ay, ay, ay.
>
> Se ciñen el talle
> esos dos galanes,
>
> ay, ay.
>
> ¡Cómo vuelve el rostro
> un galán y el aire!
>
> ay.
>
> En los arrayanes
> se pasea nadie. (*DT*: 153)

The choruses emitting 'quejío' sounds ('ay'), reproducing the typically Andalusian flamenco cry of pain and desperation but also of intense emotion in song, can be linguistic equivalents of the four galanes who one by one become absent with the progress of each of the couplets.[14] Thus, the linguistic movement implied by the verbs 'subir', 'volver', 'pasear' and the verbal phrase 'ir abajo' in four of the five couplets is reinforced by the fictive movement of the visual downwards line created by the symmetrical choruses decreasing in length (from four ays to one in the last instance). The triangle created on the page points to the bottom of the poem, where the ays stop and 'nobody' is left, whilst the meanings of 'walk up' and 'walk down' are introduced in the first two couplets, directing the reader downwards as well. The rhythmic symmetry of the couplet-chorus pattern and the fictive musical sound of the poem punctuate the progression of the poem, adding an extra element to the visual movement of the choruses downwards and the fictive movement signified in the couplets. This poetic movement bears in turn further significations.

The last couplet sees the solitary myrtle bushes on supposedly the same street as the beginning, where nobody is walking anymore. However, this last line's syntax is intentionally transposed to make 'nadie' the subject of the affirmative action of strolling (the more common construction would be the double negative 'no se pasea nadie'), suggesting that this 'nobody' is also a character, albeit one devoid of human substance, or the personification of nothingness. Nothingness is then the result of time in the poem, the state to which all the previous galanes have been subjected and the endpoint towards which their lives are inevitably bound. Time and space are thus two important forces in which the gacela is inscribed. The title already suggests the passage of time, love which is one hundred years old, so we might suppose that the poet is referencing the universality and atemporality of the sentiment. However, as the poem progresses, there is a sense that all that time does in the poem is drive the characters closer to their death, their disappearance and erasure from space and materiality. The laments interspersed with the stanzas accentuate this disappointing realisation, themselves also decreasing in number as the men do. The space, which at first sight might seem stable, mutates with the men, since the poem starts at the bottom of the street, implying a movement upwards but then returning as the now remaining three beaux walk down the street. The space of the third stanza is none other than the very bodies of the now two suitors, who ambiguously tighten their waistbands (each their own or reciprocally in a tight embrace), as the poetic voice is observing them as a voyeur of sorts. This stanza supposes a change in the poetic space, announcing the movement from the public sphere to a private, even internal realm and ending in an ambiguous setting where the location and the boundaries between self and other become blurry. At the end of the poem, the scene invoked has lost specificity: there are no spatial or time references and the poetic voice has disappeared, blurred into the disintegrating image of 'nobody'. There are no clues as to who is speaking or where they are, except for the ambiguous reference to the bushes, perhaps because 'nobody' is there and therefore it is an unknown space outside the concrete poetic space where the beaux were situated before. The disappearance of the ays and the mirrored disappearance of the galanes lead the reader to the visual nothingness that follows the end of the triangular shape formed by the choruses and the propositional nothingness implied in the last line. This nothingness refers once more to an abstract place of 'surreality', a non-place and non-time in which spatiotemporal limits can cease to exist.

Through drawing, the spatiotemporal abstraction sought in these gacelas can be more easily represented graphically. Lorca's late drawings rarely have a concrete background space, and very often they consist of objects floating in the centre of the composition, surrounded by empty space or nothingness. 'Manos cortadas', 'Rostro con flechas', 'Labios (Walking around)' and most of the calligrams contain this spatiotemporal abstraction. In the case of calligrams, poem/drawing hybrids in which the typographical organisation of letters and words creates the shape of an object sometimes relating to the content of the poem, abstraction is paired with the intricate combination of the visual and the verbal. In 'Rosa de la muerte', one of the drawings Lorca made in Argentina to illustrate Ricardo Molinari's collector's edition of *Una rosa para Stefan George*, a simplified and repetitive poetic composition is developed into a cross-like drawing creating a long-stemmed rose. Read from top to bottom and from the flower's round petals to its extending roots, the lines focus on the four elements air, water, fire and earth, but also on death, temporality, desire and the body:

> AIRE para tu boca
> Tierra Tierra Tierra
> y Madera y Madera y Madera
> cuerpo cuerpo cuerpo cuerpo
> y Nunca
> nunca nunca nunca nunca nunca nunca
> y siempre y siempre y siempre
> y siempre y siempre y siempre
> MUERTEE MU MUERTE MEU
> Muerte y Muerte
> AGUA PARA TU AMOR
> FUEGO PARA TU CENIZA
> Muerte y Muerte y Muerte
> Tierra PARA TU ALMA
> Muerte y Muerte y Muerte.

As in many calligrams, the content of the linguistic elements mirrors the graphic result of their irregular organisation. Air is placed at the very top of the composition, crowning the rose above a group of multiple fine dots that animate the petals both above and in its centre. The petals themselves are contoured by the words 'Tierra', 'Madera', 'Cuerpo', 'Nunca', 'Siempre', all of them repeated or joined by the conjunction 'y' both around the external shape of the flower and within the petals. At the centre of the flower's corolla, the capitalised word MUERTE is doubled and tripled, its letters transposed and reorganised forming a circle, which is in turn completed by a group of semicircular lines travelling along the bottom of the word. Stemming, literally, from the flower's deathly core, 'muerte' travels down the long stem creating side leaves along its course and finishing in a triangular base representing a plot of earth in the ground whose bottom ends in fine extending roots. Mirroring the 'air' above the flower at the top, the word 'earth' is inscribed linguistically and graphically within this triangle. The mid-section of the stem is traversed horizontally by two parallel undulating lines, resembling a long piece of

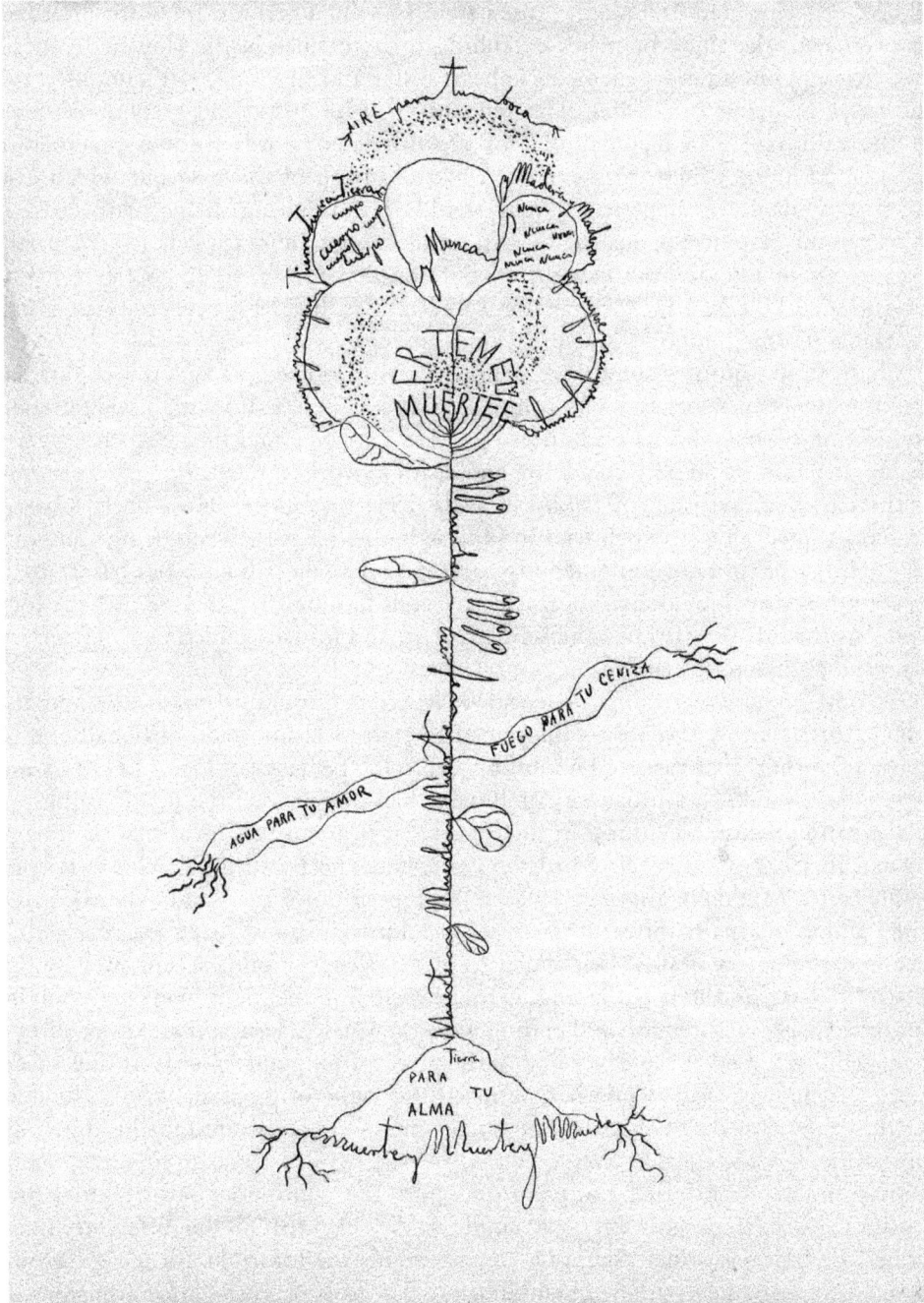

FIG. 5.2. 'Rosa de la muerte', Buenos Aires (1934).

ribbon or string tied around the rose's stem in which written lines are inscribed or even arm-like thick branches extending to both sides of the flower. In these, two further contradictory elements appear: water and fire, one nurturing love and the other reducing it to ashes. The syncretism of linguistic and graphic elements in the calligram also includes that of the unrelated words thrown together in the composition, which can be related to the image of the rose but which also work individually as lines in a poem would. The resulting image of the rose is literally and graphically formed by the four elements nurturing it (water, earth, air) or potentially destroying it (fire), but simultaneously other poetic elements are included by Lorca in the drawing, some human (madera, cuerpo, boca, alma, ceniza) and some temporal (siempre, nunca, muerte).

The rose has quintessential love connotations in poetry, and its red colour has traditionally been associated with romance and passion, but also with blood (often in connection with its thorns) and suffering. Thus it is a very apt image to encapsulate the poetic connection between desire and death at work in the calligram. As simply as the naïve composition of *Diván*'s 'Casida de la rosa' does, 'Rosa de la muerte' presents a queer object which tries to supersede the limits between being and non-being. It is a poem but simultaneously a drawing. Its object is alive but has death at its core, it is driven by desire but this desire ends in mortality, it combines the four elements that give it life but can also destroy it, and it is suspended in an uncertain time and an indeterminate space, both 'always' and 'never' existing.

A contemporaneous calligram entitled 'Mierda. Caligrama' takes an approach which differs from the rose calligram and indeed from traditional calligrams. Hispanic authors like Vicente Huidobro, Guillermo de Torre or Gerardo Diego and especially the French Guillaume Apollinaire had popularised the poetic calligram in the early twentieth century. In their works, it is usually assumed that the image created in a calligram is related to the content of the poem itself. This is not, or barely so in 'Mierda. Caligrama', where the repetition of the word 'Mierda' three times and in gradually different sizes creates an incongruous image not resembling any concrete object at all. The circularity of the composition is accentuated by the initial 'm' letter of the word, going up and developing the giant word horizontally but then changing direction and ending with the final 'a' letter upside down after a giant 'D' positioned at the other end of the circle. This giant 'mierda' is thus made illegible, but two smaller 'mierdas' also stem from the original giant 'm'. The dots on the 'i's are made of thicker dark small circles scattered around the drawing, one of them at the bottom only coloured in half, which makes it contain a small waning moon. As in other Lorquian drawings, the continuous but irregular line unifies the whole composition into a single stroke, such that all the differently sized words are joined together. Standing alone towards the top right corner is a group of small thicker sinewy lines, resembling small worms or even cartoonish signs of a bad smell (both probably results of the unseemly poetic matter from which they emanate). The irregular configuration of two of the three words (the giant one and the smaller one towards the centre-left of the drawing) suggests a scribbling process, as if the writerly hand had given up halfway through the word and decided to make

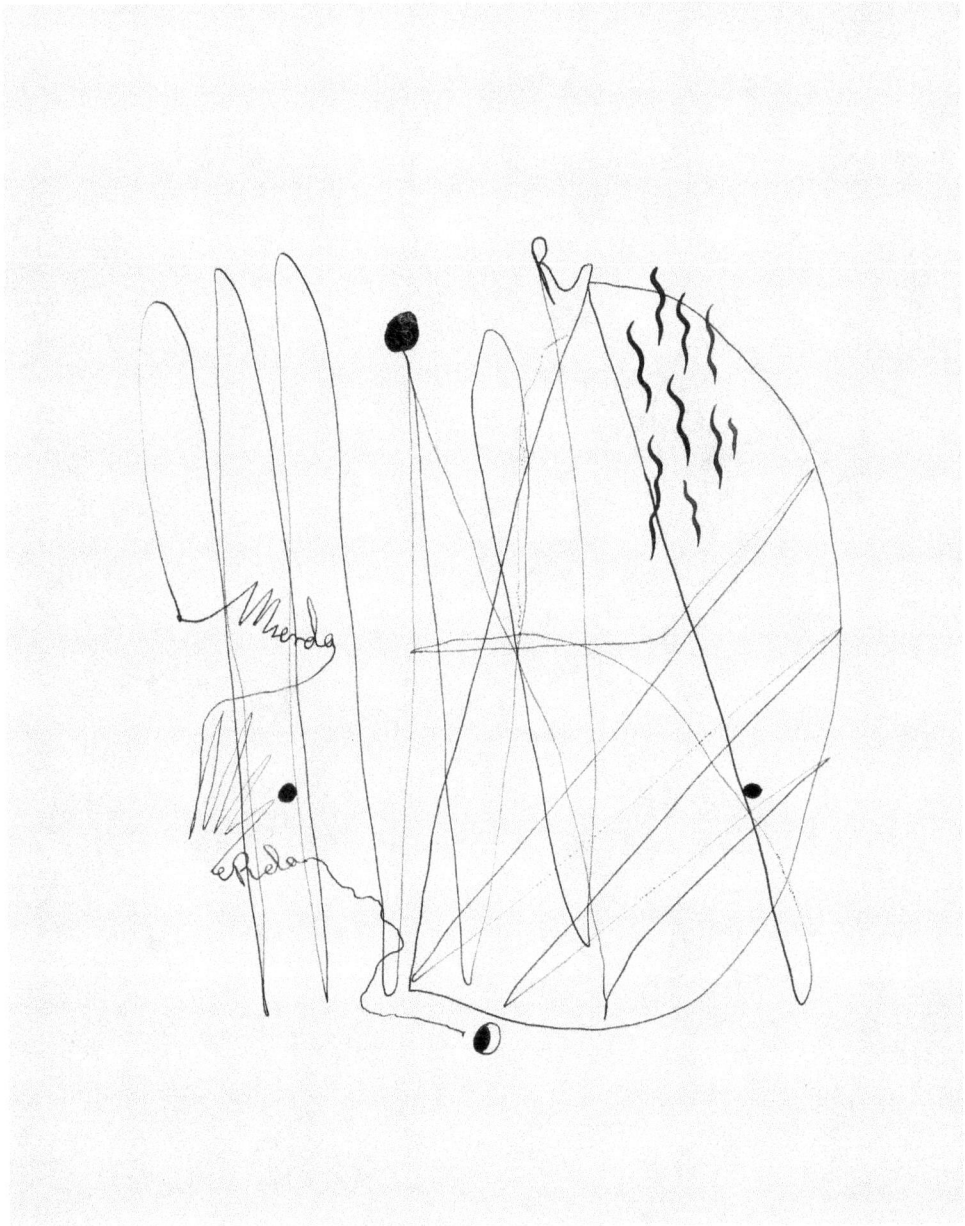

FIG. 5.3. 'Mierda. Caligrama' (ca. 1934–36).

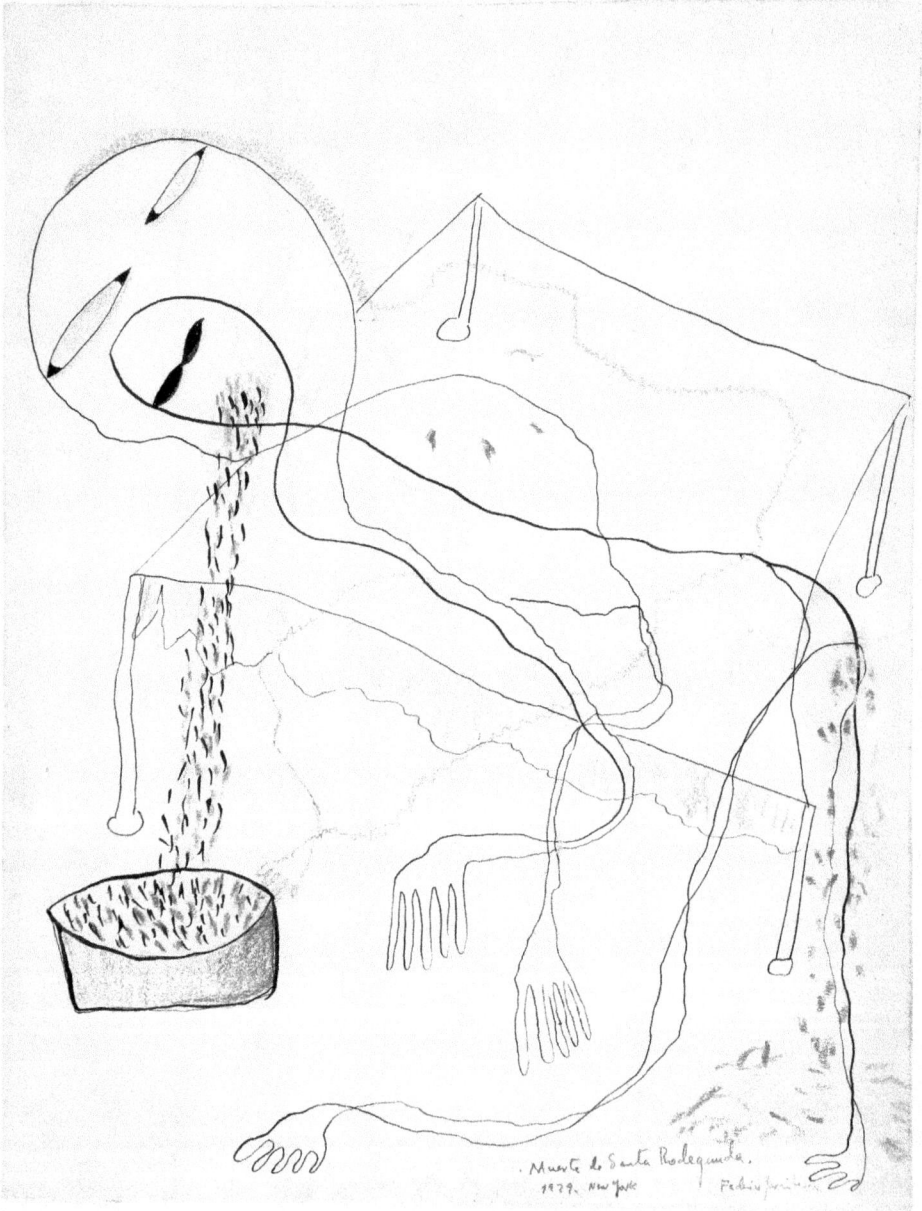

FIG. 5.4. 'Muerte de Santa Rodegunda', New York (1929).

it illegible and nonsensical, ruining the writing process and turning it into waste. The calligram thus fuses the linguistic meaning of the words repeated with the lack of meaning (or purposeful nonsense) of abstract drawings, adding a humorous or sarcastic tone in the inclusion of the politically incorrect 'shit'. This is a particularly suggestive aspect, since it remains unclear whether Lorca is subversively confronting the viewer with the very image of disgust, however abstractly, or passing judgment on his own work which has been made into literal and visual shit by his own hand.

Tying in with the subversive images of disgust that recur in the later works, especially prominent in *Viaje a la luna* and *Poeta en Nueva York*, is the drawing 'Muerte de Santa Rodegunda'. Drawn in 1929 at the beginning of Lorca's sojourn in the United States, it depicts an amorphous two-headed figure lying on a bed and vomiting violently into a brown basin while bleeding through its wounded chest and genital area. Santa Radegunda (520–87) — the different spelling in the drawing might be an error on Lorca's part or a purposeful distortion to re-appropriate the name of the saint — was a French princess canonised in the ninth century. Llera suggests that Lorca might have been interested in her biography due to her avid efforts to avoid being married to her kidnapper, the Merovingian king Clotario the First, and her subsequent refusal to relinquish her virginity (2011: 201). The deathly title, the contorted position of the vomiting figure and the intense red colour of the vomit also scattered around the edges of the drawing suggest the disturbing gushing of blood from the character's mouth and genitalia and therefore its painful agony and death.[15] However, the creature, presumably Santa Rodegunda, does not present clear human features except for two sets of eyes on each of its heads formed by disproportionate dark ovals. The bigger head, containing a smaller one, has white ovals resulting in a blank expression, while the small head has black ones, resembling an eye mask or dark glasses. Apart from the red colour of the blood, forming thick strokes that stain the drawing, and the brown colour of the basin, the rest of the contours in the drawing are made of very thin lines which accentuate the monochromatic and almost diffused aspect of the figure and the bed, both nearly blurred and fading into each other. The slender and stretched out arms and legs of Santa Rodegunda, drawn with sinewy and blurry lines, adopt a malleable shape which also confounds their contours with those of the bed. Thus, the body of the figure becomes uncertain and shapeless, doubling some of its parts like two bodies superimposed over each other.

This uneven composition contrasting the amorphous and grotesque body of the creature with the intensity of the blood and vomit emanating from it aptly evokes the fragmented bodies in *Viaje a la luna*, of which the drawing is also part. Like the juxtaposed corporeal fragments and bodily issue in the film script were animated by the rapid succession of tableaux, in the drawing the perceived intensity of the gushing fluids animates the blurry background and incidentally becomes the nexus between the limits of life and death. Whether agonising, menstruating, defecating or being disgusted, and whether male, female or neither, the creature in the drawing is made alive by the power of blood and excretion, both usually unseen but inevitably a crucial part of human bodies. The creature's mouth and its sex, both sites of interaction between the body and the outer world, also become the points of convergence of the creature's desire and its mortality. As Bakhtin posited, the limit between human bodies and the world is crossed through interactions such as eating, drinking, vomiting or defecating, since the orifices through which these actions take place become points of convergence and transformation, the confines on which 'the beginning and end of life are closely linked and interwoven' (1984: 317). Lorca's obsession with the blurring of these limits explains Santa Rodegunda's grotesque nature, almost devoid of any sign of humanity or identification but still determined by both her mortality and her living body, open through its wounds and in the throes of destructuration. Rodegunda's unique embodiment of the grotesque acts linking living and dying through bodily issue also resonates with Julia Kristeva's idea of abjection.[16] Kristeva conjures abjection as a place in which boundaries are broken down because it precedes linguistic binaries such as self/other or subject/ object. What a subject throws aside as he/she moves into the symbolic order and is constituted into a social body remains a threat to identity, a reminder of death. The abject refers to the human reaction to a threatened breakdown in meaning caused by the loss of the distinction between self and other and between life and death:

> A wound with blood and pus, or the sickly, acrid smell of sweat, of decay [...] *show me* what I permanently thrust aside in order to live. These body fluids, this defilement, this shit are what life withstands, hardly and with difficulty, on the part of death. There, I am at the border of my condition as a living being. (Kristeva 1982: 3)

The acts of vomiting and bleeding, much like in Lorca's idea of *duende* as a wound transgressing the limits of life and death, threaten the boundaries delimiting the body's finitude, discreteness and fixity, confounding what is inside and outside and what is alive and dead, thus reversing the norms of bodily interactions with the world. This powerful and shocking effect of the grotesque in 'Muerte de Santa Rodegunda' explains its inclusion among the amalgam of images similarly crossing life/death, humour/disgust and pleasure/pain boundaries in *Viaje a la luna*. In turn, the media crossover between drawing, film and poetry in which this graphic work participates unites *Poeta en Nueva York*, the film script and Lorca's *duende* aesthetics, never confined to only one medium but breaking the limits of all of them.

Focusing now on the recurrent motifs explored in Lorca's later years, the hand is one of the most prominent ones. As seen in Chapter 3, its evident reference to the craftsmanship of the writer-artist also resonates with the importance of the five senses in the poet's imagery. In addition, the inclusion of roots systems 'growing' and extending from or near hands often evokes both the relationship between man and nature as well as the limits between the living and the inert or the dead. The roots resembling vein systems or the 'arborization of nerve axoms often found in nerve cell drawings' (Cavanaugh 2003: 195) respond to Lorca's conviction that no object is too small or too ordinary to become a poetic image. Among Lorca's contemporaries the popularity of scientific studies of anatomy was growing: the works of scientists like Ramón y Cajal, usually accompanied by anatomical drawings of nerve cells or vein systems, and the fascination of artists with scientific advances and motifs extracted from scientific disciplines became a staple of the Spanish avant-garde.

Lorca believed, for instance, that a poet can create an epic poem on the exciting battle among leucocytes in the foliage of veins (*OC* III: 240), which reinforces the multidisciplinary and sensory nature of his aesthetics. His dictum 'un poeta tiene que ser profesor en los cinco sentidos corporales' (*OC* III: 225) is reassessed and expanded in the late works in order to explore how the five bodily senses can be distorted, reconfigured and transgressed.

The connection/disconnection issues explored in the drawings 'Manos cortadas' and 'Labios (Walking around)', and the incongruity and resistance to communication evoked in *Viaje a la luna* find a lyrical counterpart in the 'Casida de la mano imposible' and the 'Gacela de la raíz amarga' from *Diván del Tamarit*. In the former, the wounded hand becomes the only agent trusted by the poet in the face of human mortality:

> Yo no quiero más que una mano;
> una mano herida, si es posible.
> Yo no quiero más que una mano
> aunque pase mil noches sin lecho.
>
> Sería un pálido lirio de cal.
> Sería una paloma amarrada a un corazón.
> Sería el guardián que en la noche de mi tránsito
> prohibiera en absoluto la entrada a la luna.
>
> Yo no quiero más que esa mano
> para los diarios aceites y la sábana blanca de mi agonía.
> Yo no quiero más que esa mano
> para tener un ala de mi muerte.
>
> Lo demás todo pasa.
> Rubor sin nombre ya. Astro perpetuo.
> Lo demás es lo otro; viento triste,
> mientras las hojas huyen en bandadas. (*DT*: 165)

The poet conjures an impossible wounded hand to assist him in the process of knowing himself and making sense of his own existence and death through the poem, as well as easing him 'through his final hours of existence when the moment comes' (Anderson 1990: 121). Thus, the hand would help him be aware of his mortality ('el guardián [...] en la noche de mi tránsito'), perhaps even offer alleviation from the fear of death. Although it is unclear whether the poet's need for this wounded hand implies the call for human contact, the loneliness of the lyrical 'I' in the poem is palpable. He is ready to spend a thousand nights without a bed ('lecho' very often connotes either a conjugal or a dying bed), he compares the hand with a pale limescale lily — an ominous funereal flower made of the lime usually scattered in a grave (Anderson 1990: 122) — and with a dove clinging to his heart — which may be suggestive of hope or of a spiritual afterlife in its association with the Holy Ghost — and sees in it his deathly guardian who would forbid his entrance into the ominous moon.[17] The poet undoubtedly stands alone against all these evocative images, and concludes that 'everything else passes' and 'everything else is the other'.

This poetic voice resembles all the lonely mouths whose lips float about in 'Labios', conjoined by a single line but exuding isolation in their 'walk' around the single dark dot standing for the moon or an eye. The poet is also a reminder of the three solitary men in *Viaje a la luna* who stare up at the moon among sudden images of death and decay (45–46), and especially, of the Man of Veins whose awareness and embodiment of mortality make him a queer subject, stuck between life and death but whose open wounds suggest infinite recreations and multiple identities as opposed to 'the others', those sleepwalking customers in the bar whose disgust is provoked by desires that cannot be quenched (50). In the poem, 'the other' is a futile and transient reality, nameless and perpetually round like the moon ('Astro perpetuo'), a sad wind from whom tree leaves fly away. The final lines of the casida are strikingly similar to the ending of *Viaje a la luna*, in which the moon hurriedly appears to dominate the scene above a group of trees moved by the wind (72). Also in *Viaje*, an 'invisible hand' swiftly removes the number-ridden bedsheets in the first sequence (1–2), initiating the frenetic pace of the successive images in the film script. The hand is seen as an animator, spurring poetic images into action. It is the force that incites living roots to grow in 'Manos cortadas' and, albeit severed or wounded, it is the poet's guardian in the face of uncertainty:

> y las manos del hombre no tienen más sentido
> que imitar a las raíces bajo tierra.
> ('Gacela de la huída' *DT*: 152, ll. 12–13)

As a symbol of man's constructive and imaginative powers (Anderson 1990: 84), their purpose is to imitate growing roots underground, as they will provide nurture and 'sentido' (sense) in the midst of uncertainty. They both bridge the gap between man and the world and show the connection between them, since man emerges from the earth, desires its nurture (physical, spiritual, erotic) by merging with other bodies, and returns to earth in death.[18] However, in the poem there is also a return to the ambivalence between life and death as an ever-recurring transient cycle: 'in the midst of life we are in death' (Anderson 1990: 85).

In a similar vein, the images in 'Gacela de la raíz amarga' relate the root to the distinction between the single and the multiple and the coalescence between life and death:

> Hay una raíz amarga
> y un mundo de mil terrazas.
>
> Ni la mano más pequeña
> quiebra la puerta del agua.
>
> ¿Dónde vas? ¿Adónde? ¿Dónde?
> Hay un cielo de mil ventanas
> — batalla de abejas lívidas —
> y hay una raíz amarga.
>
> Amarga.
> (*DT*: 146, ll. 1–9)

Poema del Cante Jondo and *Romancero gitano* contained poems dedicated to the figure of 'El Amargo', an ominous gypsy character embodying fate and mortality, but in this gacela, these aspects are added to the root so that its growth and creative capabilities also announce the awareness of mortality.[19] The emphasis on a single raíz amarga, a bitter root, contrasts with the juxtaposed images of objects in groups: 'mil terrazas', 'mil ventanas' and 'abejas lívidas'. While the bitter root in the gacela is the source of pain and suffering, its confrontation with the other multiple objects instructs the poet to still embrace it as an inescapable part of his life. Despite the pain, the poet finds in this bitterness a suitable companion and calls his beloved to join him in this awareness of necessary sorrow ('¡Amor, enemigo mío, | muerde tu raíz amarga!'), in the realisation of the finitude of the body and of the inevitability of death. Not even the smallest hand, that hand which usually provides solace through the sense of touch and through creation, can in this gacela break the water door ('Ni la mano más pequeña | quiebra la puerta del agua'). This liquid door counteracts the rootedness in the poem, it seems like an inevitable flow of transience and ephemerality causing pain and heartache, and perhaps the reason that love/his beloved are seen as an enemy. His emphatic questions '¿Dónde vas? ¿Adónde? ¿Dónde?' place the poet in a place of uncertainty against multiplicity, not knowing where the flow will take him and therefore in need of roots that will anchor him to himself. Lorca had indeed tapped into this uncertainty with the sense of disorientation presented in *Viaje a la luna* through multiple slamming doors, frantic movements of superimposed images and dissolves, and verbal messages of actual disorientation:

> 14
> Caída rápida por una montaña rusa en color azul con doble exposición de letras de *Socorro Socorro*.
> 15
> Cada letrero de *Socorro Socorro* se disuelve en la huella de un pie.
> 21
> [...] Aquí un letrero que diga *No es por aquí*. (García Lorca 1994: 64)

Disorientation and uncertainty cause confusion and fear and clearly, as the poet states, this is not the way. Rootedness is now crucial to the poet, its bitterness and pain an inevitable part of his existence, just like the roots in 'Rosa de la muerte' provided nurturing, 'earth for the soul'. It is not surprising that most roots systems in the late drawings resemble human vein systems and grow from the wound, as they similarly refer to the awareness of mortality and its inextricable link with desire and creation. Faced with the instability of existence and a multiplicity of identities flowing through the open wound, the image of the root helps the poet achieve some sense of unity with the other (the beloved, reality, art), even if this comes from the awareness of death as an inherent part of life.

Emilio Peral Vega, in his study of Lorca's use of the *commedia dell'arte* figure of Pierrot in the poetry, drawings and theatre, posits that 'Pierrot is a mask, and therefore by his very nature a transient and ever-changing essence' (2015: 6). Apart from Pierrot and the Harlequin, characters explored throughout Lorca's 1920s works, further motifs are developed in his later years to deal with the idea of a transient essence. The many drawings depicting doublings and fusions, the indeterminate and reversible roles of the lovers in the late poems, and the masks and metamorphoses of characters and objects in the plays and in *Viaje a la luna*, reinforce this reversibility and fluidity of identities, to the extreme of challenging the notion that essence can be anything other than transient and ever-changing. As we have seen, throughout *Diván del Tamarit* and *Sonetos del amor oscuro*, the poetic voice articulates a state of spatiotemporal uncertainty which escapes logic and rationality, a queer fantasy in Muñoz's utopic sense (2009: 22), extending this uncertainty to the status of the subjects in the poems, usually the poet and his beloved:

> Quiero dormir un rato,
> un rato, un minuto, un siglo;
> pero que todos sepan que no he muerto;
> [...] que soy la sombra inmensa de mis lágrimas.
> ('Gacela de la muerte oscura' *DT*: 149, ll. 10–12; 15)

While the poet in 'Gacela de la muerte oscura' is taking an 'obscure' nap which may last a minute or a century, he states that he is simultaneously dead and not dead, he is but an immense shadow. Similarly, the amorphous creature depicted in 'Solo la muerte' as well as the Man of Veins in *Viaje a la luna* inhabit a space and a time in which obscurity and incongruity reveal a defiance of norms governing existence. They are simultaneously alive and dead, they possess a reversibility which impedes any stable essence, all of which requires more and more 'masks' to be created, more doubled heads and bodies to emerge. The poetic beloved is usually included in the doubling and fusing process, as both lovers' bodies and identities often tend to merge and coalesce:

> Pero ¡pronto! Que unidos, enlazados,
> boca rota de amor y alma mordida,
> el tiempo nos encuentre destrozados.
> ('Soneto de la guirnalda de rosas' *PC*: 579, ll. 12–14)

> La aurora nos unió sobre la cama,
> las bocas puestas sobre el chorro helado
> de una sangre sin fin que se derrama.
> ('Noche del amor insomne' *PC*: 586, ll. 9–11)

Trying to elude time, the lovers find their union when their bodies are destructured and become fused, in an image which also becomes double: it represents their erotic encounter as well as their encounter with mortality. They are bleeding to death but feeding off each other's blood. Their selves are superimposed. Similarly, the many doubled Pierrots and Harlequins in Lorca's graphic works depict the superimpositions and therefore fusions of personae: a man and his dual/multiple self or two lovers erotically converging. The drawing 'Marinero del "Amor"' (1934) implies that the superimposed doubled bodies are embracing or kissing each other and there is only one heart which the bodies share.[20] The heart, drawn unrealistically outside the sailor's chest, seems to be pierced by a cross and has roots coming out of it, while the word 'amor' is written across the cap the sailor is wearing on his head. The superimposed body is merely a silhouette or a shadow: only its hands are clearly drawn while the rest is a sinewy line going in and out of the sailor's body through his eyes and mouth. In 'Muerte de Santa Rodegunda', the doubling happens in the moment in which the body is bleeding and vomiting, breaking open and dying, so its limits are doubly confounded: on the one hand its body is fused with another body while on the other its wounds and orifices force it to fuse with the outside world. Lastly, one of Lorca's final drawings, 'Payaso de rostro que se desdobla', is a graphic signature dating from 1936 which depicts a doubled clown head — very similar to the figure of Pierrot — who doubly cries as its two faces look in different directions, encircled in a thick spiralling line ending in a pointed arrow. A small moon and the transposition of the name 'Federico' complete the drawing, which encapsulates the self/other and visual/verbal fluidity present in the late works. As word and image are fused in the drawing, so are the limits between Lorca and his work. The double headed portrait is dual in many ways: it is an intermedial space in which an autograph accommodates visual and verbal expressions, but it is also inhabited simultaneously by Lorca the man and Lorca the artist. The issue of authorship is mixed in with issues of selfhood and otherness, confusing the limits separating biography from artwork, poetry from drawing, the ludic element characteristic of the clown figures from the constructedness and incongruity of the grotesque, or in other words, 'Federico' from the crying heads.

In *Viaje a la luna*, several kinds of fusions take place. First, the very configuration of the film script and its adherence to the cinematic medium enables objects and body parts to merge. The fusion of tableaux through the sequencing used by Lorca in the scenario joins and doubles things at random, as the imitation of editing by the rapid succession of segments makes use of close-ups, dissolves and double and triple exposures and superimpositions to transform, dismember and recreate bodies. In parallel, fusions of bodies and the outside world are represented throughout: vomiting, open mouths, open wounds and genitalia allow Lorca to use the grotesque to play with bodily limits and mix the beautiful and the disgusting. Last but not least, the doubling of characters themselves, through masks, alter egos and metamorphoses, is a prominent part of the scenario: the Man of Veins takes off his harlequin costume before his first appearance (section 43), then transforms into a Young Man (50), takes off his mask to become the Man of Veins once more (62) and finally turns into a corpse (67); the Young Woman in the lift dissolves/transforms into a statue (63); the couple mocking the corpse transform into a Hollywood couple (71); and the Moon itself transforms into a human head (18).

All these doublings, dualities and fusions share a common aesthetic intention to represent the close interrelation of desire and death. From the lift sequence in *Viaje a la luna* in which the Man of Veins kisses/rapes/kills the young girl (sections 56–64) to the erotic and deadly reversibility and indeterminacy of the lovers in *Diván del Tamarit* and *Sonetos del amor oscuro*; from the multi-faceted shape-shifting characters and personae in the 'impossible' plays to the doubled bodies both nurturing and wounding each other in the drawings, Lorca's play with limits is reinvented through multiple media but follows a rigorous and systematic development. Paradoxically, it is not a linear development, but a fluid and circular one, open like a wound that never seals and round like the moon in which desire and death converge. Quite fittingly, the circular motifs pervading the film script and the late drawings and poems (eyes, moons, flowers, dots, tears, blood drops, wounds) mirror the cyclical transformations through which objects and bodies are constantly operating.

The fluidity of bodies and identities thus suggests the impossibility and futility of attempting to pin them down and limit them: the norms trying to govern them will always need to be rethought and reconfigured. As seen in the epigraph, Lorca believed that *duende* is never repeated, just like those shapes formed by the waves in a sea storm. This recursive metamorphosis sought in the artwork, be it through one medium or through a mix of media, helps the artist create *lo insólito*: that which breaks norms, and, in so doing, becomes something new and unprecedented; alive but open to death; which never stays still, and can never be replicated. In this ephemerality lies the special substance that *duende* makes alive through a 'forma viva' mysteriously wounded by death.

Notes to Chapter 5

1. 'El canto quiere ser luz. | En lo oscuro el canto tiene | hilos de fósforo y luna' ('[El canto quiere ser luz]', *Canciones*, *OC* I: 273); 'Verde que te quiero verde. | Verde viento. Verdes ramas.' ('Romance sonámbulo', *Romancero Gitano*, *OC* I: 400).
2. A medium is generally understood as 'a conventionally and culturally distinct means of communication, specified not only by particular technical or institutional channels (or one channel) but primarily by the use of one or more semiotic systems in the public transmission of contents that include, but are not restricted to, referential "messages"' (Wolf 2011: 2).
3. Intermediality can refer to the medium's intra-compositional aspects and/or to the relationships established extra-compositionally, that is, across media. We may speak of intermediality as 'any transgression of boundaries between conventionally distinct media', which would include relational processes taking place within or across media such as 'gestation, similarity, combination, or reference including imitation' (Wolf 2011: 3). It can be recognised that 'media do not exist disconnected from one another' and that there are different approaches to issues of intermediality: 'formal (or transmedial) intermediality'; 'transformational intermediality' and 'ontological intermediality'. Formal intermediality or transmediality is a concept 'based on formal structures not "specific" to one medium but found in different media'; 'transformational intermediality' is a model centred around the 'representation of one medium through another medium', which in turn leads to 'ontological intermediality: a model suggesting that media always already exist in relation to other media' (Schröter 2011: 2).
4. In 'Casida de los ramos', the apple tree may be a symbol of that in the Garden of Eden, the Tree of Knowledge of Good and Evil; thus the sighs or sobs felt by the apples may be due to 'the Temptation, Fall and Expulsion [which] brought evil, suffering and death into the world' (Anderson 1990: 105).
5. Lorca often discussed his reticence to Surrealist practices in his letters to art critic and close friend Sebastián Gasch: 'Gasch no es partidario del surrealismo, y esto Lorca lo sabe; en varias ocasiones insiste a su confidente catalán el intento de negar cualquier tentación de entregarse a las fuerzas del automatismo o del inconsciente' (Plaza Chillón 2008: 15). Nonetheless, the clear oneiric allusions in the poem can also be read as reinforcing Lorca's 'poetic' or 'dream' logic, and as references to *A Midsummer Night's Dream* (Anderson 1990: 116).
6. Indeed, he mentions this aspect in *Teoría y juego del duende*, conceding that *duende* is more easily transmitted through spoken poetry (see Introduction). Lorca's sensory poetics is clearly aware that aural meaning is joined to language and can be accentuated, even if the poem is not read out loud.
7. La Novia in *Bodas de sangre* is warned by the moon itself that her extramarital desires will bring fatal consequences; and Adela, Paca la Roseta and la Hija de la Librada in *La casa de Bernarda*

Alba are harshly subjected to scorn or even killed for what in their sociopolitical context are considered illicit sexual relations.

8. Ian Gibson makes these connections in the *Making of* video of Frederic Amat's filmic adaptation of *Viaje a la luna* (1998). Also, see Monegal (1994: 26), Gibson (2009: 240), Cordero Sánchez (2012: 155) and Anderson (2017: 10).

9. Concrete poetry would be the more general term encompassing calligrams and other kinds of poetic artefacts in which the formal or typographical organisation of the poem or parts of the poem creates a visual element intrinsically related to the content or meaning in the poem.

10. See Marshall McLuhan's seminal work *Understanding Media: The Extensions of Man* (1964).

11. Furthermore, Anderson relates the dark sewers (cloacas) and the toads (sapos) to affected and effeminate homosexuality, while the carnation (clavel) points to passion and sometimes specifically to virility (1990: 46–47). These images help to map the ambivalent and fluctuating emotions felt by the lovers within the fluid gender/heterodox sexuality spectrum, but failing to define or determine where exactly the lovers are located.

12. See 'El grito' (*PC*: 259–60) and 'Degollación del Bautista' (*PC*: 455–57).

13. This is reminiscent of the courting rituals alluded to in *La casa de Bernarda Alba*, with Pepe el romano wandering around the house at night as he entices and seduces Bernarda's daughters.

14. As seen in Chapter 1, a similar device was used in the sonnet '[Ay voz secreta del amor oscuro]'.

15. Llera traces the motif of the blood vomit, or *haematemesis*, back to accounts from the *Corpus Hippocraticum* and some passages of *The Iliad* (2011: 201).

16. In Llera's view, the abject in 'Muerte de Santa Rodegunda' refers to images of transgression because they introduce the ambiguous, what does not respect boundaries or norms (2011: 214). Wright and Larson both look at Kristeva's idea of the abject in relation to Lorca's *El público* (Wright 2000: 117) and to *Viaje a la luna* (Larson 2011: 311) respectively.

17. Anderson relates the dove to both Venus and the Virgin Mary and suggests an echo of the sonnet 'A Mercedes en su vuelo' (1990: 122).

18. Anderson suggests a possible reminiscence of T. S. Eliot's *The Waste Land*, specifically a passage from 'I. The Burial of the Dead' (1990: 84).

19. 'Diálogo del Amargo' in *Poema del Cante Jondo* and 'Romance del emplazado' in *Romancero gitano* both have 'el Amargo' as a protagonist. He is an ill-fated Andalusian gypsy whose imminent death is announced to him in both poems, later coming to fruition among lamenting clamours. Lorca recovered this character from his childhood recollections: el Amargo was a gypsy child who used to scare the young Lorca from his window by making faces and grinning at him (Maya 2005).

20. An earlier drawing, 'El beso' (1927) also represents doubling as a fusion of love and death. Almost a self-portrait, as the doubled character closely resembles Lorca, the doubled head consists of a face with full features and a second amorphous head superimposed, the latter with just a mouth and a collar and tie. The second head, almost like a shadow, is coloured red and yellow, with red dots resembling blood, and joins the 'main' head irregularly, both on top of it and behind it in a play of perspectives. The focal point of the drawing consists of the two heads' pair of mouths drawn next two each other, barely touching in a kiss of sorts.

CONCLUSION

❖

A Poetic Metamorphosis

My aim in this study has been to reassess Federico García Lorca's post-New York works in light of ideas of queerness. Starting with *Juego y teoría del duende* and the poetic thought Lorca put forward in the early 1930s, I have argued that two key aspects of this lecture so far overlooked — i.e. queerness and intermediality — play an essential role in his unique aesthetics. Lorca's later period was an intense (and, very fittingly, non-linear) journey across countries, genres, media and ideas. It was a climactic moment, brutally interrupted by his assassination, evidencing Lorca's continuous ability for artistic metamorphosis. In order to acknowledge the importance of Lorca's later corpus it is necessary to speak of multimodality, transgressions of limits and fluidity. *Juego y teoría del duende* is thus an apt compass to navigate his late works, since the playful and limit-breaking spirit in this prose poem on poetics embodies the Andalusian's taste for what we now know as queerness, that is, for the desire to rethink and reconfigure what seems to categorise, limit and define what we know and distinguish it from what we do not: what escapes those limits, what is different and becomes elusive, mysterious and undefinable.

Cleminson and Vázquez García's proposed 'Mediterranean model' of sexuality, the 'epenthetic' movement, in which an essentialisation of homosexuality is virtually impossible and unstable desires 'take preference over any strong expression of identity' (2007: 275), has offered a suitable framework to approach Lorca's poetics through the queer lens. Lorca's later works go beyond the binary distinctions homosexual-heterosexual and male-female and operate by means of limit transgressions, nuances, complex metaphors, literary and cultural re-appropriations and fantasies. There is at times not a clear or stable identity (sexual, of gender, or ontological) that can be ascribed to the personae in his later corpus, as there is not a clear identity between Lorca the man and Lorca the artist. In the *duende* lecture, Lorca sheds light on his play with limits by following a tricky performative route: whilst theorising about his aesthetics, he masks or disguises its complexity by also making it work as artistic creation itself, by creating poetic images that draw attention away from themselves as actual constructed images intended to transgress the very process of poetic creation. The lecture is poetry at work, but poetry which reaffirms the poet's intention to question the fabric of poetry (and of drawing, painting, dancing, acting, etc.), and their capacity to represent reality and produce meaning. He performs an act of creation while explaining his process of creation. In revealing to his audience the secrets to *duende*, he performs *duende*, battles with it, just as if he was in fact reciting poetry. Therein lies Lorca's genius, capable of presenting itself as an artistic artefact which not only emerges as aesthetic substance, but also provides a space for epistemological enquiry and, most importantly, for artistic and existential criticism.

My examination of the late poetry has shown how the language used in *Diván del Tamarit* and *Sonetos del amor oscuro* purports above all to boast its creativity and unexpectedness, to expose its ambivalences and indeterminacies and its deliberate transgressions of logic and reason. Lorca follows a poetic logic and plays with language to achieve shocking images and metaphors and unexpected meaning associations — 'lo insólito, lo inventado de la obra de un hombre' (*OC* III: 314). I have argued that the bodies and relationships among the lovers and other personae in the poems analysed are never fixed and stable. They move in a constant process of metamorphosis and cyclical reconfiguration, which allows Lorca to destabilise conventional ideas of sex, sexuality, body, soul, life, temporality and death as fixed and immutable. The fluidity of these processes is emphasised: the poem is not only language but also imagistic creation, artifice; the body of the poet is merged with the beloved's body and their desire transcends normative principles like chromosomal sex or gender. By questioning the possibility of absolute truths and stable ontologies, Lorca creates bodies that inhabit a liminal space in which spatiotemporal coordinates are suspended, unintelligible and unnameable; where the death drive signalled by the queer emerges to announce an impossible fantasy yet to come in which all limits and norms cease to exist.

I have also suggested that 'obscure' encapsulates the mysterious, inarticulable and norm-transgressing qualities of desire explored in both poetic works. The love in the gacelas, casidas and sonnets is neither clearly homosexual nor heterosexual, because precisely gender indeterminacy, fluidity and reversibility of roles recur. It is this permeability which makes the poetic subjects and objects queer, their erotic and destructive desires being as ambivalent as their elusive or epenthetic (sexual) identities. The abundance of *chiaroscuros* epitomises the pleasure/pain and being/ non-being ambivalence, while the re-appropriation and subversion of tropes taken from Spanish and European poetic traditions creates scenes in which the limits of life and death, sexual desire and spiritual suffering become destabilised and blurred. Rather than categorising Lorca's poetic discourse into a gay paradigm, I have argued that a queer lens is more suitable to approach his work in light of the ubiquitous fluidity and transgressions of (hetero)normativity that characterise his poetics.

In the 'impossible' plays, queer visibility and the exposure of the multiple levels of artificiality shaping existence imply the inclusion of the mysterious and the inexplicable in the drama, and the inclusion of death in life itself, which is what the aesthetics of *duende* ultimately seeks. Lorca's New York plays find an antecedent in the plans for a renovation of the Spanish stage during the 1920s and 1930s, when attempts were made by dramatists, stage directors, actors and intellectuals to create a new kind of 'Art Theatre' inspired by avant-garde European models which would raise the bar from more mainstream and bourgeoisie-pleasing contemporary practices. *Así que pasen cinco años* and *El público* both dramatise the transgression of conventions in theatre, be it in relation to structure, space, time and aesthetics; seeking to appeal to audiences who will have to question the limits of theatre as well as those imposed by preconceived notions about desire, identity and what constitutes reality. In portraying characters whose queerness invades the entirety of the play, Lorca proposes a dramatic space and time in which the very act of questioning established norms acquires a poetic/theatrical substance powerful enough to call for and produce change.

I have then examined the drawings from the later period in their own right, concluding that images of the body are taken to an extreme where limiting and constraining principles, such as geometrical composition, logic or rationality, are disrupted to give the metamorphic grotesque and its mysteries a leading position. Only thus will the artwork convey a sense of novelty and immediacy: what is substantial in art for Lorca. This artistic substance, though, is deeply rooted in pain and suffering, darkness and obscurity, fracture and destructuration. *Duende* represents what is mysterious in art, seeks to attack the artist, to cause a wound that resonates in the deepest spaces within the human body, bringing out the blood and the most basic instincts in it, and inevitably announcing death. Creating a 'forma viva' implies forcing that form to face mortality. Death is positivised and aestheticised, as are other disrupting elements such as blood, bodily issue, violence or physical destructuration. The late graphic works also join forces with the other media to explore fluid identities and sexualities. The gaze subjected to male figures and the veiling of sex and gender marks are paired with the coalescence of *eros* and *thanatos* to articulate Lorca's vision of heterodox desire. Considering the complexity and profundity they reveal, it is then fair to say that the late drawings were by no means a passing fad for Lorca nor unpolished and unfinished sketches: they were conceived as poetic images in their own right communicating through the immediacy and visuality of drawing some of his overarching aesthetic principles.

As for Lorca's film script, I have argued that cinema allows the poet to create an anti-narrative revelling in a spectacle of death. It is more apt to look at *Viaje a la luna* as a reference to the roller coaster ride 'Trip to the Moon' Lorca visited on New York's Coney Island than to Méliès's eponymous *Voyage dans la lune* and the linear journey on which its characters embark. Like the roller coaster, the 'trip' proposed in Lorca's film script is a disorienting and nausea-infusing one, with constant abrupt spatiotemporal breaches and corporeal jolts and transmutations that go from the grotesque and the repulsive to the humorous and the theatrical. It is no surprise that Lorca briefly situates the spectator on a roller coaster in the film script and that he also entitled a poem 'Paisaje de la multitud que vomita' (*Poeta en Nueva York*) in evocation of the aforementioned New York funfair and its dizzy visitors. The limits of corporeality are transgressed in order to challenge the norms, rationalisation and measurability that modernity introduced at the turn of the twentieth century, exemplifying the new visual means that cinema offered to create unexpected and shocking images and make them spectacular and fascinating. Corporealities and identities are unstable and multifaceted, at times fragmented and adopting unexpected forms and shapes, changing and fusing with other bodies, expressing a variety of emotions at random, and defying spatiotemporal laws and norms. The structure of the film script often resists causality and linearity. It presents a tableau narrative whose emphasis is on process, shock and display rather than on its minimal narrative continuity. Its oneiric nature mirrors other avant-garde texts and works of art of the time, being particularly close to Surrealist elements in films such as *Un chien andalou* or *Le sang d'un poète*, but it also resonates with the 'cinema of attractions' model attributed to earlier films of the 1900s in its visual unexpectedness and spectacular display. Lorca shocks and challenges the spectator with an 'attraction' that resembles poetic thought and emotion more than storytelling. In the poet's opinion, the greatness of film lies not in its rational explanation but 'in the freedom we all enjoy to interpret [it] as we will' (Morris 1980: 123).

Considering the multimedia production of Spanish and European avant-garde artists and how it influenced Lorca's post-New York years, it was also necessary to take into account ideas of multimodality and intermediality to gain a wider understanding of his *oeuvre*. A comparative analysis of the later works proves that the recurrent word-image interrelations and links within the four media examined reveal Lorca's fluid vision of the arts. His search for the unexpected requires ways of representation that fuse different levels of perception and supersede norms limiting and compartmentalising media. In parallel, some overarching aspects derived from Lorca's aesthetics are articulated in specific ways through each medium while referring to one another, particularly motifs like roots, hands, roses and circular objects and processes like doublings and fusions. The sailors, calligrams, *commedia dell'arte* characters, and complex artefacts like 'Muerte de Santa Rodegunda' also attest to Lorca's poetic fluidity, not only roaming across media limits but suggesting that identity is equally fluid and unstable. Lorca breaks media boundaries in order to show that his aesthetics goes beyond limits and restrictions: he seeks to create living poetic images worth experiencing by whichever means and channels are available. Conversely, the ways in which visuality relates to language and in which fluidity is represented in the poetry, drawings, and film script have yielded unique aspects worth exploring in their own right. If all arts are capable of *duende*, it is clear that the particular *poiesis* in poetry, drawing, and film can perform the Lorquian boundary play as well as music or theatre can.

The works studied here also share a preference for the representation of the human body and the five senses, but each destabilises this representation by destructuring bodily and sensory limits in their own particular way. In other words, they all show open wounds exhibiting the fragility of their construction and their limits broken at the seams, and therefore letting what escapes through those wounds emerge as limitless. Lorca's *duende* seeks the '*performative transmission* of artistic creativity' (Mayhew 2011b: 167), an artistic substance that will produce a deep and extreme emotion in the spectator. Redefining and disrupting ideas presumed to be stable and logical is meant to provoke this extreme reaction, questioning the possibility of true and stable identities and instead presenting them in a constant process of transformation. The heterodoxy and metamorphosis of desire and death are explored through characters who keep mutating incessantly and who embody theatricality and artificiality, as well as through spatiotemporal disruptions which avoid a synthesis of the desire/mortality dichotomy.

Desire and *poiesis* are both taken by Lorca to the edge of destruction so that they become new and reborn, communicating *duende*'s mystical and transgressive qualities when they are presented as a spectacle to watch on stage or on screen, as a poem to be read, or as a drawing to be interrogated and deciphered. Lorca's *duende* gives new meanings to avant-garde film, indeed taking the spectator on a poetic but spiralling and transformative trip to the moon. Also, in imitating and honouring the canons of love poetry, he redefines and adapts them to create obscure Lorquian metaphors and images, inscribing folkloric or Petrarchan elements in an unprecedented frame where desire and death are never again separate. Last but not least, his plastic poems or lyrical abstractions play with the literal lines that encircle his graphic compositions, picturing those bleeding wounds in actual colours which redefine in their own right the Spanish grotesque and the ever-popular sailor portraits of the early twentieth century. All these poetic artefacts should be considered on a par with Lorca's most canonical works as proof of his special embodiment of Andalusia, Spain and the European avant-garde and of his deliberate defiance of limits and boundaries. Despite their elusiveness and obscurity, *duende*'s intermedial mysteries of desire and death situate Lorca as a queer artist and thinker with legitimate relevance within Hispanic studies and cultures today.

BIBLIOGRAPHY

❖

ACTON, MARY. 2009. *Learning to Look at Paintings*, 2nd edn (London: Routledge)

AHMED, SARA. 2011. 'Happy Futures, Perhaps', in *Queer Times, Queer Becomings*, ed. by E.L. McCallum and Mikko Tuhkanen (Albany: State University of New York Press), pp. 159–82

AMAT, FREDERIC. 1998. 'Notas de *Viaje a la luna*', *Revista de Occidente*, 211: 189–94

ANDERSON, ANDREW A. 1986A. 'Federico García Lorca como poeta petrarquista', *Cuadernos Hispanoamericanos*, 435/36: 495–518

——. 1986B. 'The Strategy of García Lorca's Dramatic Composition 1930–1936', *Romance Quarterly*, 33.2: 211–29

——. 1990. *Lorca's Late Poetry* (Leeds: Francis Cairns)

——. 1992. '"Un dificilísimo juego poético": Theme and Symbol in Lorca's *El público*', *Romance Quarterly*, 39.3: 331–46

——. 2017. 'Approaching Lorca's *Viaje a la luna*: Structural Patterns, Symbolic Concatenation, and *El público*', *Hispanic Review*, 85.1: 1–21

ANDERSON, FARRIS. 1979. 'The Theatrical Design of Lorca's *Así que pasen cinco años*', *Journal of Spanish Studies: Twentieth Century*, 7. 3: 249–78

ASTRUC, RÉMI. 2010. *Le Renouveau du grotesque dans le roman du XXe siècle* (Paris: Classiques Garnier)

AUERBACH, JONATHAN. 2007. *Body Shots: Early Cinema's Incarnations* (Berkeley: University of California Press)

BAKHTIN, MIKHAIL. 1984. *Rabelais and His World*, trans. by Hélène Iswolsky (Bloomington: Indiana University Press)

BARÓN PALMA, EMILIO. 1990. *Agua oculta que llora: El Diván del Tamarit de García Lorca* (Granada: Editorial Don Quijote)

BINDING, PAUL. 1985. *Lorca: The Gay Imagination* (London: GMP)

BLACKMAN, LISA. 2012. *Immaterial Bodies: Affect, Embodiment, Mediation* (London: Sage)

BOHN, WILLARD. 2000. 'Lorca, Buster Keaton, and the Surrealist Muse', *Revista Hispánica Moderna*, 53.2: 413–24

BONADDIO, FEDERICO. 2010. *Federico García Lorca: The Poetics of Self-Consciousness* (Woodbridge: Támesis)

BORKENT, MIKE. 2010. 'Illusions of Simplicity: A Cognitive Approach to Visual Poetry', *English Text Construction*, 3.2: 145–64

BRETON, ANDRÉ. 1972. *Manifestoes of Surrealism*, trans. by Richard Seaver, and Helen R. Lane (Ann Arbor: University of Michigan Press)

BUTLER, ANDREW M. 2005. *Film Studies* (Harpenden: Pocket Essentials)

BUTLER, JUDITH. 1990. *Gender Trouble* (New York: Routledge)

——. 1993. *Bodies that Matter* (London: Routledge)

BUXÁN BRAN, XOSÉ M. 2003. '*Carne oscura de nardo marchito*: Figuras femeninas del Lorca Pintor', in *Sexualidades: Diversidad y Control Social*, ed. by Óscar Guasch and Olga Viñuales (Barcelona: Edicions Bellaterra), pp. 323–53

CABALLERO BONALD, JOSÉ MANUEL. 2016. 'La refundación del lenguaje', *El País*, 28

October <http://cultura.elpais.com/cultura/2016/10/13/actualidad/1476366198_449807.html> [accessed October 2016]

CAMACHO ROJO, JOSÉ MARÍA (ed.). 2006. *La tradición clásica en la obra de Federico García Lorca* (Granada: Editorial Universidad de Granada)

CAO, ANTONIO F. 1984. *Federico García Lorca y las vanguardias: Hacia el teatro* (London: Tamesis)

CARNERO, GUILLERMO. 2005. 'Un perro andaluz, de Dalí y Buñuel, y Viaje a la luna de García Lorca', *Arte y Parte: Revista de Arte — España, Portugal y América*, 56: 26–41

CATE-ARRIES, FRANCIE. 1992. 'The Discourse of Desire in the Language of Flowers: Lorca, Freud, and "Doña Rosita"', *South Atlantic Review*, 57.1: 53–68

CAVANAUGH, CECELIA J. 1995. *Lorca's Drawings and Poems: Forming the Eye of the Reader* (Lewisburg: Bucknell University Press; London: Associated University Presses)

——. 2003. 'Reading Lorca through the Microscope', *Hispania*, 86.2: 191–200

CLAPP, SUSANNAH. 2016. 'Yerma five-star review. Billie Piper is earth-quaking as Lorca's heroine', *Guardian*, 7 August <https://www.theguardian.com/stage/2016/aug/07/yerma-review-young-vic-billie-piper-simon-stone> [accessed December 2016]

CLEMINSON, RICHARD, and FRANCISCO VÁZQUEZ GARCÍA. 2007. *'Los invisibles': A History of Male Homosexuality in Spain, 1850–1939* (Cardiff: University of Wales Press)

CLIMENT, LAIA. 2004. 'Tradición y ruptura: El tratamiento de la literatura popular en Federico García Lorca y Maria-Mercé Marçal', in *La literatura en la literature: Actas del XIV Simposio de la Sociedad Española de Literatura General y Comparada*, ed. by Magdalena León Gómez (Alcalá de Henares: Centro de Estudios Cervantinos), pp. 335–46

COCTEAU, JEAN. 2000. *Poèmes: Appoggiatures et Paraprosodies* (Monaco: Ed. Du Rocher/J.P. Bertrand)

CONNELLY, FRANCES S. (ed.). 2003. *Modern Art and the Grotesque* (Cambridge: Cambridge University Press)

CORDERO SÁNCHEZ, LUIS PASCUAL. 2012. 'Homosexualidad y metaautores del teatro neoyorquino de García Lorca', *Bulletin of Hispanic Studies*, 89.2: 143–61

CRYSTAL, DAVID. 2008. *A Dictionary of Linguistics and Phonetics*, 6th edn (Hoboken: Wiley)

CRUZ, NILO. 2003. *Lorca in a Green Dress* (Oregon: Oregon Shakespeare Festival)

——. 2006. *Beauty of the Father* (New York: Theatre Communications Group)

DELGADO, MARIA M. 2008. *Federico García Lorca* (Oxford: Routledge)

——. 2015. 'Memory, Silence, and Democracy in Spain: Federico García Lorca, the Spanish Civil War, and the Law of Historical Memory', *Theatre Journal*, 67.2: 177–96

DE ROS, XON. 1996. 'Lorca's *El público*: An Invitation to the Carnival of Film', in *Changing Times in Hispanic Culture*, ed. by Derek Harris (Aberdeen: Centre for the Study of the Hispanic Avant-Garde), pp. 110–20

DE WITTE, BEN. 2017. 'Dramatizing Queer Visibility in *El público*: Federico García Lorca in Search of a Modern Theatre', *Modern Drama*, 60.1: 25–45

DÍAZ, EPICTETO. 1990. 'El "amor oscuro" en los sonetos de García Lorca', *Draco*, 2: 35–49

DIERS, RICHARD. 1963. 'A Filmscript by Lorca', *Windmill Magazine*, 5: 26–39

——. 1964. 'Introduction to *Trip to the Moon*. Filmscript by Federico García Lorca. Translated by Berenice G. Duncan', *New Directions in Prose and Poetry*, 18: 33–41

——. 1998. 'Un guión cinematográfico de Lorca', *Revista de Occidente*, 211: 182–85

DÍEZ DE REVENGA, FRANCISCO JAVIER. 1988. 'Federico García Lorca: de los "poemas neoyorquinos" a los "Sonetos oscuros"', *Revista Hispánica Moderna*, 41.2: 105–14

DOANE, MARY ANN. 2002. *The Emergence of Cinematic Time: Modernity, Contingency, The Archive* (Cambridge, MA: Harvard University Press)

DOBÓN, MARÍA DOLORES. 1996. '"La flor en el culo del muerto". Eros apolíneo y Eros nocturno en *El público* de Lorca', *Revista Hispánica Moderna*, 49.1: 47–58

DOBRIAN, WALTER. 2005. 'García Lorca: Los *Sonetos del amor oscuro* como expresión culmi-
nante de su vida angustiada', *Hispania*, 88.3: 456–67

DOGGART, SEBASTIAN. 1999. 'The Lorca Fiesta: Celebrating the Centenary in Newcastle',
in *Fire, Blood and the Alphabet: One Hundred Years of Lorca* (Durham: Durham Modern
Languages Series University of Durham), pp. 19–27

DOGGART, SEBASTIAN, and MICHAEL THOMPSON (eds.). 1999. *Fire, Blood and the Alphabet:
One Hundred Years of Lorca* (Durham: Durham Modern Languages Series University of
Durham)

DOMÍNGUEZ GIL, JOSÉ. 2008. *La voz de la piedra: Lorca y la "muerte oscura" del verbo* (Cáceres:
Universidad de Extremadura)

DOUGHERTY, DRU, and ANDREW A. ANDERSON. 2012. 'Continuity and Innovation in
Spanish Theatre, 1900–1936', in *A History of Theatre in Spain*, ed. by Maria M. Delgado
and David T. Gies (Cambridge: Cambridge University Press), pp. 282–309

EDELMAN, LEE. 2004. *No Future: Queer Theory and the Death Drive* (Durham, NC: Duke
University Press)

EISENBERG, DANIEL. 1988. 'Reaction to the Publication of the *Sonetos del amor oscuro*', *Bulletin
of Hispanic Studies*, 65.3: 261–71

ELLESTRÖM, LARS (ed.). 2010. *Media Borders, Multimodality and Intermediality* (Basingstoke:
Palgrave Macmillan)

FEAL DEIBE, CARLOS. 1973. *Eros y Lorca* (Barcelona: Edhasa)

FELTEN, UTA. 2005. 'El cine como generador de la escritura vanguardista en Federico
García Lorca', in *Vanguardia española e intermedialidad*, ed. by Albert Mechthild (Madrid/
Frankfurt: Iberoamericana/ Vervuert), pp. 479–88

FERNÁNDEZ CIFUENTES, LUIS. 1978. 'García Lorca: teatro del tiempo/tiempo del teatro',
Journal of Spanish Studies: Twentieth Century, 6.3: 175–92

FERNÁNDEZ MONTESINOS, MANUEL. 1988. 'Datos sobre la biblioteca de Federico García
Lorca', in *Biblioteca della Ricerca* (Italy: Schena Editore), pp. 13–23

FREEMAN, ELIZABETH. 2010. *Time Binds: Queer Temporalities, Queer Histories* (Durham: Duke
University Press)

FREUD, SIGMUND. 1961. *Beyond the Pleasure Principle*, ed. and trans. by James Strachey
(London: W.W. Norton & Co)

GALA, CANDELAS. 2011. *Poetry, Physics, and Painting in Twentieth-Century Spain* (New York:
Palgrave Macmillan)

GALLEGO MORELL, ANTONIO. 1988. 'Dimensión literaria del García Lorca dibujante',
Cuadernos para Investigación de la Literatura Hispánica, 9: 195–206

GARCÍA GÓMEZ, EMILIO. 1978. *Silla del moro y otras escenas andaluzas* (Granada: Fundación
Rodríguez Acosta)

GARCÍA LÓPEZ, MIGUEL. 2013. *A Poet/Man in Search of His Voice(s): Metapoetics and Platonism
in Federico García Lorca's* Poesía inédita de juventud (Unpublished Dissertation Royal
Holloway, University of London)

GARCÍA LORCA, FEDERICO. 1981. *Diván del Tamarit. Llanto por Ignacio Sánchez Mejías. Sonetos*,
ed. by Mario Hernández (Madrid: Alianza Editorial)

——. 1986. *Obras completas*, 22nd edn by Arturo del Hoyo, vols. I, II, and III (Madrid:
Aguilar)

——. 1987. *Dibujos*, ed. by Mario Hernández (Madrid: Herederos de Federico García
Lorca)

——. 1988A. *Diván del Tamarit. Seis poemas galegos. Llanto por Ignacio Sánchez Mejías*, ed. by
Andrew A. Anderson (Madrid: Espasa Calpe)

——. 1988B. *Poeta en Nueva York*, ed. by María Clementa Millán (Madrid: Cátedra)

——. 1994. *Viaje a la luna*, ed. by Antonio Monegal (Valencia: Pre-textos)

——. 1996. *Obras completas*, ed. by Miguel García-Posada, vols I and II (Barcelona: Galaxia-Gutenberg)

——. 1997A. *Epistolario completo*, ed. by Andrew A. Anderson and Christopher Maurer (Madrid: Cátedra)

——. 1997B. *Obras completas*, ed. by Miguel García-Posada, vols. III and IV (Barcelona: Galaxia-Gutenberg)

——. 2013. *Poesía completa*, 6th edn (Barcelona: Galaxia Gutenberg)

——. 2016A. *El público*, ed. by María Clementa Millán (Madrid: Cátedra)

——. 2016B. *Teatro completo*, 2nd edn (Barcelona: Galaxia Gutenberg)

——. 2018. *Diván del Tamarit*, ed. by Pepa Merlo (Madrid: Cátedra)

García Lorca, Francisco. 1989. *In the Green Morning* (London: Peter Owen)

Garlinger, Patrick Paul. 2002. 'Voicing (Untold) Desires: Silence and Sexuality in Federico García Lorca's *Sonetos del amor oscuro*', *Bulletin of Spanish Studies*, 79.6: 709–30

Gasch, Sebastián. 1928. 'Lorca dibujante', *La gaceta literaria*, 30: 4

George, David. 1995. *The History of the Commedia Dell'Arte in Modern Hispanic Literature with Special Attention to the Work of García Lorca* (Lewiston: The Edwin Mellen Press)

Gibson, Ian. 1987. *Federico García Lorca* (Barcelona: Grijalbo)

——. 1990. *Federico García Lorca: A Life* (London: Faber & Faber)

——. 1999. *Lorca-Dalí: El amor que no pudo ser* (Barcelona: Plaza & Janés)

——. 2009. *Caballo azul de mi locura: Lorca y el mundo gay* (Madrid: Planeta)

Gillett, Robert. 2001. 'Reading the Rose', *Hispanic Research Journal*, 2.2: 133–42

Gómez Torres, Ana María. 1999. 'El cine imposible de Federico García Lorca', in *América en un poeta: Los viajes de Federico García Lorca al Nuevo Mundo y la repercusión de su obra en la literatura americana*, ed. by Andrew A. Anderson (Sevilla: Universidad Internacional de Andalucía/ Fundación Focus Abengoa), pp. 43–68

Gubern, Román. 1999. *Proyector de luna: La generación del 27 y el cine* (Barcelona: Anagrama)

Gunning, Tom. 1993. '"Now You See It, Now You Don't": The Temporality of the Cinema of Attractions', *Velvet Light Trap*, 32: 3–12

——. 2006. 'Attractions: How They Came into the World', in *The Cinema of Attractions Reloaded*, ed. by Wanda Strauven (Amsterdam: Amsterdam University Press), pp. 31–40

Hacking, Ian. 1987. 'Was There a Probabilistic Revolution 1800–1930?', in *The Probabilistic Revolution*, volume 1, *Ideas in History*, ed. by Lorenz Krüger, Lorraine J. Daston, and Michael Heidelberger (Cambridge, Massachusetts: MIT Press)

Halperin, David M. 1995. *Saint Foucault: Towards a Gay Hagiography* (New York: Oxford University Press)

Hardison Londré, Felicia. 1983. 'Lorca in Metamorphosis: His Posthumous Plays', *Theatre Journal*, 35.1: 102–08

Harris, Derek. 1998. *Metal Butterflies and Poisonous Lights: The Language of Surrealism in Lorca, Alberti, Cernuda and Aleixandre* (Fife: La Sirena)

Hernández, Mario. 1984. 'Jardín deshecho: Los 'Sonetos' de García Lorca', *El Crotalón*, I: 193–228

——. 1990. *Libro de los dibujos de Federico García Lorca* (Madrid: Tabapress/Fundación Federico García Lorca)

——. 1991. *Line of Light and Shadow: The Drawings of Federico García Lorca*, trans. by Christopher Maurer (London: Duke University Press)

Herrero, Javier. 2014. *Lorca, Young and Gay. The Making of an Artist* (Newark, DE: Juan de la Cuesta)

Herrero, Rosario. 2005. 'Estructuras poético-narrativas en *Un chien andalou* de Luis Buñuel', in *Vanguardia española e intermedialidad*, ed. by Mechthild Albert (Madrid: Iberoamericana/ Vervuert), pp. 355–69

HIGGINBOTHAM, VIRGINIA. 1982. 'La iniciación de Lorca en el surrealismo', in *El surrealismo español*, ed. by Victor García de la Concha (Madrid: Taurus), pp. 240–54

——. 1986. '*Así que pasen cinco años*: Una versión literaria de *Un chien andalou*', *Cuadernos Hispanoamericanos*, 433–34: 343–50

HUÉLAMO KOSMA, JULIO. 1992. 'Lorca y los límites del teatro surrealista español', in *El teatro en España: entre la tradición y la vanguardia 1918–1939*, ed. by Dru Dougherty and María Francisca Vilches de Frutos (Madrid: CSIC/Fundación Federico García Lorca), pp. 207–14

HURTADO HERNÁNDEZ, MÓNICA. 2017. *Federico García Lorca: La obra de juventud, el teatro para títeres y los proyectos inconclusos* (unpublished doctoral thesis, Universidad de Barcelona)

ILIE, PAUL. 2009. *The Grotesque Aesthetic in Spanish Literature, From the Golden Age to Modernism* (Newark, DE: Juan de la Cuesta)

IRIZARRY, ESTELLE. 1984. *Painter-Poets of Contemporary Spain* (Boston: Twayne)

JEREZ-FARRÁN, CARLOS. 2000. 'Towards a Foucauldian Exegesis of Act V of García Lorca's *El público*', *The Modern Language Review*, 95.3: 728–43

——. 2001. 'Transvestism and Sexual Transgression in García Lorca's *The Public*', *Modern Drama*, 44.2: 188–213

——. 2004. *Un Lorca desconocido: Análisis de un teatro irrepresentable* (Madrid: Biblioteca Nueva)

——. 2015. 'El imperativo heterosexual y sus consecuencias en *Así que pasen cinco años* de García Lorca', *Neophilologus*, 99: 235–52

JOHNSTON, DAVID. 1999. 'García Lorca: After New York', in *Fire, Blood and the Alphabet: One Hundred Years of Lorca*, ed. by Sebastian Doggart and Michael Thompson (Durham: Durham Modern Languages Series University of Durham), pp. 57–65

JUNQUERA, NATALIA. 2014. '24 pasos y 78 años para buscar a Lorca', *El País*, 22 November <http://cultura.elpais.com/cultura/2014/11/22/actualidad/1416689210_359312.html> [accessed January 2015]

KLEIN, DENNIS A. 1975. ' "Así que pasen cinco años": A Search for Sexual Identity', *Journal of Spanish Studies: Twentieth Century*, 3.2: 115–23

KRAMER, MAX D. 2008. *The Poetry of Inversion: Queer Metaphor in Arthur Rimbaud, Stephan George, and Federico García Lorca* (Dissertation Columbia University, 2008) (Ann Arbor: UMI)

KRISTEVA, JULIA. 1982. *Powers of Horror: An Essay on Abjection*, trans. by Leon S. Roudiez (New York: Columbia University Press)

LAFFRANQUE, MARIE. 1980. 'Lectura e interpretación', in *Viaje a la luna* by Federico García Lorca (Loubressac: Braad), n.p.

——. 1982. 'Equivocar el camino: Regards sur un sccénario de Federico García Lorca', in *Hommage/Homenaje a Federico García Lorca* (Toulouse: U de Toulouse Le Mirail), pp. 73–92

——. 1986. 'Federico García Lorca, de la rosa mudable a la "Casida de la rosa" ', in *Lecciones sobre Federico García Lorca*, ed. Andrés Soria Olmedo (Granada: Comisión del Cincuentenario), pp. 279–300

——. 1987. *Teatro inconcluso* (Granada: Universidad de Granada)

LAHUERTA, JUAN JOSÉ. 2010. 'Sobre la economía artística de Salvador Dalí y Federico García Lorca en los años de su amistad', in *Dalí, Lorca y la Residencia de Estudiantes*, vol. 1, ed. by SECC (Madrid: Ministerio de Cultura/SECC/Fundación "la Caixa"), pp. 326–27

LARSON, SUSAN. 2011. ' "Cinegrafía" and the Abject in Federico García Lorca's *Viaje a la luna* (1930)', *Romance Quarterly*, 58.4: 302–15

LEÓN, JOSÉ JAVIER. 2018. *El duende, hallazgo y cliché* (Seville: Athenaica Ediciones Universitarias)

LEÓN-SOTELO, TRINIDAD DE, and FRANCISCO RUIZ ANTÓN. 1998. 'Aznar: "España hoy se llama Federico"', *ABC*, 6 June, p. 59

LEUCI, VERÓNICA. 2008. 'Eros y Thánatos: La mística del amor en los *Sonetos del amor oscuro* de Federico García Lorca', *Espéculo: Revista de estudios literarios*, Universidad Complutense de Madrid <http://www.ucm.es/info/especulo/numero40/glorca.html> [accessed 15 Nov 2013]

LIMÓN, JAVIER. 2016. '¿Es Lorca flamenco, o el flamenco es lorquiano?', *El País*, 28 October <http://cultura.elpais.com/cultura/2016/10/13/actualidad/1476366566_030544.html> [accessed November 2016]

LLERA, JOSÉ ANTONIO. 2011. 'Texto, contexto e intertexto en "Paisaje de la multitud que vomita (Anochecer de Coney Island)", de Federico García Lorca', *1616: Anuario de Literatura Comparada*, 1: 185–219

LONDRÉ, FELICIA HARDISON. 1984. *Federico García Lorca* (New York: Frederick Ungar)

LÓPEZ CASTELLÓN, ENRIQUE. 1981. *Federico García Lorca: El poeta ante la muerte* (Madrid: Ediciones Felmar)

LOUGHRAN, DAVID K. 1978. *Federico García Lorca: The Poetry of Limits* (London: Tamesis Books)

MARTÍNEZ CUITIÑO, LUIS. 2002. *El mito del andrógino en Federico García Lorca: Un Viaje a la luna* (Buenos Aires: Corregidor)

MARTÍNEZ HERNÁNDEZ, JOSÉ. 2011. 'La teoría estética de Federico García Lorca', in *Art, Emotion and Value. Proceedings of the 5th Mediterranean Congress of Aesthetics*, ed. by María José Alcaraz, Matilde Carrasco, and Salvador Rubio (Cartagena: Universidad de Murcia), pp. 91–100 <http://www.um.es/vmca/proceedings/docs/9.Jose-Martinez-Hernandez.pdf> [accessed 5 June 2013]

MARTÍNEZ NADAL, RAFAEL. 1988. *El Público: Amor y muerte en la obra de Federico García Lorca* (Madrid: Hiperión)

MARTÍNEZ, RAMÓN. 2017. *Lo nuestro sí que es mundial: Una introducción a la historia del movimiento LGTB en España* (Barcelona/Madrid: Egales)

MATAS CABALLERO, JUAN. 1999. 'Federico García Lorca frente a la tradición literaria: Voz y eco de San Juan de la Cruz en los *Sonetos del amor oscuro*', *Contextos*, 17/18.33/36: 361–84

MAURER, CHRISTOPHER (ed.). 1998. 'Preface', in *In Search of Duende*, by Federico García Lorca (New York: New Directions), pp. vii–xi

——. 2007. 'Poetry', in *A Companion to Federico García Lorca*, ed. by Federico Bonaddio (Woodbridge: Támesis), pp. 16–38

MAYA, MARIO. 2005. 'On *Diálogo del Amargo*', choreography performed at the Jardines del Generalife, Granada <http://www.juntadeandalucia.es/cultura/lorcaygranada/es/diálogo-del-amargo> [accessed October 2016]

MAYHEW, JONATHAN. 2011A. 'Was Lorca a Poetic Thinker?', *Romance Quarterly*, 58.4: 276–88

——. 2011B. 'What Lorca Knew: Teaching Receptivity', *Hispanic Issues On Line*, 8: 158–69

——. 2018. *Lorca's Legacy: Essays in Interpretation* (Oxford: Routledge)

McCALLUM, E.L., and MIKKO TUHKANEN. 2011. 'Introduction: Becoming Unbecoming; Untimely Mediations', in *Queer Times, Queer Becomings*, ed. by E.L. McCallum and Mikko Tuhkanen (Albany: State University of New York Press), pp. 1–24

McDERMID, PAUL. 2007. *Love, Desire and Identity in the Theatre of Federico García Lorca* (Woodbridge: Támesis)

McDERMOTT, PATRICIA. 1996. 'Lorca's *Viaje a la luna*: The Cinema as Sacrilegious Act', in *Changing Times in Hispanic Culture*, ed. by Derek Harris (Aberdeen: Centre for the Study of the Hispanic Avant-Garde), pp. 121–32

McLUHAN, MARSHALL. 1964. *Understanding Media: The Extensions of Man* (New York: Mentor)

MIRA, ALBERTO. 2004. *De Sodoma a Chueca: Una historia cultural de la homosexualidad en España en el siglo XX* (Barcelona: Egales)

——. 2007. 'Foreword', in *Federico García Lorca and the Culture of Male Homosexuality*, by Ángel Sahuquillo (Jefferson, NC and London: McFarland & Company, Inc.), pp. 3–10

——. 2011. 'Poetas en el cine: Paradigmas teóricos en dos narrativas biográficas (*Little Ashes* y *El cónsul de Sodoma*)', *Lectora*, 17: 123–38

MOLINA FOIX, VICENTE. 2005. '98 y 27: Dos generaciones ante el cine (Baroja y Lorca como guionistas)', *Cuadernos de Mangana*, 35 (Cuenca: Centro de Profesores y Recursos de Cuenca), pp. 9–43

MONEGAL, ANTONIO. 1994A. 'Introducción', in *Viaje a la luna*, by Federico García Lorca (Valencia: Pre-textos), pp. 7–55

——. 1994B. 'Un-Masking the Maskuline: Transvestism and Tragedy in García Lorca's *El público*', *MLN*, 109.2: 204–16

MORALES PECO, MONSERRAT. 2000. 'La imagen de España en el pensamiento y la obra de Jean Cocteau', *VII Coloquio APFUE (Asociación de Profesores de Francés de la Universidad Española)*, I: 221–34

MORÁN, FRANCISCO. 2005. '*Volutas del deseo*: Hacia una lectura del orientalismo en el modernismo hispanoamericano', *MLN*, 120.2: 383–407

MORENO JIMÉNEZ, SERGIO. 2019. 'Los arreglos del jardín sobre el texto de los *Sonetos* de García Lorca', *Boletín Real Academia Española*, 99.319: 301–25

MORRIS, C. B. 1980. *This Loving Darkness. The Cinema and Spanish Writers 1920–1936* (Oxford: Oxford University Press for the University of Hull)

MULVEY, LAURA. 1975. 'Visual Pleasure and Narrative Cinema', *Screen*, 16.3: 803–16 <https://www.amherst.edu/system/files/media/1021/Laura%20Mulvey,%20Visual%20 Pleasure.pdf> [accessed January 2015]

MUÑOZ, DANIEL. 2018. 'The Spiritual Force of Unleashed Love: Echoes of Saint John of the Cross in Federico García Lorca's *Sonnets of the Dark Love*', *Spiritus*, 18.2: 152–75

MUÑOZ, JOSÉ ESTEBAN. 2009. *Cruising Utopia: The Then and There of Queer Futurity* (New York: New York University Press)

MUÑOZ, ÓSCAR ENRIQUE. 2013. *La queja enamorada: Sobre el juego del duende de Federico García Lorca*, 3rd edn (Madrid: Mandala)

NANDORFY, MARTHA J. 2001. 'Duende and Apocalypse in Lorca's Theory and Poetics', *Revista Canadiense de Estudios Hispánicos*, 26.1/2: 255–70

——. 2003. *The Poetics of Apocalypse. Federico García Lorca's* Poet in New York (London: Associated University Presses)

NELMES, JILL (Ed.). 1996. *Introduction to Film Studies* (London: Routledge)

NERUDA, PABLO. 2000. *Residencia en la tierra* (Alicante: Biblioteca Virtual Miguel de Cervantes)

NEWTON, CANDELAS. 1992. *Lorca, una escritura en trance. Libro de Poemas y Diván del Tamarit* (Amsterdam: John Benjamins B.V.)

NICOLÁS MARTÍNEZ, PILAR. 2006. 'Análisis de las relaciones temáticas entre las obras de Federico García Lorca: *Viaje a la luna* y *El público*', *Península: Revista de Estudos Ibéricos*, 3: 263–88

OLIVARES BRIONES, EDMUNDO. 2001. *Pablo Neruda: Los caminos del mundo; Tras las huellas del poeta itinerante II (1933–1939)* (Santiago de Chile: LOM)

OPPENHEIMER, HELEN. 1986. *Lorca: The Drawings; Their Relation to the Poet's Life and Work* (London: The Herbert Press)

O'PRAY, MICHAEL. 2003. *Avant-garde Film: Forms, Themes and Passions* (London: Wallflower)

ORTEGA Y GASSET, JOSÉ. 2000. 'La deshumanización del arte', in *El sentimiento estético de la vida* <http://www.columbia.edu/cu/spanish/courses/spanish3350/05sigloxxespana/pdf/deshumanizacion.pdf> [accessed September 2013], pp. 316–28

Oxford English Dictionary (OED). 2021. *Oxford English Dictionary Online* (Oxford: Oxford University Press) <https://www.oed.com> [accessed July 2021]

PEDROSA, JOSÉ MANUEL. 1998. 'Pámpanos, Cascabeles, y la simbología erótica en *El público de Lorca*', *Teatro: Revista de Estudios Culturales/A Journal of Cultural Studies*, 13: 371–86

——. 2012. 'Federico García Lorca y la campana de la Vela (Sobre la *Gacela IV* del *Diván del Tamarit*)', *Boletín de la Biblioteca de Menéndez Pelayo*, LXXXVIII.2: 329–76

PERAL VEGA, EMILIO. 2015. *Pierrot/Lorca: White Carnival of Black Desire* (Woodbridge: Támesis)

PÉREZ PONS, MERCÈ. 2017. '...Y Belisa y Perlimplín se reencontraron en el jardín', *El País*, 12 January <http://ccaa.elpais.com/ccaa/2017/01/11/catalunya/1484169823_286369.html> [accessed March 2017]

PERRIAM, CHRIS. 2007. 'Gender and Sexuality', in *A Companion to Federico García Lorca*, ed. by Federico Bonaddio (Woodbridge: Támesis), pp. 149–69

PHILLIPS, IAN. 2000. 'The Poetry of Jean Cocteau', *The Lancet*, 356: 1117

POWELL, HELEN. 2012. *Stop the Clocks! Time and Narrative in Cinema* (London: I.B. Tauris)

PIÑERO, PEDRO. 2008. 'Lorca y la canción popular: Las tres hojas: de la tradición al surrealismo', *Culturas Populares. Revista Electrónica*, 6: 1–44

PLAZA AGUDO, INMACULADA. 2019. 'La configuración de las identidades en torno al amor en el teatro de Federico García Lorca', *Hispania*, 102. 2: 217–28

PLAZA CHILLÓN, JOSÉ LUIS. 2006. 'Degollaciones, decapitaciones, amputaciones... la poética de la violencia en los dibujos de Federico García Lorca', *La multiculturalidad en las Artes y en la Arquitectura: XVI Congreso Nacional de Historia del Arte*, 1: 831–42

——. 2008. '"Imágenes que explican poesía": para una interpretación de los dibujos de Federico García Lorca', *Terceras Jornadas Archivo y Memoria*, 1–21 <http://www.docutren.com/ArchivoyMemoria/ArchivoyMemoria2008/pdf/3J_Comunicacion_18_Jose%20Luis%20Plaza%20Chillon.pdf> [accessed October 2016]

——. 2014. 'Una proyección gráfica de la palabra: Los dibujos "abstractos" y vibracionistas de Federico García Lorca', *De Arte*, 13: 216–39

——. 2016. 'El viaje literario de Federico García Lorca a Buenos Aires y sus consecuencias gráficas. Marineros porteños: erotismo y desolación', *El Greco en su IV Centenario: patrimonio hispánico y diálogo intercultural*, pp. 531–48

——. 2019. 'La iconografía de San Sebastián en Federico García Lorca: Hagiografía y homoerotismo', *Emblecat: Estudis de la Imatge, Art i Societat*, 8: 85–108

POLANSKY, SUSAN G. 2007. 'Dos leyendas de tiempo interrumpido: *Así que pasen cinco años* por Federico García Lorca y *La familia interrumpida* por Luis Cernuda', *Hispania*, 90. 2: 215–23

PRECIADO, PAUL B. 2013. 'Pienso, luego existo', *RTVE* <http://www.rtve.es/alacarta/videos/pienso-luego-existo/pienso-luego-existo-beatriz-preciado/1986547/> [accessed January 2020]

PUYAL, ALFONSO. 2011. 'Lorca y Buñuel: de la poemática a la cinemática', *Bulletin of Hispanic Studies*, 88.7: 761–76

QUANCE, ROBERTA ANN. 2010. *In the Light of Contradiction: Desire in the Poetry of Federico García Lorca* (Cambridge: Legenda)

——. 2011. 'On the Way to 'duende' (through Lorca's Elogio de Antonia Mercé, 'la Argentina', 1930)', *Journal of Iberian and Latin American Studies*, 17.2–3: 181–94

QUESADA MARCO, SEBASTIÁN. 1997. *Diccionario de civilización y cultura españolas* (Madrid: AKAL)

REAL ACADEMIA ESPAÑOLA DE LA LENGUA. 2014. *Diccionario de la Real Academia Española de la Lengua (DRAE)*, 23rd edn (Madrid: RAE) <https://www.rae.es> [accessed 1 July 2021]

REED, CHRISTOPHER. 2011. *Art and Homosexuality* (New York: Oxford University Press)

REMY, MICHEL. 1996. 'The Visual Poetics of British Surrealism', in *Surrealism: Surrealist Visuality*, ed. by Silvano Levy (Edinburgh: Keele University Press), pp. 157–67

ROBINSON, DAVID. 1993. *Georges Méliès: Father of Film Fantasy* (London: Museum of the Moving Image)

ROMÁN LAGUNAS, JORGE. 2017. 'Orientalismo en la poesía de Rubén Darío y otros poetas latinoamericanos', *Cultura de paz*, 23.73: 33–38

ROSES-LOZANO, JOAQUÍN. 1989. 'Códigos sígnicos y discurso teatral en *Así que pasen cinco años*', *Anales de la literatura española contemporánea*, 14.1/3: 115–41

RUBIERA MATA, MARÍA JESÚS. 1982. *Ibn al-Yassab: El otro poeta de la Alhambra* (Granada: Patronato de la Alhambra y Generalife/Instituto Hispano-Árabe de Cultura)

———. 1992. *La literatura hispanoárabe* (Madrid: Maphre)

RUIZ MANTILLA, JESÚS. 2016. 'Comienza la tercera búsqueda de la fosa de Lorca', *El País*, 20 September <http://cultura.elpais.com/cultura/2016/09/18/actualidad/1474201624_945890.html> [accessed March 2017]

———. 2017. 'Dos casquillos de bala: de Lorca, nada', *El País*, 15 February <http://cultura.elpais.com/cultura/2017/02/15/actualidad/1487172181_324092.html> [accessed March 2017]

RUIZ MANTILLA, JESÚS, and TOMMASO KOCH. 2017. 'Las obras de Unamuno, Valle-Inclán, Lorca, Muñoz Seca y otros 373 autores pasan a dominio público', *El País*, 1 January <http://cultura.elpais.com/cultura/2016/12/30/actualidad/1483092260_837815.html> [accessed January 2017]

RUIZ RAMÓN, FRANCISCO. 1986. *Historia del teatro español Siglo XX* (Madrid: Cátedra)

SAHUQUILLO, ÁNGEL. 2007. *Federico García Lorca and the Culture of Male Homosexuality* (Jefferson, NC and London: McFarland & Company, Inc.)

SAID, EDWARD. 1978. *Orientalism* (London: Penguin)

SALAZAR RINCÓN, JAVIER. 1999. 'Ramos, coronas, guirnaldas: símbolos de amor y muerte en la obra de Federico García Lorca', *Revista de literatura*, 61.122: 495–519

SALINAS, PEDRO. 1962. 'Lorca and the Poetry of Death', in *Lorca: A Collection of Critical Essays*, ed. by Manuel Durán (Englewood Cliffs, N.J.: Prentice-Hall, Inc.)

SAMANIEGO, FERNANDO. 1997. 'Imágenes del 2029 en el guión de "Viaje a la Luna"', *El País* <https://elpais.com/diario/1997/12/14/cultura/882054004_850215.html> [accessed March 2020]

SÁNCHEZ, JOSÉ ANTONIO. 1998. ''The Impossible Theatre': The Spanish Stage at the Time of the Avant-Garde', *Contemporary Theatre Review*, 7.2: 7–30

SÁNCHEZ VIDAL, AGUSTIN. 1988. 'El viaje a la luna de un perro andaluz', in *Valoración actual de la obra de García Lorca: Coloquio Casa de Velázquez* (Madrid: Casa de Velázquez/Universidad Complutense), pp. 141–62

———. 1992. *El cine de Segundo de Chomón* (Zaragoza: Caja de Ahorros de la Inmaculada)

———. 1999. *Realizadores aragoneses* (Zaragoza: Caja de Ahorros de la Inmaculada/Edelvives)

SCHRÖTER, JENS. 2011. 'Discourses and Models of Intermediality', *CLCWeb: Comparative Literature and Culture*, 13.3: 1–8 <http://docs.lib.purdue.edu/clcweb/vol13/iss3/3> [accessed March 2014] (article 3)

SHAKESPEARE, WILLIAM. 1997. *Shakespeare's Sonnets*, ed. by Katherine Duncan Jones (London: The Arden Shakespeare)

SHELLEY, MARY WOLLSTONECRAFT. 1941. *Frankenstein, or the Modern Prometheus* (Cambridge, Massachusetts: Harvard College Library)

SMITH, PAUL JULIAN. 1989. *The Body Hispanic* (Oxford: Oxford University Press)

———. 1998A. *The Theatre of García Lorca: Text, Performance, Psychoanalysis* (Cambridge: Cambridge University Press)

———. 1998B. 'The Lorca Cult: Theatre, Cinema, and Print Media in 1980s Spain', *Contemporary Theatre Review*, 7.4: 65–80

——. 2014. 'Reading Intermediality: Lorca's *Viaje a la luna* ("Journey to the Moon," 1929) and *Un chien andalou* (Buñuel/ Dalí, 1929)', *Modern Languages Open* <http://www.modernlanguagesopen.org/index.php/mlo/article/view/4/51> [accessed December 2014]

SOCIEDAD ESTATAL DE CONMEMORACIONES CULTURALES SECC (ed.). 2010. *Dalí, Lorca y la Residencia de Estudiantes* (Madrid: Ministerio de Cultura/SECC/Fundación "la Caixa")

SORIA OLMEDO, ANDRÉS. 2006. ' "Me lastima el corazón": Federico García Lorca y Federico Nietzsche', in *La tradición clásica en la obra de Federico García Lorca*, ed. by José María Camacho Rojo (Granada: Editorial Universidad de Granada), pp. 113–30

——. 2009. *Federico García Lorca. Dibujos como poemas* (Barcelona: Ediciones de La Central)

SOUFAS, C. CHRISTOPHER. 1996. *Audience and Authority in the Modernist Theater of Federico García Lorca* (Tuscaloosa/London: The University of Alabama Press)

STAINTON, LESLIE. 1998. *Lorca: A Dream of Life* (London: Bloomsbury)

TALENS, JENARO. 2000. *El sujeto vacío: Cultura y poesía en territorio Babel* (Madrid: Cátedra)

TINAJERO, ARACELI. 2004. *Orientalismo en el modernismo hispanoamericano* (West Lafayette: Purdue University Press)

TORRES NEBRERA, GREGORIO. 1999. 'Del teatro inconcluso de García Lorca: apostillas a *Los sueños de mi prima Aurelia*', *Anuario de Estudios Filológicos*, 22: 425–45

TREMLETT, GILES. 2009. 'Spanish archaeologists fail to find Federico García Lorca's grave', *Guardian*, 18 December <http://www.theguardian.com/world/2009/dec/18/federico-garcia-lorca-grave-alfacar> [accessed September 2013]

——. 2012. 'Name of Federico García Lorca's lover emerges after 70 years', *Guardian*, 10 May <https://www.theguardian.com/culture/2012/may/10/name-garcia-lover-emerges> [accessed September 2013]

UNAMUNO, MIGUEL DE. 1983 [1912]. *Del sentimiento trágico de la vida: La agonía del cristianismo* (Madrid: AKAL)

VALENTE, JOSÉ ANGEL. 1976. 'Pez luna', *Trece de Nieve*, 1–2: 191–201

VÄLIAHO, PASI. 2010. *Mapping the Moving Image: Gesture, Thought and Cinema circa 1900* (Amsterdam: Amsterdam University Press)

VALIS, NOËL. 2002. *The Culture of Cursilería. Bad Taste, Kitsch, and Class in Modern Spain* (Durham, N.C. & London: Duke University Press)

VILCHES DE FRUTOS, FRANCISCA. 2008. 'El teatro de Federico García Lorca en la construcción de la identidad colectiva española (1936–1986)', *Anales de la literatura española contemporánea*, 33. 2: 283–328

WALTERS, D. GARETH. 2007. 'Introduction', in *Selected Poems* by Federico García Lorca, trans. by Martin Sorrell (Oxford: Oxford University Press), pp. ix–xxiv

WEBSTER, JASON. 2003. *Duende: A Journey in Search of Flamenco* (London: Doubleday)

WEINBERG, JONATHAN. 1996. 'Things are Queer', *Art Journal*, 55: 11–14

WHITTOCK, TREVOR. 1990. *Metaphor and Film* (Cambridge: Cambridge University Press)

WOLF, WERNER. 2011. '(Inter)mediality and the Study of Literature', *CLCWeb: Comparative Literature and Culture*, 13.3: 1–9 <http://docs.lib.purdue.edu/clcweb/vol13/iss3/2> [accessed March 2014] (article 2)

WRIGHT, SARAH. 2000. *The Trickster-Function in the Theatre of García Lorca* (Woodbridge: Támesis)

——. 2007A. 'Theatre', in *A Companion to Federico García Lorca*, ed. by Federico Bonaddio (Woodbridge: Támesis), pp. 39–62

——. 2007B. 'The Reluctant Don Juans: Lorca, Marañón, Amiel', *Anales de la literatura española contemporánea*, 32.2: 447–61

Filmography

Battleship Potemkin. 1925. Dir. by Sergei Eisenstein (Soviet Union: Mosfilm)

Bones of Contention/Pero que todos sepan que no he muerto. 2017. Dir. by Andrea Weiss (USA/ Spain: Jezebel Productions)

Entr'acte. 1924. Dir. by René Clair (France: Société Nouvelle des Acacias/Criterion Collection)

Excursion dans la lune. 1908. Dir. by Segundo de Chomón (France: Pathé Frères) <https:// www.youtube.com/watch?v=QwvVnXtobwU> [accessed May 2017]

La Grenouille. 1908. Dir. by Segundo de Chomón (France: Pathé/Les Archives du Film du CNC) <https://www.youtube.com/watch?v=ed1kBEO1bPs> [accessed May 2017]

La mala educación. 2004. Dir. by Pedro Almodóvar (Spain: El Deseo)

La novia. 2015. Dir. by Paula Ortiz (Spain: Get in the Picture Productions/Mantar Film/ Cine Chromatix KG/TVE)

Le sang d'un poète. 1932. Dir. by Jean Cocteau (France: The Criterion Collection)

Little Ashes. 2009. Dir. by Paul Morrison (United Kingdom: PT Films/Aria Films/Met Film/Factotum Barcelona)

Making of Viaje a la luna. 1998. Dir by Frederic Amat <http://www.youtube.com/ watch?v=CpahIqIoknA24> [accessed September 2013]

Métamorphoses. 1912. Dir. by Segundo de Chomón (France: Pathé/Cinémathèque Française) <https://www.youtube.com/watch?v=zDafGw5PGHw> [accessed May 2017]

Metropolis. 1927. Dir. by Fritz Lang (Germany: UFA)

Muerte en Granada (*The Disappearance of García Lorca*). 1997. Dir. by Marcos Zurinaga (Spain/ USA: Antena 3 TV/Canal +/Enrique Cerezo)

Todo sobre mi madre. 1999. Dir. by Pedro Almodóvar (Spain: El Deseo)

Un chien andalou. 1929. Dir. by Luis Buñuel. Screenplay by Luis Buñuel and Salvador Dalí (France: Grands Films Classiques)

Viaje a la luna. 1998. Dir. by Frederic Amat (Spain: Comunidad de Herederos de Federico García Lorca/ Frederic Amat/ Canal Sur Televisión/ Ovideo TV)

Voyage dans la lune. 1902. Dir. by Georges Méliès (France: Star Film Company) <https:// www.youtube.com/watch?v=_FrdVdKlxUk> [accessed September 2013]

INDEX

❖

www.ingramcontent.com/pod-product-compliance
Lightning Source LLC
Chambersburg PA
CBHW081131090426

42737CB00018B/3300